ELLEN SHIPMAN
AND THE AMERICAN GARDEN

LALH
Library of American Landscape History

ELLEN SHIPMAN

AND THE AMERICAN GARDEN

Revised and Expanded Edition

JUDITH B. TANKARD

UNIVERSITY OF GEORGIA PRESS

ATHENS

LIBRARY OF AMERICAN LANDSCAPE HISTORY

AMHERST, MASSACHUSETTS

Published by the University of Georgia Press
Athens, Georgia 30602
www.ugapress.org

Designed and typeset by Jonathan D. Lippincott
Set in Sabon
Printed and bound by Thomson-Shore

The paper in this book meets the guidelines for
permanence and durability of the Committee on
Production Guidelines for Book Longevity of the
Council on Library Resources.

Printed in the United States of America
18 19 20 21 22 C 5 4 3 2 1

Library of Congress Control Number: 2017959200
ISBN 978-0-8203-5208-4

Frontispiece. Stan Hywet Hall & Gardens. Photo by Carol Betsch.

Ellen Shipman and the American Garden was made possible with the generous support of the following individuals:

Anonymous
Kelly Comras, FASLA, and Michael Lofchie
William H. Frederick, Jr.
Cynthia Hewitt and Dan Holloway
Carolyn Marsh Lindsay
James Turner and Dede Delaney, Impact Assets–The Blackhaw Fund

Mr. and Mrs. Craig Barrow III
Joanne W. Blokker
Thomas Lemann, Azby Art Fund
Janine Luke
Richard and Augusta Turner, Westchester Community Foundation-
    Esplanade Fund, in honor of Nancy R. Turner

Jeff Allen, ASLA, Jeff Allen Landscape Architecture
George W. Curry, FASLA
Nora Mitchell, ASLA, and Rolf Diamant, ASLA
W. Scott and Jean Peterson, Vanguard Charitable–The Peterson Family
    Advised Fund
Gil Schafer III, G. P. Schafer Architect
Thomas Woodward and David LePere

Sandra Clinton, FASLA, Clinton & Associates
David Coleman
Mr. and Mrs. Joseph H. McGee
Keith Morgan
Darwina Neal, FASLA
Nancy Newcomb
Carl R. Nold
Elizabeth Barlow Rogers

To the late Nancy Angell Streeter
whose memories of her grandmother
made this book possible

CONTENTS

PREFACE

The field of twentieth-century landscape studies has grown considerably since *The Gardens of Ellen Biddle Shipman* was published in 1996. At the time, monographs on American practitioners were rare, and the classic gardens of England and Europe still cast such long shadows on this side of the Atlantic that few historians were tempted to tackle the subject. But over the course of the 1990s, increasingly rigorous research began to illuminate both the range and the quality of the accomplishments of long-forgotten designers throughout North America, Ellen Shipman among them. Judith Tankard's monograph—among the first to apply art historical methodology to an American practitioner—deftly returned to us one of the very best of the period.

In the two decades since Shipman's biography appeared, there has been an explosion of interest in the American "pioneers," as they have come to be identified. Monographs on individual practitioners and firms (including new books on Fletcher Steele and Beatrix Farrand, and first-time treatments of Innocenti & Webel, Warren H. Manning, John Nolen, Arthur Shurcliff, and Ruth Shellhorn, to name a few) have laid the groundwork for a field of inquiry that continues to expand and to deepen. Each of these books has contributed to our understanding of individual practitioners' oeuvres, and each has also provided insight into the comprehensive history of the field, so our understanding of the whole has evolved too.

Other important developments have occurred as a consequence of burgeoning scholarship in American landscape studies. Primary among these is the revitalization, rehabilitation, and restoration of historic cultural landscapes across the country, from gardens and parks to city centers. When we decided to pursue a revised edition of Shipman's biography, it seemed an apt occasion to round up several examples of recent preservation work in her gardens, particularly those projects inspired and supported by the scholarship in the first edition.

The impressively varied but by no means exhaustive survey in Tankard's new introduction reveals a growing passion for Shipman's work and, less expected, great robustness in the designs that are still extant. While Shipman is often regarded as a masterful plantswoman whose gardens featured imaginative combinations of successive bloom, photographs of the recently restored places highlight as well the strength of her handling of architectural form and spatial layout. Even when plantings have been simplified to adjust to contemporary conditions—including, in most cases, much smaller gardening staffs—Shipman's designs retain their character and artistic strength.

We believe that today's landscape practitioners in particular will find much of interest in these pages. Styles shift from one period to the next, but the essential components of the art of landscape design remain constant. In Ellen Shipman's hands, these coalesced into some of the era's most remarkable achievements. We are pleased to be able to publish an expanded and updated edition of her work so that readers can better comprehend the elements that made her gardens the superlative places they were and, in some cases, still are.

I thank all the generous individuals who make the work of LALH possible—a comprehensive list of underwriters of the new volume appears on page v. My thanks also go to the board of directors of LALH, who provide vital financial and intellectual support for our publishing program; our talented staff—Sarah Allaback, Neil Brigham, and Carol Betsch, who edited the new edition and created the index; and the staff of the University of Georgia Press, particularly our acquiring editor James Patrick Allen and art director Erin New. My deepest thanks go to Jonathan Lippincott for his creation of the superb new design and to Judith B. Tankard for her willingness to jump back in after twenty years.

Robin Karson
Executive Director
Library of American Landscape History

ELLEN SHIPMAN

AND THE AMERICAN GARDEN

Italian Garden, Cummer Museum of Art & Gardens, Jacksonville, Fla. Photo by Mick Hales.

INTRODUCTION

When *The Gardens of Ellen Biddle Shipman* was published in 1996, it found a broad-based readership. Eventually selling more than five thousand copies—to home gardeners, students, landscape practitioners, historians, and preservationists—the biography brought a long-forgotten landscape architect out of the shadows into the pantheon of influential, early twentieth-century American practitioners. The publication has had other far-reaching influences, too, particularly in the realm of preservation.

Although Ellen Shipman (1869–1950) was one of America's most accomplished and prolific garden designers of her day—she out-produced both Beatrix Farrand and Marian Coffin—by the time of her death, her maintenance-intensive gardens had gone out of fashion, and during the second half of the twentieth century, most of these designs were altered beyond recognizable form or demolished to make way for expanding house footprints. Some, however, were left to their own devices, and these have proved a rich basis for a remarkable number of restorations, many of which were inspired by the appearance of the 1996 book. Excited about the accomplishments of this deft and inventive practitioner, stewards of her gardens have taken on the tasks of researching original design principles and bringing these important cultural landscapes back to life. In this sense, *The Gardens of Ellen Biddle Shipman*, like other titles published by LALH, has had a pervasive impact on the preservation and restoration of historic landscapes throughout the country.

One of the most dramatic Shipman "rediscoveries" occurred in Jacksonville, Florida, home of the Cummer Museum of Art. Shortly after its publication, Carolyn Marsh Lindsay, former chair of the American Horticultural Society and a noted garden designer, was given a copy of *The Gardens of Ellen Biddle Shipman* by LALH director Robin Karson. She was startled to discover the name of Arthur Cummer, once a prominent resident of Jacksonville, in the client list. Lindsay was intrigued because she had recently moved to Florida and was becoming involved in activities at the Cummer Museum. She ordered a complete set of the original garden plans from Cornell University, where Shipman's archives are housed, and spent the next six months researching the extensive plant palette they indicated.

Historic photos of the garden came to light in the museum's archives and family collections, and these, too, provided invaluable guidance in the recovery effort that was soon under way. In addition to rebuilding brick walkways, benches, and crumbling walls, the revitalization focused on the restoration of the garden's centerpiece, a large marble fountain purchased by Ninah and Arthur Cummer during a 1930 tour of Italy, the same trip that had inspired Ninah to seek out Shipman's design services in the first place. The fountain was cast by Marble Studio Stagetti in Pietrasanta, using old photos, drawings, and molds of the original. In time, Shipman's beds were replanted, using horticultural species that as nearly as possible replicated those in the original plans.

My subsequent research commissioned by the museum revealed that Ninah Cummer had hired the Chicago-based landscape architect Ossian Cole Simonds to lay out a landscape plan for the estate grounds in 1903, well before Shipman's work there. Further developments occurred in 1910, in what came to be known as the English Garden, designed by the well-known Philadelphia nursery of Thomas Meehan & Sons. Additional research revealed that Olmsted Brothers had advised on the grounds in 1922 and again in 1931.

The task of unifying these disparate garden areas into a cohesive museum campus was carried out over several years with assistance from the well-known Belgian landscape architect François Goffinet. These restoration projects have brought national recognition to what is now the Cummer Museum of Art & Gardens, reflecting the historic gardens' appeal both to the Cummer's own constituency and to garden lovers generally. Many visitors come to Jacksonville to see these outstanding examples of early twentieth-century garden design—works of art as surely as the painting and sculpture on view inside the museum.

Other Shipman gardens in the South have been restored since the appearance of the 1996 biography. Among the most significant of these is Longue Vue House & Gardens, in New Orleans, Shipman's most ambitious mature design, initiated in 1935 for Edith and Edgar B. Stern. As was the case with many of Shipman's designs, the gardens and grounds were changed over the

Italian Garden. Photo by Judith B. Tankard.

Portico Garden (*top*) and Wild Garden, Longue Vue House & Gardens, New Orleans, La. Photos by Amy Graham.

years, in part by Edith Stern, who commissioned William and Geoffrey Platt to alter the grounds after Hurricane Betsy in 1965.

In 1997, Longue Vue commissioned a far-ranging preservation plan from Heritage Landscapes of Charlotte, Vermont. The document guided a large-scale restoration that brought Shipman's design principles back into focus, and it also included a recovery of the estate's extensive wild garden designed by the southern naturalist Caroline Dorman. The work, comprising tree removal and replanting and substantial structural repairs, continued into the early 2000s. The grounds of Longue Vue were badly damaged when Hurricane Katrina swept through New Orleans in August 2005, felling hundreds of trees and killing nearly two-thirds of the new plantings. But plans were quickly put in place for yet another restoration, thanks in large measure to support from The Garden Conservancy. Since then, the tree canopy has been restored and new, more accurate plantings are thriving.

Another Shipman design in the South that has been revitalized in recent years is the Moonlight Garden at the Edison & Ford Winter Estates in Fort Myers, Florida. Mina Edison (wife of Thomas Edison) commissioned the garden on the advice of her friend Clara Ford, who had hired Shipman for work at Fair Lane, the Fords' Dearborn, Michigan, estate. Designed in 1929, the plan of the Moonlight Garden resembles others by Shipman, with a central reflecting pool surrounded by turf and densely planted flower borders.

Moonlight Garden. Photo by Manfred Behr. Courtesy Edison & Ford Winter Estates, Fort Myers, Fla.

In 1947, Mina Edison deeded the property to the City of Fort Myers. By the early 2000s, however, it had seriously deteriorated as a consequence of high visitation and deferred maintenance and many of the original plants had disappeared. Shipman did not well understand the demands of Florida's climate, and her plant palette included many choices that proved unsuitable to the heat and humidity of the Gulf Coast, one of many circumstances that contributed to the landscape's decline.

As more information became available about Shipman's significance, thoughts turned to a restoration, and in 2002, the work began. The landscape architect Ellen Goetz of Naples, Florida, oversaw a restoration plan that made horticultural substitutions to replace some of the less successful species Shipman had recommended, although an emphasis on sweet-scented plants remained central to the plan. Today old roses and gardenias (in variety) add perfume to the secluded, predominantly blue-and-white scheme, which also features Queen's Wreath (*Petrea volubilis*). The Moonlight Garden has become a favorite spot for weddings and painting classes, and it also, of course, draws garden lovers.

In Durham, North Carolina, the Sarah P. Duke Gardens at Duke University also benefited from the publication of the biography. Commissioned by the university at the urging of Dr. Frederick M. Hanes, Shipman's imaginative design of 1936 featured curving stone terraces planted with a mix of Japanese cherries, crabs, shrubs, and perennials, the uppermost of which was crowned by a latticework structure draped in Chinese wisteria. Over

Sarah P. Duke Gardens, Durham, N.C. Wikimedia Commons.

time, the maintenance demands associated with the public space (one of the very few Shipman designed) led to a simplification of her plant palette and a widening of walkways. A series of interventions to bring the design back to its prime began in the late 1990s. In 2014, the original wisteria vine was removed from the gazebo—it had completely engulfed and severely damaged the structure—and a less aggressive, native variety planted in its place.

In 1928, Shipman designed a trim boxwood parterre garden for Eugene du Pont in Wilmington, Delaware, and this, too, was the site of successful, recent restoration by the current owners of the property, the Greenville Country Club. When the club acquired the property in 1961, the boxwood was so overgrown that it was impossible to walk down the paths. But the garden layout had never been altered, and the main features, including the teahouse and fountain, remained in place and intact. In 1979, a young groundskeeper discovered several of Shipman's garden plans in the garage, but it was not until 2005 that head gardener Leslie Bottaro was able to implement a full-scale restoration of the garden using Shipman's planting plans as well as

Owl's Nest, Eugene du Pont estate, Greenville, Del. Photo courtesy Archives of American Gardens/Smithsonian Institution.

Owl's Nest. Photo by Leslie Bottaro.

archival photographs. The overgrown boxwoods, which had been nursed along for decades, were removed and the stone paths relaid. The following year new compact boxwood (*Buxus* 'Green Velvet') was planted and shade plants installed under the original ornamental trees, some of which had grown to thirty feet. Flowering shrubs, including azaleas, summer sweet, and oak leaf hydrangea were planted outside the borders. Today the garden serves as an intimate, lush setting for outdoor social events.

The Midwest provided Shipman with a greater concentration of commissions than any other region in the country, so it is not surprising that some of the finest examples of Shipman's extant work can be found there. The Gertrude and F. A. Seiberling estate, Stan Hywet (now Stan Hywet Hall & Gardens), in Akron, Ohio, was, in fact, the site of one of the earliest restorations of a Shipman-designed garden. The enclosed English Garden had been designed c. 1911 by the landscape architect Warren H. Manning and the architect Charles S. Schneider, but, on Manning's recommendation, in 1928, Gertrude Seiberling engaged Ellen Shipman to redesign it to bold effect. After Stan Hywet became a public landscape in 1957, stewardship of the English Garden did not always reflect the spirit of original design intentions, and, as shade conditions deepened, groundcovers, impatiens, and hosta gradually replaced the jewel-toned colors of Shipman's unusually vibrant plantings.

Recovery work in the English Garden got under way in mid-1990s, just as research for the Shipman biography was turning up new information about her significance. Supported by the Akron Garden Club, the restoration was overseen by the landscape architects Christine and Gerald Doell and Stan Hywet president John Franklin Miller. The meticulous replanting of the garden beds (described in an afterword by Miller in the first edition) was guided by Shipman's original plans, accompanied by extensive tree thinning and repairs to infrastructure, including work on the garden's sculptural centerpiece, *Garden of the Water Goddess* by Willard Paddock.

There are cases where Shipman's gardens were never entirely lost, and private owners, some of whom had lavished decades of care on their land-

English Garden, Stan Hywet Hall & Gardens, Akron, Ohio. Photo by Carol Betsch.

Halfred Farms, Windsor T. White estate, Chagrin Falls, Ohio. Photo by Carol Betsch.

Halfred Farms. Photo by Carol Betsch.

scapes—unaware of Shipman's stature—became more knowledgeable as a result of the Shipman book. Clara M. Rankin, of Chagrin Falls, Ohio, surely counts as one of the most devoted and conscientious Shipman garden stewards. She spent long hours deliberating about how best to care for the enclosed garden that Shipman designed for the original clients, the Windsor Whites, in 1921. As the effects of time and weather took a toll on the elegant Chinese Chippendale architecture, Clara and her husband regularly repaired fences, gates, and the pool house. More perplexing was the question of whether to replace the great arborvitae that add vertical heft and structure to the beds. She continued to resist the urge to replace the great specimens with smaller trees that might be more in scale with the garden's proportions because the originals brought a sense of age and mystery into the garden. They stand there still, now cared for by new owners.

The formal garden of Gwinn has also received careful stewardship

Gwinn, Elizabeth and William G. Mather estate, Cleveland, Ohio. Photo by Carol Betsch.

Crab Tree Farm, William McCormick Blair estate, Lake Bluff, Ill. Photo by Judith B. Tankard.

through the years from family descendents of the original owners, William and Elizabeth Mather. Originally laid out in 1907 by Charles A. Platt, the Cleveland garden was redesigned by Shipman in 1935, who added Japanese cherries and tree lilacs to surround the central pool and vines on the loggia and teahouse. She also reconfigured the beds, adding pale pink and apricot tones to the original color palette of blue, yellow, and white. Shipman returned to Gwinn in 1940 to create a parterre of interlocking initials *W* and *E*, and again in 1946 to design new plantings for the beds in front of the loggia. Although some of these features proved too elaborate to maintain (the parterre, for example), the Ireland family kept alive the spirit of Shipman's plantings for many decades. New owners of Gwinn continue the tradition of stewardship.

On the North Shore of Chicago, Shipman's intimate dooryard garden at Crab Tree Farm, the former William McCormick Blair estate overlooking Lake Michigan, was sympathetically reinterpreted by Neville and John Bryan, who have lived there for decades. It retains the hallmarks of Shipman's design of the 1920s—a boxwood-edged parterre filled with seasonal flowers, a tiny pool with an ornamental tree arching overhead, and a small gate to ensure privacy. Shipman's garden complements both the handsome house by David Adler and the extensive, naturalistic landscape on the beautiful property, designed, in part, with advice from Warren Manning in 1928.

Fair Lane, Historic Ford Estates, Dearborn, Mich. Photo by Clare Pfeiffer.

Shipman's 1927 design for the formal garden at Fair Lane, the estate of Clara and Henry Ford in Dearborn, Michigan, has also been the subject of recent restoration efforts, and an extensive rehabilitation of the design is planned for the future. The initiative, under way in 2017, focuses on restoration of the elaborate teahouse and the central pool. Shipman-era plantings will also be reintroduced, to be blended with Clara Ford's original palette of roses.

An updating of Shipman's list of clients for the new edition yielded many surprises, including several significant commissions for the Knox family. Among these are Seymour Knox's estates in New York and South Carolina as well as an important commission for his sister, Marjorie Knox Campbell, in East Aurora, near Buffalo. When he purchased Orchard House in

Orchard House, Marjorie Knox Campbell estate, East Aurora, N.Y. Photo by Robin Karson.

the 1980s, James Prise found that the gardens Shipman had designed for Marjorie Knox and J. Hazard Campbell in 1931 had not been maintained. With the assistance of a team of stonemasons and a head gardener, Prise rebuilt the entire infrastructure, including the walls, paths, balustrades, and garden gates, keeping in mind the integrity of the original design. The estate has since been acquired by new owners who are no less committed to its stewardship.

Another discovery since the publication of the book was Shipman's collaboration with the architect Frank Lloyd Wright at Graycliff, Isabelle and Darwin Martin's lakeside summer retreat outside of Buffalo. In 1997, the Graycliff Conservancy was founded to rescue the derelict property, which had functioned for years as a religious retreat. In 1998, Graycliff was designated a New York State Landmark and is now managed under the auspices of the University of Buffalo. Thanks to generous funding, Graycliff was able to initiate a full-scale multiyear restoration. As part of a phased restoration, Heritage Landscapes was commissioned to prepare a cultural landscape report and treatment plan in 2008; an additional treatment plan was prepared by Pressley Associates in 2011.

While Wright's landscape rendering of 1928 concentrated mainly on the entrance water garden, Shipman's detailed plans of 1929–31 encompassed areas adjacent to the house as well as eight acres of grounds. Archival photos and family letters, however, revealed that the Martins had their own ideas about plant selection, so not all of Shipman's proposals were implemented. Wright's water garden, which Shipman later filled in with apple trees, was restored in 2012 to reflect Wright's original conception. In 2016, Shipman's borders in front of the house and the sunken garden adjacent to the sunroom were replanted following Shipman's detailed plans, although the plantings evolved from evergreens to beds of summer annuals (such as *Zinnia elegans*). Restoration of Shipman's plans for the cutting border off the entry drive is currently under way.

A particularly dramatic private restoration effort catalyzed by *The Gardens of Ellen Biddle Shipman* occurred in Middlebury, Connecticut, at Tranquillity Farm, a bucolic three-hundred-acre estate laid out for the J. H. Whittemore family by Charles Eliot, John Charles Olmsted, and Warren Manning in the late 1890s under the auspices of Olmsted, Olmsted & Eliot. In 1923, Ellen Shipman was commissioned to design a new garden for an area that sat below the massive stone retaining wall, with an arresting view to Lake Quassapaug. Shipman's characteristically detailed drawings recorded an almost impossibly long list of plants, but Whittemore's great-great-granddaughter, Thyrza Whittemore, became entranced with the idea of having a Shipmanesque garden of her own. For a parcel across the road, she created one from scratch, modeling a toolhouse/dovecote on

Tranquillity Farm, J. H. Whittemore estate, Middlebury, Conn. Photos by Carol Betsch.

prototypes she found in the 1996 book. Two decades later, inspired by her daughter's upcoming wedding, Whittemore took on the even more demanding project of renovating the original Shipman flower garden on the historic site. She followed the plans closely but allowed judicious plant substitutions when old varieties were impractical or impossible to locate. Jean and W. Scott Peterson, who own the well-preserved core of Tranquillity Farm, continue to care for these plantings and many others on the estate that date to its nineteenth-century origins.

A more liberal interpretation of Shipman's ebullient plantings has guided a striking revitalization of High Court, in Cornish, New Hampshire, Charles A. Platt's first private commission and the site of a Shipman design in 1914 for the second owners, Mary and A. Conger Goodyear. Shipman recalled that it was at High Court, looking over Platt's sunken garden of lilies bathed in moonlight, that she first realized that the garden was the most essential part of a home. She dated her decision to become a landscape designer to this moment. The enclosed garden's fountains, walls, and pavilion, as well

High Court, A. Conger Goodyear estate, Cornish, N.H. Photo by Carol Betsch.

High Court. Photo by Carol Betsch.

as the 1890 house (designed by Platt for the art patron Annie Lazarus), were thoroughly restored over several years, beginning in 1995, by the new owners. Plantings in the two long borders were simplified, and today *Hydrangea* 'Annabelle' convey the luxuriant fullness that is the hallmark of Shipman's planting approach.

Shipman's gardens for Evander B. Schley in Far Hills, New Jersey, were rescued and replanted in 2008 as the centerpiece for "Mansion in May," a local fundraiser of historic house tours. A team of landscape architects and contractors revitalized the gardens by following Shipman's original 1926 plans and historic photographs published in the Shipman book. Tile-capped whitewashed walls were rebuilt, the stonework repointed, and Moorish tiles reinstalled in the paved patios to set off Shipman's plantings.

In Milton, Massachusetts, Shipman's gardens for Mrs. Holden Mc-Ginley are in the early stages of restoration after decades of benign neglect under several previous owners. The once-majestic views to the Great Blue Hills that informed Shipman's design have been lost to development, and the original statuary has vanished, but the three garden terraces and pools

Froh Heim, Evander B. Schley estate, Far Hills, N.J. Photo by Judith B. Tankard.

Froh Heim. Photo by Judith B. Tankard.

Mrs. Holden McGinley estate, Milton, Mass. Photo by Thomas Wedell.

Saint-Gaudens National Historic Site, Cornish, N.H. Photo by Judith B. Tankard.

remain unaltered. The present owners made essential repairs to the low garden walls (with their sculptural niches) and other structures, and new trees, shrubs, and perennials have recently been planted.

Many of the sites of Shipman gardens are now on the National Register of Historic Places and local historic registers, and some have been designated regional landmarks. The National Park Service has become the steward of several, including the former Devore garden at Chatham Manor in Virginia, Marsh-Billings-Rockefeller National Historical Park in Woodstock, Vermont, and the Saint-Gaudens National Historic Site in Cornish, New Hampshire. All have gardens designed, in part, by Shipman, and some have been restored in large measure.

One of the most thorough restorations undertaken by the National Park Service is the small garden at the Longfellow House on Brattle Street in Cambridge, just steps from the Harvard campus. Originally designed in 1904 by Martha Brookes Hutcheson (who created the distinctive pergola and trellises), the gardens served as a private retreat for the Longfellow family. In 1925, Alice Longfellow asked Shipman to revitalize them for use by Radcliffe College students. The landscape architect retained Hutcheson's original layout and features but redesigned all the plantings. Over the years the gardens were simplified and lost their original essence.

In 2001, the National Park Service initiated a full-scale rehabilitation plan to restore and rebuild the architectural features and reinstall Ship-

Longfellow House, Cambridge, Mass. Photo courtesy National Park Service, Longfellow House National Historic Site.

man's plantings. Substitutions had to be found for the Shipman-era cultivars that had long since been lost, but efforts were made to retain their essential character. The present challenge, according to NPS gardener Mona McKindley, is addressing climate change issues such as drought, flooding, and insect infestations, all of which require plant substitutions for the original heirloom varieties. Thanks to a three-year capital campaign to provide funding for the rehabilitation, the garden now serves as a fitting setting for the historic house and a welcome oasis in a busy urban environment.

Shipman's gardens for the Devore family at Chatham Manor in Fredericksburg—now part of the expansive Fredericksburg and Spotsylvania National Military Park—may turn out to be the most extensive of all the recent restorations. Designed in 1921, at the height of Shipman's career, the gardens surrounding the house were characteristically labor intensive—beds of densely packed annuals in boxwood-edged configurations, as well as vine-

Chatham Manor, Col. Daniel B. Devore estate, Fredericksburg, Va. Photo by Frances Benjamin Johnston / Library of Congress.

draped pergolas. Recent efforts have been directed to stabilizing the outlines of her design. A new cultural landscape report provides the first important step in bringing back Shipman's renowned gardens for the future.

❧

In many cases, "Friends" groups have helped spearhead restoration projects at these sites. Thanks to newly formed local organizations such as the Tregaron Conservancy, Shipman's only surviving wild garden at the former Parmelee estate in Washington, D.C., is now undergoing restoration. Long overgrown with invasive plants and disfigured by graffiti-scarred stone bridges, Shipman's garden is taking on a new life. The Conservancy has planted new trees and underwritten a multiyear meadow project to establish a new habitat for native plant communities. Under the direction of the preservation landscape architect Glenn Stach, the extensive naturalistic woodlands, including bridle paths and a pond, are undergoing thoughtful renewal. Shipman's detailed plant list of 1919 has been cautiously measured against species that are currently considered invasive. When the restoration is complete, Tregaron Estate, which is listed on the National Register of Historic Places, will be a national treasure.

In the course of my travels I have also found many slumbering Ship-

Tregaron Estate, Washington, D.C. Photo by Kristin Dill / Tregaron Conservancy.

man gardens that still retain their distinctive architectural features. These include Hamilton Farms, the James Cox Brady estate in Gladstone, New Jersey; the Samuel Salvage estate on Long Island with its dovecote-inspired toolhouses; the Ralph Hanes garden (now the university president's home, Wake Forest University) in Winston-Salem, North Carolina, which features the same diminutive toolhouses; and Cave Hill, the De Waal estate in Lexington, Kentucky, with the original pool house and network of radiating brick paths. In other cases, the architectural outlines of Shipman's original gardens, such as those of the Superintendent's Garden at the U.S. Military Academy at West Point, are still visible and ripe for preservation treatment.

In 2010, the landscape architect Janice Parker contacted me about a garden in Ridgefield, Connecticut, for Mrs. Alonzo Barton Hepburn (the wife of the chairman of Chase National Bank of New York) that she had been asked to restore. In the absence of any documents at Cornell, Parker sought out local historical societies for information. The property, known as Altracraig ("high ridge"), was in a degraded condition and the house had burned in 1994, but many of the original garden features remained, including a pool pavilion and a dolphin fountain. The plantings had disappeared, with the exception of several original magnolias. Working with a postcard view and other resources, Parker was able to successfully reconstruct Shipman's design.

For every Shipman garden that has survived, however, many others have

Tregaron Estate. Photo by Lynn Parseghian / Tregaron Conservancy.

Ralph P. and DeWitt Hanes estate, Winston-Salem, N.C. Photo by Judith B. Tankard.

Altracraig, Mrs. Alonzo B. Hepburn estate, Ridgefield, Conn. Photo by Neil Landino, courtesy Janice Parker.

been swallowed up by institutions, destroyed by new additions to buildings, obliterated by the work of subsequent designers, or simply razed to the ground. Rose Terrace, for example, the majestic Anna Thompson Dodge estate in Grosse Pointe, Michigan, was torn down in the 1980s to make way for a new housing development. Countless suburban gardens have been replaced by new houses or with simpler, contemporary designs, while others have simply vanished without a trace. Most of Shipman's early gardens on Long Island, where development has been especially intense, such as the Pruyn garden, have long since disappeared.

❧

Research on Shipman's gardens has been enriched by numerous scholarly publications, articles, and seminars in recent years. *A Genius for Place: American Landscapes of the Country Place Era* by Robin Karson (2007) includes a chapter on Shipman's life and work which contextualizes her contributions to the field in relation to her female cohorts, particularly Beatrix Farrand and Marian Coffin. My publications on women landscape architects, including *Beatrix Farrand: Private Gardens, Public Landscapes* (2009), have also helped to shed light on the challenges women faced in the early years of the profession. Cynthia Zaitzevsky's *Long Island Landscapes and the Women Who Designed Them* (2009) and Thaisa Way's *Unbounded Practice: Women and Landscape Architecture in the Early Twentieth Century* (2009), among others, have expanded our knowledge of the subject as well. Some of the women who worked in Shipman's New York office, such as Eleanor Roche, have been the subject of new inquiries. Gaiety Hollow, the Oregon home and garden of Edith Schryver, who worked in Shipman's office in the 1920s and later opened the first West Coast firm of women landscape architects, has been preserved and managed by the Lord & Schryver Conservancy.

In addition, the digitizing of period slides and photographs by the Library of Congress, Smithsonian Institution, and other collections offers accessible visual testimony of Shipman's gardens in their heyday. The Archives of American Gardens, an initiative of the Garden Club of America, comprises thousands of glass lantern slides that in some cases provide the only record of long-vanished projects. The collection (now held at the Smithsonian) includes more than sixty photographs of Shipman gardens. Among them are several images of Bonaire, Mrs. Robert A. Franks's garden in Llewellyn Park, New Jersey, with its dazzling color borders. Other images record Mrs. Edward D. Shumway's garden in Lake Forest, Illinois, Mrs. John S. Newberry's garden in Grosse Pointe, and Shipman's own garden at Brook Place, in Plainfield, New Hampshire. The Library of Congress's extraordinary collection of hand-colored lantern slides by Frances Benjamin Johnston includes a dozen depicting Chatham Manor at its peak. Sam Watters's *Gardens for a*

Beautiful America, 1895–1935: Photographs by Frances Benjamin Johnston (2012) reveals the scope and extent of this important resource.

Shipman's town house on Beekman Place in New York City recently sold for $35 million—an amount that would have astonished her—arguably a striking measure of her renown. Described in the real estate offering as the "Shipman house," the elegant residence put Beekman Place on the map as a fashionable destination for wealthy city dwellers. She would also be pleased to know that her beloved Brook Place in Plainfield, New Hampshire, is still intact as well, cared for privately and enjoyed to this day.

Chatham Manor. Photo by Frances Benjamin Johnston / Library of Congress.

Mrs. Edward D. Shumway garden, Lake Forest, Ill. Photo courtesy Archives of American Gardens / Smithsonian Institution.

The growing interest in American garden history and the preservation movement has enhanced our understanding of many long-lost gardens. The Library of American Landscape History, The Garden Conservancy, The Cultural Landscape Foundation, the Foundation for Landscape Studies, the National Association of Olmsted Parks, and numerous regional and local organizations have helped give visibility to historic landscapes through lectures, tours, oral histories, and exhibitions, and these, in turn, have inspired the preservation and revitalization of significant gardens and parks. *The Gardens of Ellen Biddle Shipman* provided the foundational knowledge that supported more than two decades of research and preservation activity. The new edition of this landmark publication will undoubtedly spur new rounds of interest and, we hope, new preservation initiatives throughout America.

Ellen Shipman in the garden at Poins House, Plainfield, N.H. Streeter collection.

ONE

EARLY YEARS

Warren H. Manning considered her "one of the best, if not the very best, Flower Garden Maker in America." In 1933, *House & Garden* hailed her as the "dean of American women landscape architects." *House Beautiful* regularly featured her projects in their column "Gardens in Good Taste." A 1950 obituary in the *New York Times* identified her as "one of the leading landscape architects of the United States."[1] At the peak of her career, Ellen Shipman worked on projects as far-flung as Long Island's Gold Coast and Seattle, York Harbor, Maine, and New Orleans. Her clients included Fords, Astors, Edisons, du Ponts, and Seiberlings, captains of industry, financial leaders, and patrons of the arts. At her death, she had completed more than six hundred projects.[2]

After a period of informal apprenticeship with the architect Charles A. Platt, Ellen Shipman established her own practice. Throughout her career, she continued to work both independently and in collaboration with Platt and other prominent architects and landscape architects. Shipman designed plantings that "softened" the architectural "bones" laid out by her partners, but in many circumstances her artistic achievements were considerably more extensive. In the hundreds of gardens for which she designed both plantings and architectural elements, Shipman arrived at her own distinctive style. In her solo work her imagination found freer, arguably more vital expression.

Domesticity, intimacy, and sensual seclusion characterized the best of Ellen Shipman's landscape designs, distinguishing them from the grander, self-consciously European schemes many of her colleagues created. Shipman's own experiments with large-scale European-influenced estate design generally do not figure among her most memorable work. Her more original aesthetic derived from the simplicity of traditional Colonial Revival spatial layout, the convention of the outdoor room, an artist's approach to planting, and a sense of the garden as a lush, green, and—above all—private world. Her debt to the British designer Gertrude Jekyll is unmistakable, but Shipman's gardens were American in their robust, spirited inventiveness.

Shipman's career was propelled by the same booming economy that kept her colleagues busy with prominent, large-scale jobs. And like her colleagues, she was well aware of the fundamental task at hand: to create settings for her wealthy clients' social lives which evoked a sense of high culture and privilege. But Shipman was first and foremost a gardener, and it was from personal experience that she approached landscape design. "The renaissance of the art," she once wrote, "was due largely to the fact that women, instead of working over their boards, used plants as if they were painting pictures and as an artist would."[3]

Shipman wanted all homeowners to experience the excitement of gardening firsthand and lectured widely on topics ranging from maintenance to planting design. Late in her career, she wrote a gardening book that was intended for a middle-class audience, but postwar shifts in taste and homeowners' attitudes precluded its publication. Shipman's view of gardening was emphatically democratic, as one passage in her preface eloquently expresses: "Gardening opens a wider door than any other of the arts—all mankind can walk through, rich or poor, high or low, talented and untalented. It has no distinctions, all are welcome."[4]

Shipman was also an active advocate for women in the profession. For over thirty-five years she ran an all-women office where she trained many successful designers. She also served as an adviser to the Lowthorpe School of Landscape Architecture and Horticulture for Women in Groton, Massachusetts, and frequently in her lectures and in interviews emphasized the role of women in the profession. She believed that women were crucial to the gardening revival that enlivened the century's early years. "Before women took hold of the profession," she wrote, "landscape architects were doing what I call cemetery work. . . . Until women took up landscaping, gardening in this country was at its lowest ebb."[5]

Shipman viewed home and garden as an almost hallowed sanctuary, perhaps as a result of her own geographically dislocated childhood. Vivid recollections reveal an image of the garden as the very essence of domesticity. "Our memory of our childhood home is not the architecture of the house, but the fragrance of the lilac, lily of the valley, jasmine, or the blooming of the rose," she later noted. About one such early moment at her grandparents' house, she reminisced: "Looking through a high white washed paling fence, I saw a white lilac in bloom with rose, tulips and forget-me-nots at its feet.

The picture remains with me still and I only have to call it to mind to feel again the thrill of that May morning."[6] The impression left by the image would inspire her to create a lifetime of such garden pictures for her clients.

The apparent contradiction inherent in this formative garden scene—at once unassuming and "thrilling"—reflects paradoxes in Shipman herself. She was, on the one hand, a down-to-earth, at times even deferent designer, eager to satisfy her clients' most specific horticultural requests and to create gardens that blended seamlessly with the landscape beyond. She accepted tightly constrained commissions that most of her colleagues would have refused, jobs that were limited to planting only or to borders within larger landscapes by other landscape architects. But Shipman's bearing was commanding, her presence determined, charismatic, even regal, according to some clients. Handsome, articulate, and deeply confident of her own design capabilities, she ran one of the most successful practices in New York City. Despite Shipman's reputation and the exactitude of her design schemes, however, most of her gardens proved ephemeral. That their character derived so specifically from horticultural rather than architectural determinants made them especially vulnerable to the ravages of time, disease, and changing tastes. Shipman watched most of her designs disappear within years of their implementation.

As a divorced, working mother at a time in history when societal support for neither circumstance existed, Ellen Shipman faced a set of extraordinarily difficult challenges. And as her career gained momentum, professional aspirations forced a series of decisions that jeopardized the very domestic pleasures her gardens so idyllically expressed. She triumphed against great odds to make beautiful gardens, but that success did not come without its personal price.

⟿

Ellen McGowan Biddle was born on November 5, 1869, in Philadelphia, the daughter of Ellen Fish McGowan Biddle from Elizabeth, New Jersey, and Colonel James Biddle, a career soldier from the Philadelphia branch of the family, a large and powerful clan who counted among their houseguests the Prince of Wales.[7] Ellen's parents and two brothers were living at a military outpost in Brenham, Texas, when Mrs. Biddle returned east to give birth to her daughter. Despite an early bout of enteric fever, the baby thrived, and mother and daughter soon rejoined the rest of the family.

Ellen's adventurous childhood was spent at frontier outposts in Nevada, Colorado, and the Arizona Territory, where she rode horses and played with children in the local tribes. Mrs. Biddle remembered her daughter during these years as "happy as a bird."[8] On family expeditions through canyons and valleys, the family camped in the desert, where Ellen saw mesquite and

Ellen McGowan Biddle and Colonel James Biddle. From
Reminiscences of a Soldier's Wife (Philadelphia, 1907).

acacia trees of commanding size and cactus of every description. Buffalo
and antelope grazed western plains flooded by crimson sunsets, while sud-
den storms and plagues of grasshoppers offered reminders of nature's ca-
priciousness. Vegetation on the desert edge was especially precious. Ellen
remembered "the excitement of seeing water that my father had ordered
brought for miles to a Nevada post . . . to feed the trees he had planted along
the driveways—the only trees in our vicinity."[9]

Not all Shipman's early memories were of wilderness, however. She also
reveled in the glitter of military balls and festive dinners during the Colonel's
leaves in San Francisco and, when an uprising of the local tribe threatened
the family's safety, she went east with her mother and brothers for an extended visit with her grandparents. As the train approached the McGowans'
New Jersey farm, four-year-old Nelly pointed out the window to the "beautiful stones growing out there." She had never seen grave markers before and

assumed they had sprouted in the grass.[10] Her children's excitement at seeing cultivated fruit and real gardens for the first time delighted Mrs. Biddle.

The family was reunited on the frontier once tensions were quelled. At the age of six, when her older brothers were sent to school in Connecticut, Ellen was left to amuse herself in Fort Whipple, Arizona Territory. Ellen's mother noted that her daughter "was quite tall for her age, rode well, and was perfectly fearless, also hearty and strong, owing to the outdoor life in that wonderful climate."[11] Four years later, she too was dispatched east for school, as her parents felt she should find companionship of girls her own age. She went reluctantly.

Life in New Jersey offered lasting though comparatively tame pleasures and a more traditional social environment. Ellen's grandmother was "a lover of flowers, plants and shrubs, and of working among them." Shipman later recalled the joy of "finding a real garden" at her grandparents', where "it was impossible not to pick flowers and to break fast rules—a rose to hold all the way to school seemed well worth the punishment." She credited both her father and her grandparents for instilling in her "a great love of growing things."[12] The contrast between the starkness of the West and the green fertility of New Jersey made a strong impression on the young girl. While her earliest memories were set against the backdrop of mountains and desert, her first sense of a "garden" came from trips east, where cultivated flowers and white picket fences must have seemed almost toylike in comparison to the grandeur of the West. Throughout her career, Shipman retained a notion of the garden as artifice and haven, an embellishment, rather than an abstraction of nature.

During her teenage years, Ellen was sent to finishing school at Miss Sarah Randolph's in Baltimore, where her strong artistic gifts emerged and were celebrated. After finding the margins of Ellen's school notebooks "full of house plans and garden plans of all descriptions," Miss Randolph gave her an architectural dictionary. Shipman later remembered the importance of the gesture. Miss Randolph had seen her talent years before she recognized it herself.[13]

In 1887, when Ellen was eighteen, her parents moved to Washington, D.C., where Colonel Biddle was reassigned to the War Department. Mrs. Biddle's reminiscences offer little information about this period, other than noting that her daughter had "tasted to the full during the two years in Washington all that a society life could give her."[14] How she spent the intervening years is unknown, but by the early 1890s Ellen was living in Cambridge, Massachusetts, in a rented house with a group of women friends, an unconventional arrangement that would likely have been discouraged in more conservative Baltimore. Among these friends were Mary Lucy Wilkins Rogers, Louise Emory, and Marian Nichols, who later provided important

Ellen Biddle in Boston, c. 1890. Photo by Marshall. Streeter collection.

connections for Shipman's subsequent career as a landscape architect. (Marian's older sister, Rose Standish Nichols, was to become a well-known landscape architect and writer; Margaret Nichols, Marian's youngest sister, would marry the landscape architect Arthur Shurcliff, whose professional path would intersect with Shipman's.)[15]

Only one record of Ellen's 1892–93 enrollment at Radcliffe, then known as Harvard Annex, survives to document a rather undistinguished and short-lived academic career.[16] Family lore suggests that she may have been involved in suffrage activities during this time.[17] Perhaps she was distracted from her studies by her housemate Mary Rogers's cousin, Louis Evan Shipman.[18] Louis was charming and lively with literary aspirations, the son of a New York City contractor, descended from a well-established upstate New York family.[19] He had attended Brooklyn Polytechnic Institute before his only recorded term at Harvard. Like Ellen, he was twenty-three when he enrolled as a special student; also like Ellen, he withdrew after one year, in 1893.[20] The unlikely couple were married that October at Ellen's parents' new home in Berkeley Springs, West Virginia.[21] Soon after, the newlyweds moved to Connecticut, where Ellen gave birth the following August to a daughter, named Ellen Biddle Shipman.

Ellen and Louis Shipman at Poins House, Plainfield, N.H. Streeter collection.

TWO

LIFE IN THE
CORNISH COLONY

In the summer of 1894, Ellen and Louis visited Cornish, New Hampshire, a small village nestled in the mountains cradling the Connecticut River Valley.[1] Augustus Saint-Gaudens, uncle of Ellen's former housemate Marian Nichols, had discovered the village in 1885 and found its rural beauty irresistible. Imagining that it would be an ideal setting for his summer home and studio, he bought and "classicized" an old farmhouse there. Other artists soon followed, most of them fleeing the summer heat of New York City, where their artistic lives centered. Charles Platt came in 1889, and Thomas Dewing and his wife, the painter Maria Oakey Dewing, arrived in 1890; in 1893, Platt's friend Stephen Parrish, the Philadelphia painter and etcher, moved to the village community. The artists were followed by the literary glitterati and, over the years, by more ordinary folk.[2]

Ellen Shipman vividly remembered her first night in Cornish, during which she had attended a party at High Court, the home of the art patron Annie Lazarus, designed in 1890 by Charles Platt. "The valley was still filled with rolling clouds . . . in the distance was Ascutney Mountain, . . . [and] just a few feet below, where we stood upon a terrace, was a Sunken Garden with rows bathed in moonlight of white lilies standing as an altar for Ascutney. As I look back I realize it was at that moment that a garden became for me the most essential part of a home. But," she added, "years of work had to intervene before I could put this belief, born that glorious night, into actual practice."[3]

For Ellen and Louis, then a promising playwright, life in an artists' colony offered freedom and stimulating exchange with other creative souls.

Their social life among the close-knit group of painters, sculptors, illustrators, writers, and musicians revolved around dinner parties and amusements such as charades, there being little in the way of formal entertainment in the New Hampshire countryside. They particularly enjoyed masques, allegorical dramatic performances with costumed actors that provided opportunities for collaboration and high-spirited expression. The most memorable of these was *A Masque of "Ours," The Gods and the Golden Bowl,* put on in 1905 in the pine grove below Saint-Gaudens's home, Aspet. Ellen Shipman played the part of Minerva, goddess of the arts and wisdom.[4]

But business took precedence over play in Cornish. Social calls were not encouraged before four o'clock, when the day's labors were complete. The only exceptions were "visits of state," when one artist invited another over for a critique or consultation. As one journalist observed in 1907, the atmosphere in Cornish was "one of culture and hard work."[5]

During their first two years there, the Shipmans shared a farmhouse with the writer and editor Herbert Croly, and his wife, Louise. They then moved to nearby Plainfield, where they rented an old brick tavern, which they named Poins House after a character in one of Louis's stories (revenue from which apparently paid the rent). Ellen made their attachment to the artists' colony obvious by playfully marking her calling cards "Geographically in Plainfield, Socially in Cornish."[6] "No one else thought of trying to live in [the house]," recalled one neighbor, "but the Shipmans, with their instinct for what could be made charming, saw its possibilities." Ellen had a knack for finding old furniture to outfit "rooms that seemed made for it."[7] She also created her first real garden there, a simple New England country garden with a dirt path lined with borders of traditional summer flowers. She later lamented that she never again had "such marvelous annuals." The ebullient borders set an informal, regional tone that was echoed in the low stone wall separating the garden from the road. The early, Colonial Revival design found a permanent place in Shipman's imagination and served as a prototype for many later projects.[8]

Much of the artistic energy in Cornish was devoted to horticulture, resulting in extraordinary gardens that affected not only Ellen Shipman but American garden design as a whole. She was well aware of the significance of what one critic identified as "the most beautifully gardened village in all America."[9] "Here," Shipman later wrote, "was the renaissance of gardening in America, the first effort in this country to return to early traditional gardening." She applauded the changes from a Victorian approach whose stiff artificiality grated against her deepest aesthetic impulses: "The intricacy of the forms of beds, lying out in the lawn, was the predominant feature. These beds were filled with brilliantly colored small annuals—perennials and shrubs played no part. Frequently broken glass and colored pebbles were used to simulate flowers, as the flowers themselves could not be held permanently low enough to show the distorted designs. Privacy, imagination, and beauty had fled. This era of gardening almost, but not quite, killed the love of gardens."[10]

While many Cornish gardener-artists "hardly knew the commonest flowers by name," they were nevertheless thoroughly conversant with the principles of design—and their gardens showed it, attracting national attention as "livable, lovable spots, on very intimate terms with their owners."[11] The charm of these gardens lay in their unpretentious individuality, close visual and spatial ties to local vernacular architecture, and careful, sometimes passionate, maintenance. "One night when a number of us were dining with Maxfield Parrish," Shipman later remembered, "the talk had been so continually upon plants and diseases that he rose, put his hands on the table, and leaned over, said in a deep voice, 'Let us spray.'"[12]

Cornish artists had their English counterparts in Broadway, a picturesque village in the Cotswolds, made famous in the United States by Edwin Austin Abbey and other American illustrators for *Harper's Magazine*.[13] As in Cornish, many of the best Broadway gardens were designed by the artists who lived there, including several by Alfred Parsons, who portrayed them in paintings of winding walks, country cottages, and beds of old roses, hollyhocks, poppies, phlox, and other hardy plants growing in elegant, haphazard profusion.[14]

At the turn of the century the rediscovery of hardy plants for American gardens was chronicled in many popular books, including *A Woman's Hardy Garden* by Helena Rutherfurd Ely and Alice Morse Earle's *Old Time Gardens*.[15] Old-fashioned gardens flourished throughout the northeastern United States, from summer communities on Nantucket and in Easthampton, Long Island, to artists' colonies such as that at Old Lyme, Connecticut. Some were immortalized in paintings by resident artists, such as Maria Oakey Dewing, Stephen Parrish, and Edith Prellwitz in Cornish, and Childe Hassam, who painted gardens on Long Island and in Gloucester, Massachusetts. The quintessential old-fashioned flower garden was the tiny one created by the poet Celia Thaxter on Appledore, in the Isles of Shoals off the coast of Maine, made famous by Hassam's paintings and Thaxter's book, *An Island Garden*, published in 1894, just as Ellen Shipman arrived at Cornish.

The Cornish version of the "grandmother's garden" helped shape Ellen Shipman's aesthetic, while the highly sophisticated artists, architects, and critics she came to know there exposed her to the design techniques she needed to create it. Of these, the multitalented Charles Platt exerted the most significant influence, but there were others, too, including Rose Standish Nichols, whose several books on travel and garden design remain classics;

Herbert Croly, who became editor of the influential magazine *Architectural Record* and founder of *The New Republic;* the painter Stephen Parrish; and his son Maxfield Parrish, who illustrated Edith Wharton's book *Italian Villas and Their Gardens.*[16] Shipman also learned how to garden from her Cornish friends; Thomas Dewing's, Stephen Parrish's, and other Cornishites' experiments with new varieties of hardy plants were avidly discussed by all.

Of the many gardens that were undoubtedly important in Shipman's development, two in particular stand out. Aspet, the summer home and studio of Augustus Saint-Gaudens, combined a classicizing renovation of a New England farmhouse with several formal gardens. Their strict axial geometry and lush plantings sounded two themes that later appeared in Shipman's own designs. Long after Saint-Gaudens's death, when Shipman had become a highly successful designer, she was commissioned by the Saint-Gaudens Memorial to create a planting plan for the terrace gardens at Aspet.[17]

Shipman would also have known Northcote, Stephen Parrish's eighteen-acre estate sited on a steep Cornish hillside. Parrish had begun the garden in 1893 at the same time that he commissioned the residence from Wilson Eyre and just as the Shipmans were settling in the valley. "And such a

Edith Prellwitz, *Saint-Gaudens Garden*, oil on canvas, 1898. Saint-Gaudens National Historic Site.

ELLEN SHIPMAN AND THE AMERICAN GARDEN

Augusta Saint-Gaudens in the garden at Aspet, July 1906. Saint-Gaudens National Historic Site.

garden!" one critic exclaimed. "Landscape painter for the fun of it, Stephen Parrish is a gardener for the love of it."[18] The horticultural elements of Parrish's rigorously studied design were subject to continual improvement and change, but the formal layout near the house, carefully framed views, and paths that meandered through the outlying shrubbery gave the garden its permanent structure. A garden enclosed on three sides by the vine-covered walls of the house was devoted to old-fashioned flowers, with raised beds featuring hardy roses, peonies, hollyhocks, and sweet william, interspersed with drifts of annuals. A blend of traditional and innovative elements made Parrish's garden one of the most memorable of the era.

The Shipmans were part of the small group of "chickadees" who lived year-round in Cornish. Henry and Lucia Fuller, Stephen Parrish, his niece Anne Parrish and son, Maxfield, and, later, the Saint-Gaudenses shared in the more intimate, more "truly Cornish" spirit that characterized the colony then. During long winter evenings, the release from gardening duties

Stephen Parrish, *Northcote, Cornish, N.H.*, oil on canvas. Private collection.

gave rise to active socializing. Frances Grimes, a sculptor who worked with Saint-Gaudens, remembered the Shipmans at one of many dinner parties they hosted: Louis, "the picture of hospitality . . . rotund, beaming, with set phrases of greeting which could be anticipated. Ellen had a trace of southern manner; there was a sparkle in the gleam on her face which made her smile peculiarly hers. Nothing else was ever in their minds but your arrival." In October 1903 the couple celebrated their tenth anniversary at a surprise party planned by their friends, who came in costume with hand-made gifts.[19]

Louis's career took a promising turn when his play *D'Arcy of the Guards* opened to critical acclaim in San Francisco in 1901.[20] The saga of the dramatization was the subject of one of his best books, *The Adventures of a Play*. Despite their richly creative life and the idyllic setting, however, problems began to surface in the Shipmans' household. The apparent root of these difficulties was financial—though he was enjoying critical success, Louis was not making much money as a writer. That Louis's life was increasingly centered in the literary world of New York while Ellen's interests were focused in the country may also have been a source of conflict. As Ellen grew closer to her Cornish neighbors, Louis alienated many, particularly those who did not know him well. Margaret Nichols Shurcliff's vivid memory of Louis during a tennis game captured the writer's intensity and self-absorption: a "fat roly-poly author and playwright . . . dripping with perspiration . . . and pouring forth a continuous line of boasting and teasing." His "absurdity is his safety," another friend recalled, adding, somewhat ominously, "he is one that would bludgeon a lily before breakfast and be proud of it all day." Yet another pegged Louis as "the warmest and most deleterious of friends, the bitterest and most innocuous of enemies."[21] Rumors of Louis's wandering eye began to circulate.

Anne Parrish in the garden at Northcote. Photo by by Stephen Parrish, 1898. Saint-Gaudens National Historic Site.

Louis Shipman near the tennis court, Brook Place. Streeter collection.

His absences from home became more frequent. Within a few years, the marriage deteriorated beyond repair.

While running the household increasingly on her own, Ellen continued to garden and to dream about "innumerable houses for desirable and unprocurable sites." She undoubtedly was encouraged by an event that had taken place in 1899, when she and Louis were spending the winter in the home of Charles and Eleanor Platt while awaiting the completion of renovation work at Poins House. On returning from their yearly seasonal move to New York, Platt discovered some house plans Shipman had inadvertently left behind on the drawing board in his studio. He wrote her a note saying, "If you can do as well as I saw, you better keep on," and made her a gift of a drawing board, T square, and drafting implements.[22]

None of Shipman's plans for "dream houses and dream gardens" was realized until she and Louis purchased the John Gilkey farm in Plainfield, around 1903. The late-eighteenth-century homestead on Meriden Stage Road consisted of a cottage and a barn and was bordered by a mill brook that gave the property its name, Brook Place. The couple planned to remodel the farmhouse, located near the road, and live there until a new house was built farther back on the property to overlook Mt. Ascutney, but the Panic of 1907 killed the "grandiose idea," and instead, Ellen concentrated on a renovation that nearly doubled the modest size of the existing house.[23] Her plans were realized through Platt's office, but there is no evidence that Platt himself had any design involvement.[24]

The emotional significance of the project for Shipman was recorded in her unpublished Garden Note Book: "If you are planning to build a home, you are embarked on man's greatest achievement—it is for its protection that wars are fought; and for its beautification that other arts have been developed. It was the building of a home, one stone upon another, and the cultivation of the surrounding land that differentiated man from beast more than any other one thing. . . . Do not take this great experience casually—give it all the consideration such a momentous undertaking should receive."[25]

Shipman's orchestration of the architecture, interiors, and layout of the grounds at Brook Place—which eventually comprised about two hundred acres—bore the mark of the refined, imaginative sensibility that friends and clients would soon seek out for their own properties. A substantial addition transformed the modest farmhouse into a special dwelling with unusual charm. She added a large picture window with 120 curved panes

Entrance hall, Brook Place. Photo by Mattie Edwards Hewitt, 1923. Streeter collection.

of glass imported from England and paneling salvaged from a Vermont church. In the library a secret door led to Louis's private study overlooking the tiny brook, horse pastures, and hills beyond. In front of the house stretched a wide tree-lined lawn and, secluded from view, a tennis court. To the side of the house, beyond the pergola-shaded veranda, was Ellen's garden.

In her garden, Shipman refined and formalized the simple concepts she had explored at Poins House. It was the landscape's "charm, seclusion, and informality" that caught the eye of one writer, who observed that it harmonized "entirely with the dwelling."[26] Photographs by Mattie Edwards Hewitt taken in 1923 reveal the property at the peak of its development, but likely the plan began simply and evolved slowly in accordance with its maker's maturing tastes and her budget.[27] The garden functioned both as a setting for outdoor family life and as a learning laboratory for Shipman. "Working daily in my garden for fifteen years," she later wrote, ". . . taught me to know plants, their habits and their needs."[28]

Many Cornish gardens were featured in both the local and national press in those early years, but Shipman's was rarely among them. One mention in 1906 was confined to a notice of the "fragrant flowers of our grandmother's

Pergola overlooking the garden, Brook Place. Photo by Mattie Edwards Hewitt, 1923. Saint-Gaudens National Historic Site.

day" growing alongside the front path. The gardens most often singled out for praise were those more architecturally determined—the Dewings', Stephen Parrish's, Maxfield Parrish's, Saint-Gaudens's, and Annie Lazarus's High Court by Charles Platt.[29]

Platt was a landscape painter when he first arrived in Cornish as a summer resident in 1889, seeking solace after the tragic death of his young wife and their newborn twins. His first ideas about architecture were sparked by a trip to Italy in 1892 with his brother, William, a landscape architect and apprentice to Frederick Law Olmsted, who warned William to ignore the "fine and costly gardens of Italy" in favor of the roadside scenery.[30] Nonetheless, the brothers visited several villas and gardens, which Platt recorded in a brief text and haunting black-and-white photographs. These were first published as a series of articles, then, in 1894, as a book, *Italian Gardens*. The strong resemblance of the Cornish hills to the Tuscan landscape explains

Thomas W. Dewing, *Portrait of Charles A. Platt,* oil on canvas, 1893. Private collection.

Flower garden at Villa Pamphili, 1894. From Charles A. Platt, *Italian Gardens* (New York, 1993).

in part the colony's attraction for Platt.[31] But, from the beginning, Platt's intention was not to reproduce what he had seen in Italy but to adapt its spirit to an American context. As Royal Cortissoz noted in his introduction to his 1913 monograph on Platt: "A really typical Platt design has nothing alien about it. The old Italian idea is so tactfully and with such sincerity adjusted to local conditions that the completed work becomes part and parcel of a veritable characteristic American home."[32] Others, also convinced of the originality of Platt's designs, championed his work. Among these influential writers was the Shipmans' neighbor Herbert Croly, for whom Platt would also design a home.

Platt's first professional Cornish commission was a house for Annie Lazarus, whose garden so inspired Shipman on her first visit.[33] No doubt

Charles A. Platt, *Larkspur (Garden at High Court, Cornish)*, oil on canvas, c. 1895. Private collection.

Platt's training as a landscape painter helped him to visualize and control the all-important views, especially the one to Mt. Ascutney, which he hid behind walls of hemlock until the visitor reached the rear courtyard. Terraces contained the sloping site, and a modest flower garden was located near the house. As at many Cornish houses, a grapevine-draped loggia was positioned for greatest enjoyment of the view to the mountains.

Over the years Platt also created houses for Herbert Adams, Winston Churchill (the novelist), Mary Banks Smoot, and other Cornishites. In 1890 he began his own simple clapboard house and studio, just below High Court, nestled in the Cornish hills and overlooking the Connecticut River Valley. On his return from Italy in 1892, he added a loggia and gardens to enhance the visual connection with the landscape. Platt's integration of house and garden set the tone for a Cornish-based style that merged Italian concepts with vernacular form.

Platt's first commission outside Cornish, landed in 1897, was in Brookline, Massachusetts, where he designed a large walled garden at Faulkner Farm for Charles and Mary Sprague. In addition to classical garden architecture—a pergola, a casino with flanking curved loggias, columns, and ornament—Platt introduced a flower garden, with overflowing beds of lilies, poppies, and phlox. A still grander commission for Platt followed in 1900 at The Weld, the home of Larz and Isabel Anderson. Though only one of several gardens on the large estate, the "Italian" garden was the most dramatic. A contemporary critic, Wilhelm Miller—the influential gardening editor of *Country Life in America*—quickly sensed the importance of Platt's achievement. To Miller's eye, Platt's garden was distinguished from other "Italianized" examples by the dominance, rather than the "merest incident," of flowers.[34]

The two-tiered arrangement of beds flanking the grassy central mall in the walled garden contained more than 17,000 square feet of bloom, providing continuous color from March to October. The combination of bold architectural framework and waves of flowers proved very photogenic and vaulted Platt to national prominence.[35] From then on, all his residential landscapes would feature lush, floriferous gardens. That his own talents did not include planting design scarcely mattered; he would collaborate with specialists—such as Ellen Shipman—to oversee this aspect of a project.

Like Platt, Shipman brought to her art a lively interest in gardening and architecture and a self-nurtured creative vision. And like Platt, her timing was fortuitous. Wealthy Americans throughout the country were seeking designers for their new homes and gardens. And landscape architecture was one of the few professions open to women. Women had recently gained access to new training programs. The first of these was the Lowthorpe School of Landscape Architecture for Women founded in 1901. Nine years later, the Pennsylvania School of Horticulture for Women at Ambler opened. The Cambridge School of Architecture and Landscape Architecture for Women was founded in 1916. But Shipman benefited from none of these or from grand tours of Europe. In addition to her constrained finances, Shipman was a wife and mother, unlike most women in the profession. Her Cornish neighbor Rose Nichols was more typical of those who pursued careers in landscape design in that she had the money and freedom to secure a formal education and travel as she wished. After studying drawing with Platt and other architects and visiting Europe, Nichols was admitted as a special student to the Massachusetts Institute of Technology, where Marian Cruger Coffin, an even more prominent woman in the field, was also trained.[36]

By 1908, Ellen and Louis had three children—young Ellen was followed

"Italian" garden at The Weld, Larz and Isabel Anderson estate, Brookline, Mass. Photo by Thomas E. Marr, c. 1904. Courtesy Historic New England.

by Evan in 1904 and Mary four years later. Shipman tutored her children at home, not finding any of the eleven country schools in the Plainfield area suitable for them. Her theories of education, recorded in a lone article on the subject, reveal a firm sense of purpose and practicality: to inspire curiosity and to direct a child's reasoning, rather than to supply the answers. She found the work gratifying, and later recalled that for no other activity was she "so repaid as for the few minutes each day that I have given to teaching my children."[37] During these years Shipman was also active in the Plainfield Mothers' and Daughters' Club, founded in 1897 to help needy families through the winter. The club also offered companionship to women and spearheaded a nationally recognized arts and crafts industry.[38]

In 1910 or thereabouts, despite these pulls on her time, Ellen Shipman decided to become a professional landscape architect. Her precise career motivations are not recorded, but Louis's departure for London that year left the family without visible means of support. Other factors undoubtedly also played a role. Many of the women of Cornish worked in design- and art-related fields; additionally, landscape design was one of few professional

Ellen Shipman with her son, Evan, at Brook Place, c. 1906.
Streeter collection.

Ellen Shipman with Ellen, Evan, and Mary at Brook Place, c. 1910. Streeter collection.

options open to women at the time, and Shipman had friends and neighbors who were deeply involved in it.

After Louis left, Ellen continued to maintain close friendships with many of her summertime Cornish neighbors, particularly Charles Platt. It is likely that she also developed friendships with her clients, both men and women, but none are recorded from these early years. She does not appear to have found another significant love relationship, at this or any other point in her life.[39] Shipman undoubtedly worked hard and spent considerable time alone as she was trying launch her business. Years later she wrote to a friend, "Each year—each day you spend alone only makes you see the future—I know—I have found work to be the only help—except my children and grandchildren."[40] As business consumed increasing amounts of Shipman's time, responsibility for running the household and caring for her two younger children, both still under ten years, fell to adolescent Ellen.[41] Had the Shipmans' elder daughter been unable to meet the emotional demands of the situation, her mother's professional life may well have taken an entirely different turn. Despite the cozy domesticity captured in the old photographs of Brook Place, Ellen Shipman had few opportunities for the more tranquil pleasures of motherhood.

View from terrace, Fynmere, James Fenimore Cooper II estate, Cooperstown, N.Y., 1912. Cornell.

THREE

COLLABORATION WITH CHARLES PLATT

Shipman's work with Platt began when he told her that "he liked the outcome of [her] efforts at Brook Place" and asked her "to do the planting for the places he was building." He well understood the importance of imaginative planting design to his own success, and Shipman had no doubts about the value of a Platt connection for her future career. But she was not quite prepared to take the leap: "I felt I could not [proceed] without further knowledge of expert drafting. He was good enough to permit one of his assistants to give me instruction." Shipman acknowledged that "it was working with Charles Platt and with his office that gave me the foundation for my future knowledge of design."[1]

The precise dates and details of Shipman's instruction are unknown, but correspondence indicates that she was actively working with Platt by 1913.[2] Given that the earliest surviving drawings from Shipman's own Cornish practice date from 1912, and that a letter from a friend that year referred to her happy engagement in the profession, it is likely that she began her apprenticeship about 1910, when she was forty-one.[3] Platt had achieved considerable national fame by that time; among his clients were wealthy industrialists such as Harold F. McCormick, William G. Mather, and Russell Alger, and in 1913, the lavish monograph introduced by Royal Cortissoz was published, showing examples of Platt's architectural and landscape work.

Under the architect's tutelage, Shipman was soon preparing construction drawings for walls, pools, and small garden buildings Platt seems to have inspired her curiosity and encouraged her to provide her own design solutions. He likely gave her access to his professional library and encouraged her to build one of her own—by the 1920s, Shipman had assembled a large collection of books related to the profession. Like thousands of gardening enthusiasts across the country, she would have been eager for the information and images offered in the heavily illustrated new volumes. The combination of Platt's technical instruction and encouragement and her exposure to a superb body of gardening literature accounts for Shipman's unusually strong start as a designer.

Among the British volumes that would have been available to her were *The Wild Garden* (1870) and *The English Flower Garden* (1883) by William Robinson, both of which emphasized the use of hardy plants. Gertrude Jekyll's *Colour Schemes for the Flower Garden,* published in 1908, demonstrated an approach to planting design that stressed, for the first time, artistic arrangement—in Jekyll's words, "careful selection and definite intention." Inigo Triggs's books and Thomas Mawson's *The Art and Craft of Garden Making* (1900) were also widely available.[4]

Accessible, too, were significant books on Italian design, more relevant to Shipman for their plans and architectural embellishments than for their plantings. Platt's own book, *Italian Gardens,* appeared in 1894 and was followed ten years later by Edith Wharton's *Italian Villas and Their Gardens,* illustrated by Maxfield Parrish. Shipman could also have turned to many American publications for design and horticultural information. A tide of sophisticated gardening magazines bridged popular and professional concerns: *Garden and Forest, Country Life in America, House & Garden*, and *House Beautiful* had wide readerships. One of the most important American garden books of the day was Guy Lowell's *American Gardens* (1901), which featured work by Charles Platt, among others.

The first documented collaboration between Platt and Shipman took place at Fynmere, the summer home of James Fenimore Cooper II in Cooperstown, New York. (Cooper was a lawyer who practiced in Albany and grandson of the famous author.) Platt was hired in 1913 to design an addition to the Frank P. Whiting house constructed three years previously and to enlarge the gardens. According to the historian Keith N. Morgan, primary responsibility for the garden design was assigned to Shipman, who was supervised by her mentor.[5] By this stage of his career, Platt was interested in garden commissions only when he was also given jurisdiction over the design of the house.

The small walled garden featured a broad terrace and a view of the Susquehanna River from an outlook of patterned brickwork that recalled the terraces at Brook Place. Low stone walls framed views to the distant hills and served to define the edge of the garden. Its interior was filled with rectangular beds of flowers (specific varieties are not known) and a path system for circulation among them. A focal point was provided by fellow Cornishite

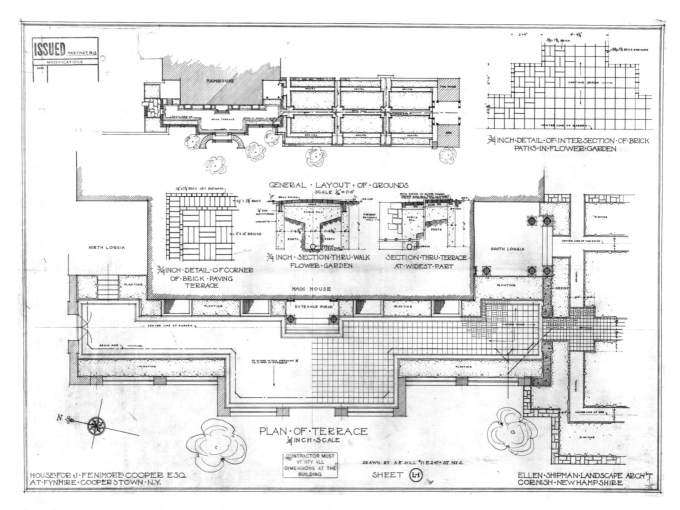

Plan of terrace, Fynmere, drawn by Albert E. Hill, ink on linen, 27 March 1913. Cornell.

Herbert Adams, who sculpted *Nymph of Fynmere* for the garden. Shipman designed a toolshed-teahouse in the style of the residence and its material, local fieldstone. The building gave the gardener access to tools while the other side was left free for socializing. In subsequent projects, Shipman frequently used such garden houses to define and focus space.

Apparently all did not go smoothly during the course of the commission—while the garden was under construction, Cooper declared that Shipman "had ruined" the place. "I had a feeling myself that I had," she confessed many years later. "There is an awful sinking feeling you can have." Given her neophyte status, the substantial budget, and the fact that her mentor was looking over her shoulder, perhaps literally, Shipman must have been self-conscious. Cooper demanded a driveway with room for a turnaround directly behind the house, where an existing road made the feature almost impossible. Even after she resolved the problem, Cooper would not acknowledge Shipman's input, claiming that he had "had all the ideas about doing it

Nymph of Fynmere by Herbert Adams, 1916. Photo by Slote Studio. Cornell.

Garden houses under construction, Fynmere. Cornell.

before [she] came."[6] The Coopers' son, however, expressed admiration for Shipman's work, remarking on the quality about it that would prove most enduring: "I think it was the most beautiful place I have ever seen—not grand but home-like and heart-warming."[7]

Still, Shipman had not yet mastered the skills that would eventually enable her to create more authoritative three-dimensional spaces. The stone walls that defined the garden's edge were low in relation to the wide expanse of beds and walks and did not give the garden the sculptural form necessary to achieve a distinct sense of place. The garden seemed almost a footnote to the big view beyond, its drafting-room genesis all too evident.

In 1914, Platt asked Shipman to design plantings for The Causeway, the James Parmelee estate near Washington Cathedral, in Washington, D.C., where two years earlier he had designed the house and adjacent walled garden.[8] Period illustrations show that Shipman's plantings—boxwood-edged beds filled with perennials, arborvitae, and standard roses—did little to subdue Platt's architectural framework. It almost seems that Shipman was following Platt's lead, emulating the formal rhythms of the architecture rather than counterbalancing it, as she soon would begin to do, with a richer, less orderly but more original planting style.[9]

Shipman faced other problems as a beginner. April 1914 found her in

Ohio consulting with Platt's client William Gwinn Mather, who was displeased with the original plantings in the formal garden of his estate, Gwinn. Mather thought that the colors—determined by Paul Rubens Frost, Platt's young assistant—were too startling. Platt had recommended that Shipman visit Cleveland to rework the scheme. (Shipman was to receive several commissions to revise early planting designs.) Her suggestions for drift plantings in cool tones may have delighted Mather but they were disregarded by his gardener, as she discovered, to her exasperation, several weeks after her initial visit. By her next visit in June, Mather had managed to assuage Shipman's frustrations, but even so, nothing came of the scheme. It would be two decades before Shipman returned to Gwinn.[10]

One of the first artistically successful collaborations between Platt and Shipman was the garden for William F. Fahnestock in Katonah, New York.

Walled garden, The Causeway, James Parmelee estate, Washington, D.C. Photo by Frances Benjamin Johnston, c. 1917. Cornell.

Vista from pavilion, William F. Fahnestock estate, Katonah, N.Y. Photo by Jessie Tarbox Beals, c. 1912. Cornell.

Pool and pavilion, Fahnestock garden. Photo by Jessie Tarbox Beals, c. 1912. Cornell.

Olmsted Brothers were originally hired to carry out planting plans in 1911 but were dismissed by the client in 1912, and Platt, who was architect for the house, suggested Shipman as a replacement. Splendid photographs of the garden in maturity reveal that Shipman's planting composition was, this time, muscular enough to stand up to Platt's powerful architectural frame work, dominated by an ornate, pedimented garden house.[11]

The interiors of the boxwood-bordered beds were filled with a rich mixture of perennials, flowering shrubs (including rhododendron), fruit trees, and conifers. These plantings balanced the proportions of the broad walks, pool, and long vistas. One of the most evocative landscape passages on the property was an informal area developed behind the pavilion which resembled an Edwardian-era English kitchen garden. Rose trellises arched over a long path flanked by unruly borders of iris, poppy, lupine, and dianthus. By following this path, visitors could find the orchard and more naturalistic landscape beyond. Shipman and Platt were discovering a steady balance of purpose in their collaborations; their design skills were proving increasingly complementary.

When Platt was hired in 1915 to remodel the Georgian country home of Isaac T. Starr in the wealthy Chestnut Hill section of Philadelphia, he again called on Shipman. Platt's symmetrical design used a loggia to link house and garden. Across a fifty-foot cruciform of two broad strips of turf stood a pergola of precisely the same dimensions as the loggia. It seems likely that Platt and Shipman decided together on the placement of architectural features and the overall planting scheme, for here dogwood, cedar, cherry trees, and shrubs were combined with groups of perennials to control views out of the garden and provide enclosure to a degree that Platt's independent designs did not. Again, Shipman's lush, loose plantings successfully evoked the spirit of Cornish gardens, even in this most formal of settings.

The same year, 1915, found Shipman in Seattle, Washington, working on the Merrill garden Platt had designed six years before. The walled formal garden was a development of the style and layout Platt had introduced at The Weld and Faulkner Farm, but its general impression was less elaborate and less insistently architectural. Early photographs in the Platt monograph document the same rigorous geometric plantings used at Gwinn. Shipman's charge, once again, was to enliven the display. No photographs survive to record her work, but the Merrills retained Shipman's services over the next decade and a half.[12]

In the working methods they had forged, Platt and Shipman resembled their British contemporaries Edwin Lutyens and Gertrude Jekyll, whose partnership was well publicized and certainly known to Shipman. By 1912, Lutyens and Jekyll had completed many important projects that had been published in *Country Life* magazine, from which Shipman often clipped gardening articles. In 1913, the year the Platt monograph appeared, Country Life Library published a large folio on Lutyens's work, which elicited the comment from Shipman that the architect's "interesting and intricate patterns" for steps emphasized the stonework more than plantings.[13] Lutyens and Jekyll's division of responsibilities varied from project to project, depending on the parameters of the job. Sometimes they worked together on design concept, frequently debating the placement of architectural features. At other times, they worked independently on separate tasks for the same project, but Jekyll always did the plantings. The Platt-Shipman partnership was not so collaborative but rather more reflective of the traditional, gendered division of labor in this country by which men oversaw architectural tasks and women tended to planting design.[14]

In 1917, a pivotal opportunity for Shipman to work on one of Platt's projects emerged in Grosse Pointe, Michigan, the first of forty-four design

Fahnestock garden. Photo by Jessie Tarbox Beals, c. 1912. Cornell.

Pool and loggia with *Pan*, Laverock Hill, Isaac T. Starr estate, Chestnut Hill, Pa. Photo by Mattie Edwards Hewitt, c. 1924. Cornell.

projects she would eventually do there. Her charge at the Russell A. Alger Jr. estate, The Moorings, was to revise Platt's c. 1908 planting scheme for the entrance court and a small pool garden. Photographs of the mature garden show mixed herbaceous and shrub plantings cradled in a dense evergreen backdrop and Platt's grapevine-covered pergola focusing a view to Lake St. Clair. They also record Shipman's interest in linking the garden to the larger landscape. Platt's notes reveal his painterly orientation to plants. In specifying wild grape for the pergola, for example, he commented that it had "a quality our domestic variety fails to possess; the leaves are very large, thin and translucent; they are lighter, brighter, more cheerful, and form . . . a more graceful shelter."[15]

A fieldstone path alongside the residence was flanked by rich double herbaceous borders, and here the old-fashioned garden of Shipman's early years

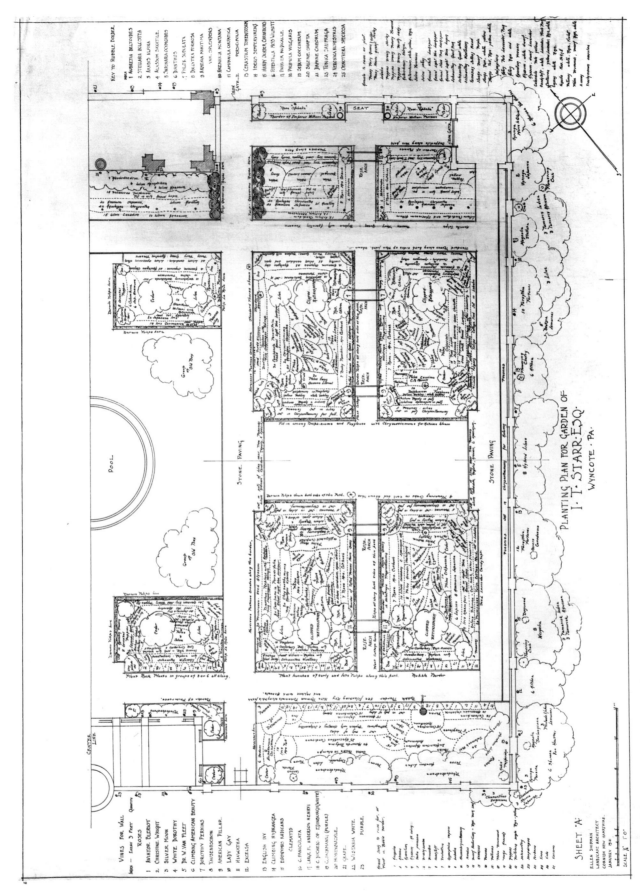

Planting plan, Laverock Hill, ink on linen, January 1916. Cornell.

assumed greater sophistication. Tea rose standards were backed by two varieties of lilies, white Japanese anemone, columbine, two varieties of monkshood, delphinium, and gas plant. By the late 1910s, Shipman routinely used the drift-style plantings promoted by Jekyll instead of the grid plantings she had specified in previous designs, such as those at Fynmere.

Around the rectangular pool, Shipman played groups of perennials against ascending layers of greenery to create a serene enclosure. The scale of plantings progressed from miniature to grand. At the pool edge, tiny lustrous leaves of cotoneaster, then a recent import from China, provided a foreground for loose clumps of summer perennials and fruit tree standards. The setting deepened with small-scale ornamental shrubs and a backdrop of conifers.[16]

Path beside house, Laverock Hill. Photo by Mattie Edwards Hewitt, c. 1924. Cornell.

Garden wall, Laverock Hill. Photo by Mattie Edwards Hewitt, c. 1924. Cornell.

"Whatever type of garden," Shipman once observed, "in the background there should be a traditional copse or bosquet." Such a backdrop made the garden an intimate world-unto-itself. "This point cannot be too strongly stressed, and will be reiterated and reiterated," she elaborated in her Garden Note Book, "until the reader grasps the point, that privacy is the most essential attribute of any garden, whatever type or period."[17]

By 1920, Shipman had collaborated with Platt on at least ten projects for which evidence exists.[18] Her client list provides nineteen additional names who were also Platt clients: Vincent Astor, John Jay Chapman, George R. Dyer, Allen F. Edwards, Dr. John Elliot, David M. Goodrich, A. Conger Goodyear, John Henry Hammond, Meredith Hare, Erskine B. Ingram, L. C. Ledyard, Arthur McGraw, William Gwinn Mather, Eugene

Lake vista, The Moorings, Russell A. Alger Jr. estate, Grosse Pointe, Mich. Photo by Thomas Ellison, 1930s. Cornell.

Pool garden, The Moorings. Photo by Thomas Ellison, 1930s. Cornell.

Meyer, Richard D. Merrill, R. D. Pruyn, Lansing F. Reed, W. Hinckle Smith, and Francis M. Weld. Shipman would continue to work with Platt through the 1920s, although with less frequency. But the precise extent of their collaboration remains elusive. To one client Shipman later wrote, "For some years I did all of the gardens related to Charles Platt's houses." Another client claimed that Platt "would not build a house unless Ellen Shipman did the landscaping."[19] Neither statement was accurate. Platt may have preferred to work with Shipman, but occasionally he collaborated with other landscape architects, including the Olmsted Brothers firm. Neither was Shipman tied to Platt's practice; she would also work with many other architects during her active career—Roger H. Bullard, Clark & Arms, Delano & Aldrich, Alfred Hopkins, Harrie T. Lindeberg, Mott

B. Schmidt, John F. Staub, and Horace Trumbauer, among others. She also designed gardens for estates that had been laid out by other landscape architects; she was often recommended by Warren Manning. But she would do some of her most interesting work on her own.

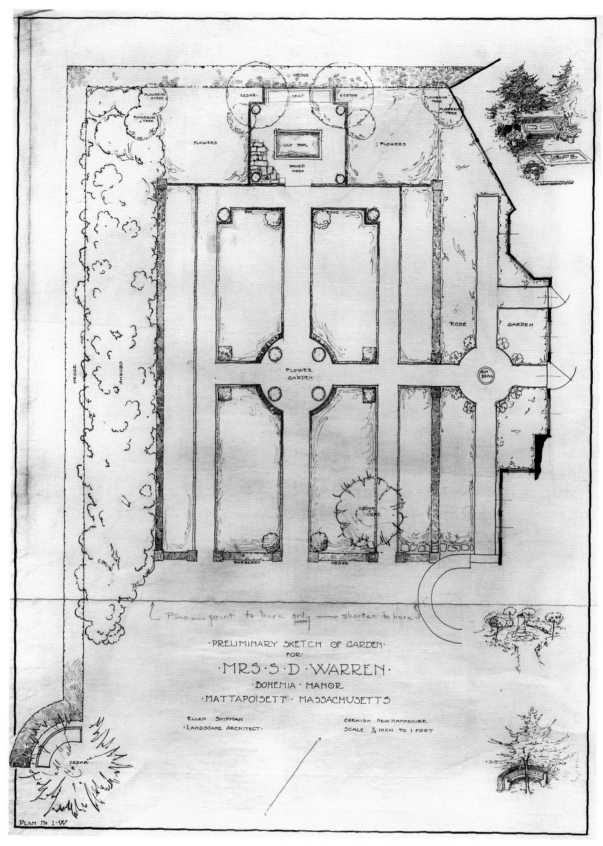

Preliminary sketch of garden, Bohemia Manor, Mrs. Samuel D. Warren estate, Mattapoisset, Mass., ink on linen, 1912. Cornell.

FOUR

A STYLE OF HER OWN

Between 1912 and 1919, Shipman's solo work progressed from cautious competence to inventive expression. Pivotal collaborations with Platt during these years sharpened her design sense while they established a firm base for an expanding network of contacts and clients. Shipman mastered architectural skills, engineering specifications, and the intricacies of large-scale planting schemes. From the first, she grasped the importance of an intimate relationship between house and garden, whereby the garden becomes a "shadow of the house," relying on the same principles that had so often led Platt to success: axial layouts, careful proportional relationships between house and garden architecture, strong visual and physical connections between house and garden and garden and setting. As did Platt, Shipman preferred to see house and garden develop as a single integrated unit. Her advice to one client, to "see me before you see your architect, or even buy the grounds," was likely repeated many times.[1]

In some respects, however, Shipman's gardens diverged sharply from those of her mentor. Whereas Platt's approach often called for substantial regrading and replanting, Shipman explored the advantages of keeping to the original lay of the land: "Design as nearly as possible to the existing grades," she advised in the Garden Note Book.[2] Shipman's independent, early ideas about grading and architectural intervention are especially apparent in the small seaside garden she designed in 1912 for Mrs. Samuel D. Warren, in Mattapoisset, Massachusetts. Defined on one side by a wall of evergreens, the garden consisted of beds of phlox and lilies and converging stone walks. A sundial and a Lutyens bench—at that time new in America—appear to

Fieldstone path, Bohemia Manor. Photo by Edith Hastings Tracy. Cornell.

have been the design's two ornaments. Breezy, unstudied, romantic, the design incorporated several existing trees and stopped at a distance from the shoreline, opening to a broad expanse of informal lawn. Here Shipman was responding to elements that preceded her involvement: the big trees, the flat grades, and, most significant, the summery, seaside character of the site.

The horticultural interests of her clients would also play an influential role in Shipman's work throughout her career. "When I am planning a garden," she wrote, "I always feel that it should be according to the owner's desire," and, elsewhere, "I feel strongly that each garden that I do is like a portrait of the person and should express their likes and dislikes."[3] Shipman sometimes used plants she actively disliked when a client specifically requested them. But such acquiescence may not have enhanced Shipman's artistic reputation. Many of her colleagues were more inclined to argue with their clients' opinions if disagreements came up. For instance, when a dis-

ELLEN SHIPMAN AND THE AMERICAN GARDEN

Bohemia Manor, three months after construction. Photo by Shipman office. Cornell.

Bohemia Manor, 1912. Photo Edith Hastings Tracy. RMC-Cornell Univ. Library.

pute erupted between Warren Manning and William Mather, Manning did not yield to Mather but made it his duty to "educate" his client about the subtleties of the native palette he proposed instead.[4] Less flexible artistic personalities, such as Manning's or Platt's, often appealed to prospective clients. Shipman's more frequent contact with women clients, who were often extremely knowledgeable and informed gardeners themselves, almost certainly helped to shape her collaborative design approach.

Shipman's March 1913 design for Alanson Daniels, on Boston's North

Old Farms, Alanson L. Daniels estate, Wenham, Mass., 1913. Photo by Edith Hastings Tracy. Cornell.

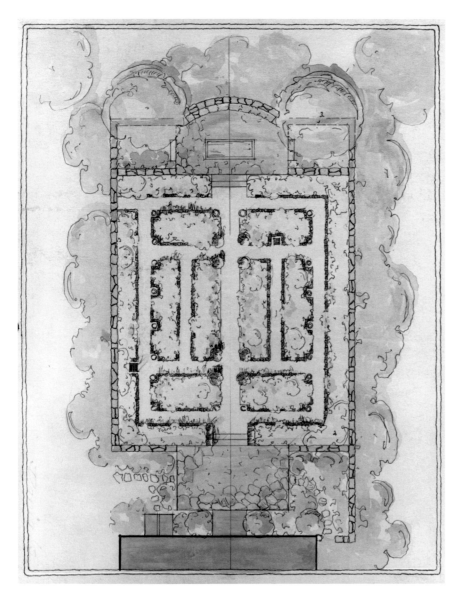

Sketch plan for walled garden, Old Farms, ink and wash on paper, March 1913.
Cornell.

Shore, harmonized with its country setting and a seventeenth-century house. Her layout of a Colonial Revival dooryard garden of hardy plants juxtaposed an existing orchard with a new design—a series of rectangular beds and walks culminating in a pool and semicircular apse. The character of the garden derived directly from its setting: the old orchard and its evocation of the larger agricultural landscape. By combining traditional New England landscape forms—such as the orchard and stone walls—with "modern" Jekyll-inspired plantings, Shipman's design signaled a move into new territory. This was one of the first instances where she used bold foliage, such as hosta, *Bergenia,* and iris, to strong sculptural effect. (Hosta quickly became a mainstay of Shipman's; she claimed she could not make a garden without it: "like the charity of the Bible—it covers the shortcomings of many

Walled garden, Old Farms. Photo by Edith Hastings Tracy. Cornell.

other plants.")[5] The deliberateness with which the plants were arranged and the careful relationships between them and the architectural elements was quietly revolutionary.

Although Shipman's planting experiments transcended Cornish tradition, she remained true to the gardening fundamentals she had learned there. She continued to rely on her own experience, using her horticultural acumen to visualize each plant "in the picture." Shipman once commented that she used plants "as a painter uses the colors from his palette." Her recommendation to "eschew all outlandish plants" was an extension of this orientation.[6] Big horticultural budgets and competition among clients sometimes led to collections of dwarf, oddly pigmented, weeping, and otherwise-altered horticultural wonders, but Shipman had no taste for oddities that would draw attention away from the larger picture or undermine her goal of a unified design.

Shipman advised would-be garden makers to "remember that the design of your place is its skeleton upon which you will later plant to make your picture. Keep that skeleton as simple as possible."[7] Her sketch for the Dora Murdocks garden, likely a pre-professional effort, which she later identified as her first plan, shows the essence of the Platt-derived, axial approach from which she only occasionally deviated.[8] The herringbone-patterned brick paths, vine-covered garden walls, fruit tree standards, flanking perennial beds, and central fountain provided a generic working vocabulary for many future projects.

A country garden for Philip B. Jennings was typical of the basic spatial arrangement that guided Shipman's best solo work for the first decade of her practice. Detailed plans prepared in 1914 by Shipman's first assistant, Elizabeth Leonard Strang, with evocative thumbnail sketches in the borders, show the intended development of the Bennington, Vermont, project. Shipman designed two large rectangular gardens—one for flowers, one for vegetables—in axial alignment with the end of the house by the architect Harrie T. Lindeberg, whom Shipman knew through Cornish connections.[9] An informal lawn bounded by screen plantings lay on the other side of the house. Later that year construction drawings were prepared; planting plans followed in 1915.

Access to the flower garden was across a house terrace and down a flight of steps. The area was structured by a series of brick-paved walks that broke the rectangle into eight beds. A fountain basin marked the central intersection. The two walks continued beyond the walled formal garden into the adjoining, much larger (160 x 100') vegetable garden, where they terminated in a semicircular loop at the far end. There a small, apselike space was set aside for annuals. The major circulation pattern of the two-part garden was, in other words, a long rectangle. The starkness of the plan would not have been obvious to visitors distracted by the charms of the diminutive teahouse, dovecote (soon to appear in many Shipman gardens), two-story birdhouse, and Chippendale-style gate. Shipman also noted masses of "iris, paeonies, funkia, hemerocallis, larkspur, hollyhocks, achillea, anthemis, anchusa,

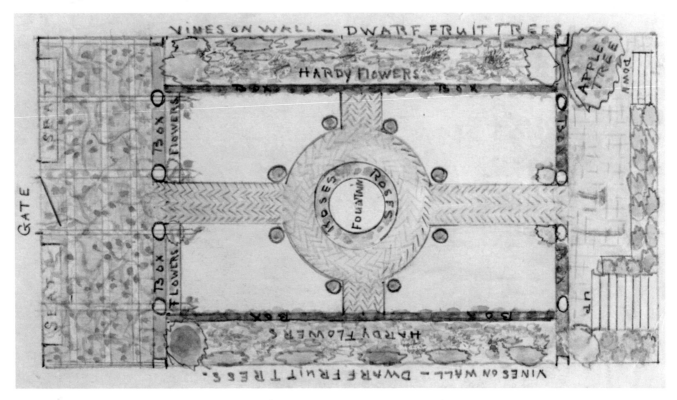

Plan for Dora Murdocks garden, Baltimore, Md. Streeter collection.

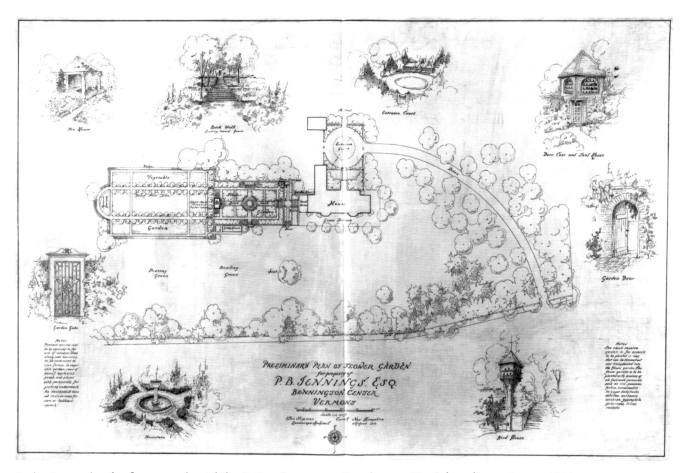

Preliminary plan for flower garden, Philip B. Jennings estate, Bennington, Vt., ink on linen, August 1914. Cornell.

Detail sketches of gate and dovecote-toolhouse.

gypsophila, primroses, lilies, rockets" that would have made the picture considerably more luxurious than the plan's skeletal geometry suggests. The scheme captured Shipman's basic approach: keep the plan simple—almost always rectangular, in axial relation to the house—and make it interesting with plants and garden architecture.

The distinctive style of the Jennings presentation drawings developed by Elizabeth Leonard Strang soon characterized other material from the office. Long after Strang had left Shipman's employ, the style was continued by others.[10] Though the concept was not entirely original, these drawings differed subtly from those of other offices in their graphic style. They routinely combined plans with charming pen-and-ink illustrations that figuratively took viewers on a walk through the garden, striking a more informal note than did the Beaux-Arts–style watercolors produced by Beatrix Farrand's office, for example, or the highly detailed pencil sketches done by Henry Hoover in Fletcher Steele's office. The graphic style is similar to Inigo Triggs's *Formal Gardens in England and Scotland,* a large folio with plans and thumbnail sketches of architectural features, and to illustrations in Thomas Mawson's

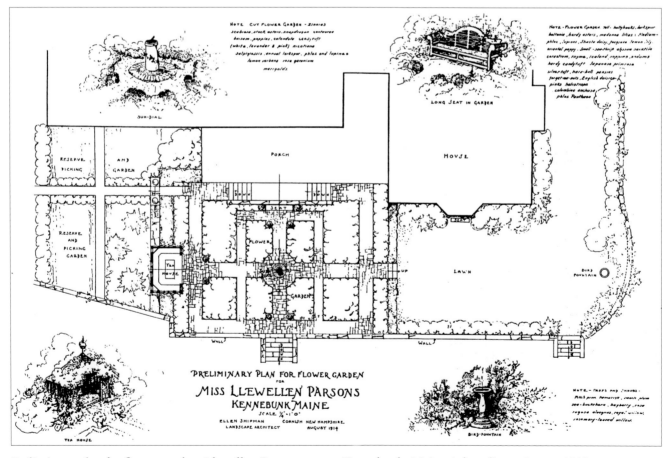

Preliminary plan for flower garden, Llewellyn Parsons estate, Kennebunk, Maine, ink on linen, August 1914. Cornell.

The Art and Craft of Garden Making. The sketches also resemble the renderings and perspective drawings of country houses found in *American Architect and Building News.*

Shipman's elaborate plans also carried horticultural instructions, written in meticulous, somewhat informal language, almost as a letter to the client. Her instructions on the Jennings plan are typical: "The small reserve garden is for annuals to be planted in rows that can be thinned out and transplanted into the flower garden. . . . In the vegetable garden, rows of dwarf apple, crab, peach and plums with perennials for picking underneath. As designed it does not include room for corn or hubbard squash."

In 1914, Strang drew the plan for the Llewellyn Parsons commission in Kennebunk, Maine, a flower garden on axis with a large porch overlooking the ocean view. Visitors entered the garden by descending either of two short flights of steps. Brick walkways divided the rectangular area into eight beds. The small teahouse (rendered in the plan's lower left-hand corner) provided a stop to the long axis. The similarities between this and the Jennings plan, also dated 1914, reveal a decidedly "Shipmanesque" style emerging in both garden and graphic design.

Few of the circumstances of these early commissions are known. Shipman had been called in to design the Parsons landscape four years after the Olmsted Brothers firm had subdivided the extensive Kennebunk family compound. She returned once more, sometime after that date, to add to plantings along the entry drive and develop a garden of native plants.[11] An enthusiastic though somewhat restless client, Llewellyn Parsons also hired Arthur Shurcliff for work there in 1916 and again in 1931. Fourteen years later, she hired Fletcher Steele for still more development.

More spatially complex—and sensually rich—than any of these early projects was the garden at Grahampton, the Henry Croft estate in Greenwich, Connecticut. A grading plan and site and planting plans confirm Shipman's involvement beginning in 1917. The intricacy of the design may have been prompted by the unusual circumstances of site. Her task seems to have been to develop new gardens beyond those already in place—the original design, by James Leal Greenleaf, had been conceived to form an integrated whole.[12] Shipman elected to give three new areas, none of which was visible from the earlier garden, a diminutive scale and a sense of enclosure. An evergreen garden, a flower garden, and a pool garden were attached in an L shape. The fourteen-foot drop in elevation allowed Shipman to set up plunging and rising views across the two main axes. One of these views led to a sculpture of Diana, added in 1927.

The new area was planted so that the three gardens were not all visible from any single vantage point. A sense of mystery was heightened by the seclusion of each, as though the outside world, including the rest of the

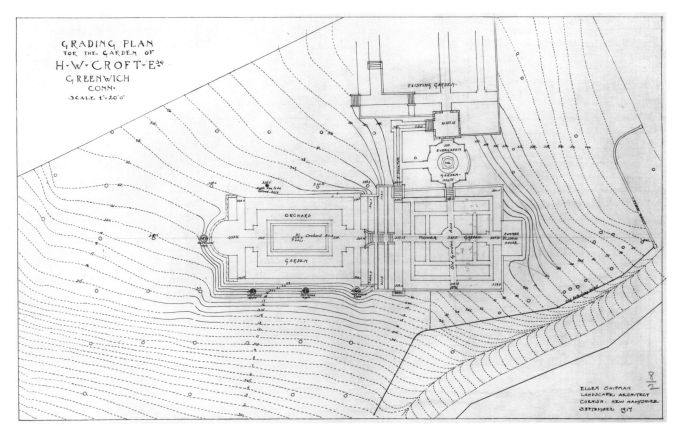

Grading plan for Grahampton, H. W. Croft estate, Greenwich, Conn., ink on linen, September 1917. Cornell.

Flower garden, Grahampton. Photo by Mattie Edwards Hewitt, c. 1922. Cornell.

Pond garden, Grahampton. Photo by Mattie Edwards Hewitt, c. 1922. Cornell.

Stone bench, Grahampton. Photo by Mattie Edwards Hewitt, c. 1922. Cornell.

property, had ceased to exist. Shipman held an unswerving belief in the importance of privacy: "Planting, however beautiful, is not a garden. A garden must be enclosed . . . or otherwise it would merely be a cultivated area."[13] In this she differed somewhat from Platt, who tended to utilize walls and hedges to establish spatial separation but one that rarely offered the sense of seclusion provided by tall walls of foliage. "Some gardens, like some homes, afford little more privacy than a shop window. Better one room that is your own," Shipman advised, "than a whole house exposed to the world, better a

Vista to *Diana*, added in 1927, Grahampton. Photo by Mattie Edwards Hewitt, c. 1928. Cornell.

tiny plot where you can be alone than a great expanse without this essential attribute of the real garden."[14]

In her first plan for Philip Gossler's estate in New Canaan, Connecticut, Shipman experimented with a complex spatial organization that transcended any of her earlier designs. The initial 1919 design shows an extensive and somewhat arbitrary arrangement of individual garden rooms, whose proportions bore little relation to the house. Although the placement of these rooms was determined by existing trees and shrubs, the number and size of the areas would have overwhelmed the rather modest home. The failure may have guided her back to her early principles and strengthened her adherence to them in the process. On her second try, Shipman produced a less ambitious and more successful design. Years later, a *House Beautiful* critic noted that "nothing seems to equal the enclosed garden in friendliness."[15] Gossler

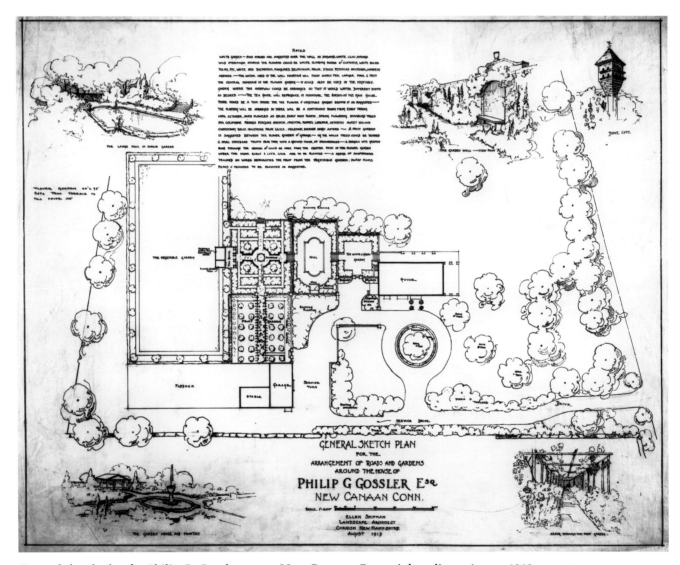

General sketch plan for Philip G. Gossler estate, New Canaan, Conn., ink on linen, August 1919. Cornell.

was obviously pleased, too; when he moved to Long Island in 1925, he commissioned a new garden from Shipman there.

❧

Three examples from the late 1910s show the range of Shipman's experiments with planting design. At Wampus, the John Magee estate in Mount Kisco, New York, she balanced an unconventional scheme of architectural elements—one of her most developed to date—with a particularly rich combination of plants.[16] Because she was commissioned to design the architectural and spatial frameworks and the plantings, her imagination could tackle both simultaneously—a far more complicated charge than simply enlivening a preexisting frame.

At Wampus, Shipman's intricately detailed brick walks, terraces, and pergola were an unexpected mixture of Italian, British, and traditional American motifs. Corinthian columns supported a wood trellis that cast intricate shadows on the herringbone brick terrace beneath. Antique urns, tank, and benches stood next to cast concrete ornaments that recalled classical prototypes. Shipman's lyrical plantings served to emphasize the architecture rather than counterbalance it. Mattie Edwards Hewitt's photographs

Pergola and fountain terrace, Wampus, John Magee estate, Mount Kisco, N.Y. Photo by Mattie Edwards Hewitt, c. 1918. Cornell.

Terrace overlooking Wampus Pond. Photo by Mattie Edwards Hewitt, c. 1918. Cornell.

Pergola, Wampus. Photo by Mattie Edwards
Hewitt, c. 1918. Cornell.

from c. 1918 show a mature garden awash with June-blooming plants. Shipman's wisteria-covered pergola bordered a small, hedged enclosure and a riot of cottage garden flowers. Dense clumps of rhododendron and green shrubbery on an adjacent terrace were reflected in a small pool and provided a lustrous green counterfoil.

The same year, 1916, Shipman began a summer garden for Julia Fish in Greenport, Long Island, as simple as Wampus was complex. The garden's main features were double perennial borders, nearly four hundred feet in length, set against a backdrop of cedars and shrubbery. The color-graded borders ranged from lavender to pink to blue on one side, from blue to white on the other. A wide turf path separated the beds, as was common in British gardens of the period. Shipman kept the defining walls and floor of the area green; the one slight change in elevation was negotiated by inconspicuous turf steps. The centerpiece, a small reflecting pool, made the garden sparkle from every side. Each view across it terminated in a different focal point:

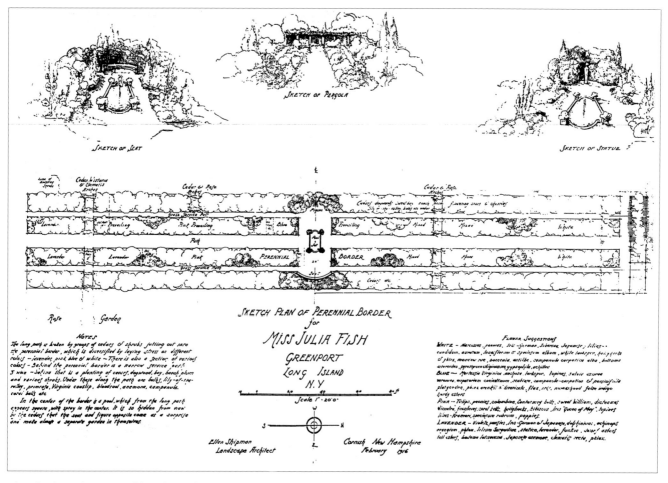

Sketch plan of perennial border, Julia Fish garden, Greenport, N.Y., ink on linen, February 1916. Cornell.

(left) **Fish garden under construction.** Photo by Shipman office, c. 1916. Cornell.

Pool and borders, Fish garden. Photo by Mattie Edwards Hewitt, August 1927. Cornell.

Perennial borders, Fish garden. Photo by Mattie Edwards Hewitt, August 1927. Cornell.

Pool, Fish garden. Photo by Mattie Edwards Hewitt, August 1927. Cornell.

sculpture, a bench, a garden house. Rare construction photographs in Ship-man's records, dating to about 1916, reveal the extent to which the garden was pure invention. Mattie Edward Hewitt's photographs, taken ten years later, show the transformation of the open field that confronted Shipman on her first visit to the site.

Shipman's inspiration may have come, in part, from Gertrude Jekyll's *Colour Schemes for the Flower Garden,* a copy of which was in her private library.[17] The book detailed Jekyll's pioneering efforts in blending colors and contrasting textures so as to evoke the billowing effect of an Impressionist painting. Shipman's borders for the Fish garden were spectacular, but in fact were atypical in her oeuvre. Most of her later color borders—such as the one at Stan Hywet Hall in Akron, Ohio—juxtaposed jewel-like colors to create a stained-glass-window effect rather than an impressionistic wash.

Shipman's planting and design skills are also in evidence in her 1919 garden in Easthampton, Long Island, for the artists and volunteer social workers Mary and Neltje Pruyn. The referral undoubtedly came from

Platt, who had recently remodeled the modest cottage. In his introduction to the 1926 *House Beautiful Gardening Manual*, Fletcher Steele wrote appreciatively of Shipman's design: "Part of the unusually successful Colonial feeling here is due to the fact that stiff accuracy has been avoided. Note even that one side of the path is edged with brick—the other with a board."[18]

As Shipman's confidence grew, her handling of plants and materials became more relaxed and intuitive. The inspiration for the Pruyns' tiny garden was the Colonial Revival; however, Shipman eschewed the haphazard mix of color and bloom of the traditional dooryard garden in favor of more sophisticated plant combinations. Comparison with Stephen Parrish's Northcote sheds light on the artistry of Shipman's plant choices.

At Northcote, the general impression of abundant, healthy bloom and

Mary and Neltje Pruyn garden, 1920, East Hampton, N.Y. Photo by Mattie Edwards Hewitt, c. 1923. Cornell.

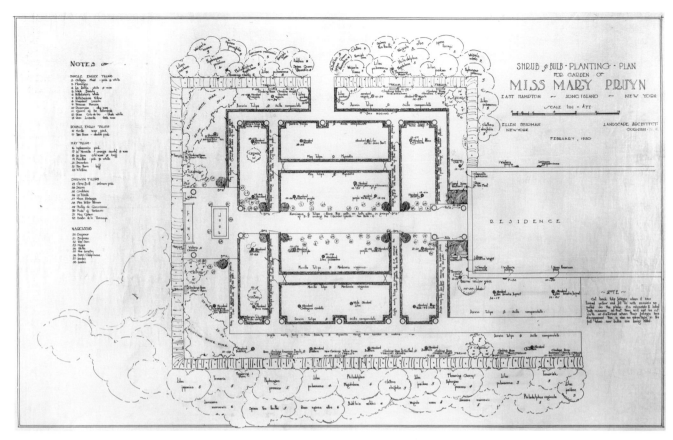

Shrub and bulb planting plan, Pruyn garden, ink on linen, February 1920. Cornell.

unstudied, horticultural confusion bespoke the care of a dedicated amateur and from this derived its sense of joy and naiveté. Each robust perennial clump maintained its identity as an individual block. Shipman, by contrast, arranged abstract drifts of plants of varying sizes, in varying shapes, in response to each plant's character and habit. Edges disappeared. Symmetry was avoided in favor of unexpected pairings and contrast. Bold-foliaged plants, such as peonies and anchusa, abutted ephemeral clouds of baby's breath and astilbe. Iris swords penetrated the less insistent, deeply lobed foliage of delphinium. Everywhere the eye rested new combinations were revealed. The prim layout and profligate planting could scarcely have sounded two more different stylistic notes; in combination, they created something quite new.

Ellen Shipman at Beekman Place. Photo by Bradley Studio, 1920s. Streeter collection.

FIVE

THE NEW YORK OFFICE

In the early 1920s, Ellen Shipman decided to move to New York City. She may have been encouraged by the success of her brother Nicholas Biddle, who ran a successful law office there. (Nicholas was trustee for the Astor Estate Office, commercial clients of Charles Platt; Vincent Astor was a client of Ellen's.) Years of separation from her husband, ending in divorce in 1927, may also have provided her strong emotional as well as financial motivations to move. She probably anticipated that her business would function much more efficiently from New York than from rural New Hampshire, particularly given the complexities of train travel. Additionally, Ellen's youngest child, Mary, had just turned twelve—old enough, in her mother's view, to attend boarding school.[1]

After considering other properties, Shipman bought a town house on Beekman Place, at the corner of East 50th Street. Sited on a high bluff overlooking the East River, the street had once looked down on slaughterhouses, but she saw great possibilities in the view and the location. The house was one of several older brick buildings that had recently been purchased by writers and actors who hoped to transform the former working-class neighborhood into a stylish enclave. Shipman later noted, "There is not in all New York another piece of property like it, for it has seclusion . . . southern exposure, beauty of architecture, combined with the extended view of the East River." By 1932, when William Bottomley's River House and its private landing were constructed, Beekman Place had become one of the city's most desirable addresses.[2]

Shipman engaged the architects Butler & Corse to assist her in remodel-

19–21 Beekman Place, New York, N.Y. Photo by Samuel H. Gottscho, c. 1927. Streeter collection.

ing the house, as she wrestled with the challenge of creating separate quarters for the office, her residence, and two apartments on the upper floors. Her ability to integrate interior design with architecture served her well here (and proved to be an asset in later years, when she generated more income from interior work than from landscape design).

The renovations put the office door on Beekman Place and the entrance to Shipman's private quarters on the East 50th Street side. Photographs in a 1927 *House Beautiful* article record English Georgian furniture, Lowestoft china, decorative paneling, carvings, and wall coverings from Chinese screens. Childe Hassam's view of Gloucester, a pastoral landscape by Willard Metcalf, and drawings by Maxfield Parrish brought reminders of the

Dining room with Chinese screen wall coverings (*top*) and bay window, Beekman Place. Photo by Samuel H. Gottscho, c. 1927. Streeter collection.

Office reception room, Beekman Place. Photo by Samuel H. Gottscho, c. 1927. Streeter collection.

Cornish colony to Manhattan. A bay window created the setting for a small shelf garden. Work quarters included a large drafting room and Shipman's private office, which overlooked the river. The walls of the reception room held photographs of the Fahnestock, Starr, Morris, and Cooper commissions. Copies of *House Beautiful, Historic Gardens of Virginia,* and other publications, many of which undoubtedly contained images of Shipman's gardens, were spread on the table for waiting clients.[3]

Shipman's would prove to be one of the most durable of several New York offices run by women landscape architects.[4] Increasing publicity, the photogenic quality of her gardens, strong relations with garden club networks (particularly the Garden Club of America), and Shipman's congeniality as a speaker, houseguest, and artist attracted scores of clients as the widespread demand for country houses kept the pool of prospective customers full. Shipman built up geographic networks of clients, often returning to do jobs for other family members, neighbors, and friends. She worked for twenty-four clients in Greenwich, Connecticut, for example, seventeen in Mount Kisco, New York, and fifty-seven on Long Island. Other areas with significant client clusters were Houston, Buffalo, and Winston-Salem. In Grosse Pointe Shores, Michigan, she completed forty-four projects. In Ohio she had forty-five commissions, mostly on estates outside Cleveland and Toledo.

Like Beatrix Farrand, Shipman employed women exclusively, relying heavily on graduates from the Lowthorpe School because she thought the training there "unsurpassed."[5] No documents reveal the basis for her policy, but at least two different circumstances could explain it. Certainly Shipman wanted to give women opportunities for training and jobs not otherwise available in a male-dominated field. She once wrote, "There is no profession so suited to [women], so needed and so repaying in every way—nor any that at once gives so much of health, wealth and happiness."[6] It is also likely that male applicants for positions in female landscape architectural practices were scarce.

By the late 1920s, Shipman's staff comprised up to five draftsmen, with as many as ten working on a temporary basis, and two secretaries.[7] Drainage and grading work were almost always subcontracted to engineering consultants. Among Shipman's most important assistants besides Elizabeth Leonard Strang were her designer and office manager, Louise Payson, who, like Strang, initially worked in Cornish, and her draftsman Eleanor Hills Christie. Dorothy May Anderson and Mary P. Cunningham also worked for Shipman, as did Agnes Selkirk Clark. Clark and Edith Schryver became two of the best-known landscape architects trained in the office.[8]

One assistant who did not go on to open her own office was Frances Mc-Cormic, a longtime associate of Shipman's and a close personal friend of her family. Shipman had quickly offered McCormic a job after she won a prize for model making at Lowthorpe in 1926; McCormic abandoned her formal studies and went to work for Shipman full-time. For two decades she was Shipman's office head, chief draftsman, and model maker. When she left in 1945 to take a job with Condé Nast, Shipman was slow to forgive her.[9]

Shipman's office procedures were conventional, although her involvement in every stage of development was not characteristic of the largest practices of the period. Most jobs began with a site visit and consultation. "I never have done and never expect to do a piece of work without seeing the place and making the plans especially for it," Shipman wrote to a client who had suggested that one of her plans for another project would do.[10] Initial visits were recorded in copious notes and photographs. These, along with a survey plan, rough sketches, and her broad recommendations, would be forwarded to her office with instructions for several alternative design solutions. Eleanor Christie recalled that on receiving rough sketches that were often not drawn to scale, she and other assistants would work to "make it fit together." Several schemes would then be fleshed out for presentation to the client. For larger estates, watercolor designs were prepared. Only after the concept was approved and detailed construction drawings under way were planting plans drawn up. Shipman relied on her draftsmen to generate finished drawings and in some cases to supervise installation.[11]

Office correspondence from before the mid-1940s is sparse, so little information is available about the fees Shipman charged for her work. According to an invoice for a job in 1946, however, her fee was one hundred dollars, plus travel, for a consultation, and from twenty-five to one hundred dollars each for construction and planting plans.[12] As her workload increased, Shipman juggled numerous jobs simultaneously, spending much time traveling between distant geographic areas. For longer journeys she traveled by overnight train (always on a lower berth) and in later years by plane.

Many of Shipman's clients eventually became her personal friends. As did Platt, she often stayed in their homes rather than in hotels. She ate with the family and was entertained lavishly at luncheons where friends and neighbors—all of them prospective clients—could tap her for garden-making advice.[13] Not all practitioners were so inclined. Warren Manning and Beatrix Farrand, for example, enjoyed hotels and the respite they offered from round-the-clock socializing. Shipman had her limits, too; she made it clear that cats were not welcome in her quarters and that she required a one-hour nap after lunch.[14]

According to one employee, Shipman "took endless trouble to see that her clients had all the information needed to execute her plans successfully."[15] Most plans included copious horticultural notes that explained what, how, and when to plant, how to stake, and what to replace plants with when they started to fade. The instructions penned into the margins of her plan for the superintendent's gardens at the U.S. Military Academy at West Point were typical in their specificity and rigor:

> STAKING—After the preparation of the soil and the planting, the next most important thing for the success of the garden is proper staking. This should be attended to most diligently, as most plants, if not staked from the beginning, form roots on their stems and spread out, leaving no room for less hardy and less vigorous adjacent plants. Small stakes should be used at first and replaced with larger ones as the plants increase in size. The plants must not be tied to the stakes. The stakes should be placed around the plant or group of one variety and raffia tied to the stakes, leaving the plant or plants free in the center. Asters, chrysanthemums, and other large plants can be trained or staked carefully about September first, to lean forward and cover any vacant place where plants have died down.

Shipman's horticultural standards were exacting and her tolerance of inferior work limited. She advised on seasonal maintenance, making once- or twice-yearly visits to her gardens to monitor their condition. This procedure was not unusual—most of the era's other designers also suggested it to their clients. Less common was Shipman's practice of administering an annual discretionary sum to purchase plants. A request from her to a client for one such arrangement began, rather exasperatedly, "quite frequently you are away and the time for planting then goes by, and we sometimes lose a whole year."[16]

Shipman's recommendations about regular visits may have been less insistent when women gardeners or caretakers were involved. In a letter to William and Elizabeth Mather, her Cleveland clients at Gwinn (ironically, one of the few estates that ever employed a female superintendent), Shipman stated, "I never secure men for any place unless I see it at least twice a year, because I have never found any man who is able to keep a garden or place in the condition that I thought it should be unless I supervise it twice a year."[17] Shipman's British contemporary Viscountess Wolseley confessed a similar prejudice to her students at the Glynde School for Landscape Gardening in Sussex: "We want to banish once and for all the inferior, rule-of-thumb, slow-thinking, inartistic man-gardener whom we have tolerated for so long and in his place require intelligent, educated ladies, who will direct and supervise as ably and in some cases even better than the very best type of male gardener."[18]

Despite Shipman's advice to her clients, her own gardener at Brook Place was male. John Hathaway, an Englishman, also served as Shipman's super-

Brick-paved terrace, Brook Place, Plainfield, N.H. Photo by Mattie Edwards Hewitt, 1923. Streeter collection.

Loggia, Brook Place. Photo by Mattie Edwards Hewitt, 1923. Streeter collection.

Front garden, Brook Place. Photo by Mattie Edwards Hewitt, 1923. Streeter collection.

intendent on an important commission for Samuel Salvage during the late 1920s. He later went to work for Shipman's clients the Ormsby Mitchells in Greenwich, Connecticut, and then the Ralph Haneses, in Winston-Salem, at which time Charles Meyette took over Hathaway's duties at Brook Place. Shipman enjoyed a warmly satisfying relationship with both Meyette and his wife, and remembered her caretaker handsomely in her will.[19]

Each summer until World War II, Shipman removed her practice to New Hampshire, where work continued at a more leisurely pace. Frances Mc-Cormic, who spent many summers at Brook Place, remembered the annual packing of the office paraphernalia and moving to the country as a "big production"—and not one of her own choosing, since she found little to do in the country when she was not working. McCormic lived in an apartment above the garage at Brook Place, while the other employees boarded else-where.[20] The seasonal move, in addition to the taxing travel associated with

Stone wall and plantings, Brook Place. Photo by Mattie Edwards Hewitt, 1923. Streeter collection.

the job, would have made it difficult for an employee to maintain a marriage or family responsibilities. It is not surprising, then, that many of Shipman's were single.

In Cornish, Shipman entertained lavishly, with the help of four servants and the cook she brought from New York. She continued as an active member of the Mothers' and Daughters' Club in Plainfield, where she gave slide-illustrated lectures. She also held annual competitions for the colony's most artistically designed garden, the prize a twenty-dollar gold piece.[21] During these years, her daughter Mary became an accomplished equestrian. Evan also developed an interest in horses, but preferred to watch them race. By 1925, he was routinely spending summers at Brook Place and wintering in Paris, where he wrote poetry and befriended several writers, including Ernest Hemingway.[22]

During the 1920s, the gardens at Brook Place were in their prime. The moment recorded by Mattie Edwards Hewitt in 1923 and featured in *House & Garden* the following year shows a country landscape of great charm.[23] A brick terrace laid in a basketweave pattern kept tune with the traditional New England farmhouse and the millstone at the doorstep. Old wooden buckets filled with conical hemlocks performed the same decorative role as Charles Platt's bay trees had in his gardens, but in a country vernacular. The brick-paved terrace continued around to the covered porch alongside the pergola, where the tea table was set on another millstone. The vine-covered porch, seen from the middle of the garden, was cloaked to provide a shady retreat. A small pool, closely modeled on one designed for a client, provided a flicker of reflected light.

Phlox, peonies, delphiniums, and other hardy perennials filled the big beds, just as in Shipman's design for the Pruyn garden; dianthus and hardy geranium bordered plank-lined dirt paths. The billowing perennials were bolstered by hemlock cubes topped by topiaried globes. At the far end of the garden, a low stone wall separated the private compound from the road. Birch and other trees tied the garden to the outer landscape. Two large vegetable gardens kept the larders full, and a cutting garden supplied fresh flowers for the house. One year's autumn seed order included calendula, candytuft, alyssum, *Centaurea Americana,* delphiniums, and mixed Shirley poppies.[24] At Brook Place, Shipman was both designer and dirt gardener. The garden's mix of sophistication and unpretentiousness resonated with her own.

Garden at Edgehill, Samuel Morris estate, Chestnut Hill, Pa., 1922. Photo by Mattie Edwards Hewitt, c. 1924. Cornell.

SIX

ARTISTIC MATURITY

Shipman's client roster was rapidly growing thanks to publicity in popular magazines and books. Gardens planted during the previous decade were reaching their peak by the early 1920s when images by Mattie Edwards Hewitt, Jessie Tarbox Beals, Frances Benjamin Johnston, and other superb photographers were published with articles about Shipman's work. Beginning in 1921, a flood of photo essays chronicling her gardens appeared in *The Garden, House & Garden,* and *House Beautiful,* as well as in professional journals showing collaborative work with architects. By 1924, for instance, the Magee garden of 1916 had been featured in all three popular magazines, in Elsa Rehmann's book *Garden-Making,* and in the 1923 annual exhibition of the Architectural League of New York.[1]

Shipman's fame spread rapidly during the early 1920s. Many new commissions resulted from word-of-mouth recommendations; in addition, news of her talent was circulated by organizations such as the Garden Club of America, whose members became clients. Noticeably absent from Shipman's growing list of clients, however, were referrals traceable to her family, where they might normally be expected to have originated.

Shipman's gardens from this decade were ever more assured and varied in style, according to the requirements of site, client, and budget. Often the new designs incorporated traditional architectural motifs illustrated in Shipman's library; her collection included as many books on architecture and interiors as on horticulture.[2] Large folios depicting Majorcan houses, English cottages, and French provincial architecture as well as several on English Georgian architecture and interiors provided a wealth of detail. She also owned several British reference books on garden architecture: Gertrude Jekyll and Lawrence Weaver's *Gardens for Small Country Houses* (1912), Weaver's *Small Country Houses* (1914), and Jekyll and Christopher Hussey's *Garden Ornament* (1927). These titles presented a strong visual case for a vernacular Arts and Crafts approach to design, as opposed to the Beaux-Arts philosophy promoted in the leading schools of landscape architecture at Harvard, Cornell, and elsewhere. Two other influential books by the English architect H. Inigo Triggs, *The Art of Garden Design in Italy* (1906) and *Garden Craft in Europe* (1913), allowed Shipman to examine in detail historical examples of garden design. Fletcher Steele's *Design in the Little Garden* (1924) and Wilhelm Miller's *What England Can Teach Us about Gardening* (1911) were among the few representations of works by American landscape architects. Standard horticultural reference works by Taylor and Liberty Hyde Bailey as well as monographs on lilies, roses, and clematis stood alongside volumes of garden writing by Neltje Blanchan, Helena Rutherfurd Ely, and Louise Beebe Wilder. Shipman also owned several titles by Louisa Yeomans King and Mabel Cabot Sedgwick's practical book *The Garden Month by Month* (1907); both writers were also clients.

Three of Shipman's largest commissions from the 1920s—for Carll Tucker, Samuel Salvage, and Ormsby Mitchell—came to her near the end of the decade, when her design powers were at their height. But modest jobs were more common, circumscribed by budget, site size, or preexisting designs by other landscape architects. Shipman's availability to work up an elaborate planting scheme for a few hundred dollars proved irresistible to dozens of clients whose resources were limited or who already owned grand gardens that simply needed to have their plantings rejuvenated. These smaller jobs usually involved new plantings and designs for pools, terraces, flights of steps, and other architectural features; most did not include site design or extensive grading.

Typical of the decade was the commission for the Windsor Whites in Chagrin Falls, Ohio, a small village outside Cleveland where Shipman would eventually complete a dozen jobs. The Halfred Farms project began in 1919 while Shipman was still in the Cornish office; construction and planting continued through the early 1920s. Warren Manning, whose professional path crossed frequently with Shipman's, also began working for the Whites that year. It may have been their first of many professional intersections.[3] Manning oversaw the layout of the general plan, which necessarily included existing features—such as the 1860 farmhouse and several farm buildings that supported a thriving apple business. Shipman was asked to create a design specifically for a formal garden. Certainly, the two would have communicated with each other about ongoing development.

In Shipman's plan, a large rectangular lawn stretched beside the farmhouse on a lower terrace reached by a flight of flagstone steps. Directly op-

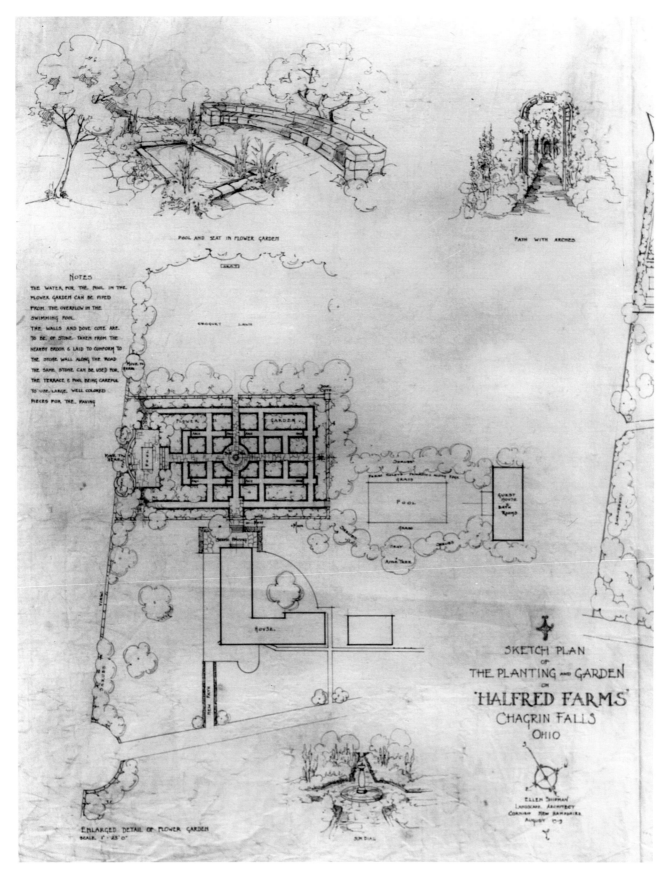

Sketch plan of Halfred Farms, Windsor T. White estate, Chagrin Falls, Ohio, ink on linen, August 1919. Cornell.

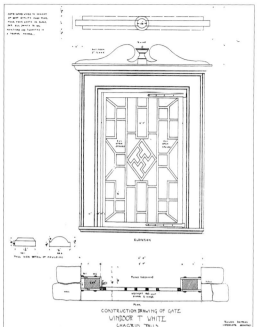

(right) Construction drawing of gate,
Halfred Farms, ink on trace, April 1919.
Cornell.

(below) View through flower beds,
Halfred Farms. Photo by Tebbs & Knell,
1920s. Cornell.

posite the steps was a Chinese Chippendale–style gate, a formal answer to the guest house designed by Bryant Fleming, which was probably part of the Manning plan. At the foot of the garden were a semicircular stone terrace and small rectangular pool. Large square beds of perennials, flowering shrubs, arborvitae, and rose arches filled the central garden space. Around the pool, unexpected contrast erupted between the formal juniper spires that recalled the upright forms of Italian cypress and the naturalistic treatment of the plantings that merged into surrounding woods. The untamed aspect of this planting may have reflected the subtle influence of Manning, whose informal tastes had undoubtedly imbued the general layout with the robust spirit of nature. Adjacent to the square garden, delineated by a low stone wall, was a rectangular iris garden with a small oval pool at its center. The ornamental garden areas nestled closely to house; through the small complex of farm outbuildings, winding roads led to apple orchards and meadows filled with bobolinks.

Shipman developed a close friendship with the Whites, who helped her

Garden under construction, Halfred Farms. Photo by Shipman office, 7 May 1922. Cornell.

Pool, Halfred Farms, 1919. Photo by Parade Studio, 1920s. Cornell.

career by recommending her services to friends and relatives and, years later, donated money to a scholarship fund Shipman oversaw for the Lowthorpe School. In 1942, she thanked them for making Cleveland "one of the bright spots" of her professional career. (The Cleveland area was also unusually rich in Shipman trainees, many of whom had flourishing practices.) According to one source, Shipman met Charles Lindbergh during one of her many stays at Halfred Farms and caught a plane ride home to New York with him.[4]

Shipman's charge for the Mrs. Robert S. Brewster Jr. estate, Avalon, in Mount Kisco, New York, was also characteristic of her more modest jobs. Avalon's extensive grounds had been designed originally by Charles Delano of the firm Delano & Aldrich in 1912 according to Beaux-Arts principles

Pool vista, Avalon, Mrs. Robert S. Brewster Jr. estate, Mount Kisco, N.Y. Photo by Mattie Edwards Hewitt, c. 1923. Cornell.

Stone arch and plantings, Avalon. Photo by Mattie Edwards Hewitt, c. 1923. Cornell.

Pergola, Avalon. Photo by Mattie Edwards Hewitt, c. 1923. Cornell.

of spatial layout; much of the surrounding woodland had been left intact.[5] Shipman was hired in the early 1920s, probably in response to aging or otherwise unsatisfactory plantings, to redesign the central, ornamental part of the scheme. The original planting designer is not known; Delano, an architect, was probably not much involved on a horticultural level.

In Delano's design, a sunken garden and pool were revealed to visitors as they emerged from beneath a circular pergola to descend a wide flight of steps onto the garden's "carpet," a broad stretch of lawn surrounded on three sides by dense woods. The oval pool provided Shipman a setting for what was, essentially, a border wrapped around its perimeter. June photographs record iris, lilies, dianthus, hosta, and Wichuraiana rose spilling into the water. The delicate texture of Shipman's border was repeated on a bolder scale by flanking beds that echoed the pool's curve.

Shipman told one interviewer that she used no more than six to eight main flowering plants in each design and "let each, in its season, dominate the garden. For the time one flower is the guest of honor and is merely supplemented with other flowers." There were exceptions to this approach, of course, but Shipman used it to guide most of her planting decisions. The strategy had several practical implications. First, because there were fewer numbers of varieties in bloom at any one time, color harmonies were less complex and therefore easier to control. It was also possible to achieve a more cohesive overall impression. In Shipman's view, too, a well-placed grouping of flowers against a green background produced a more dramatic effect than unrelieved blocks of color did; she had discovered that green shrubbery was useful for "lending lights and shadows" to bloom, increasing their impact and beauty. Last, because only a small number of flowers burst into bloom at any given moment, Shipman could spread out the show and thereby achieve a longer season of color.[6]

The wisteria-draped pergola at Avalon offered a different sort of plant-

Sketch for brick walk, Philip B. Jennings estate, Bennington, Vt., 1914. Cornell.

Garden steps, Picket Farm, A. Ludlow Kramer estate, Westbury, N.Y. (1920). Photo by Mattie Edwards Hewitt, 1923. Cornell.

Terrace steps, Clark Williams garden, Greenwich, Conn. (1925). Photo by Harry G. Healy, 1935. Cornell.

ing opportunity altogether: two cascades of white Wichuraiana rose cushioned the curving stairs, emphasizing the delicate proportions of the steps. A mixed scheme, such as that surrounding the pool, would have undermined the delicacy and focused simplicity of the picture. Few of Shipman's step plantings achieved this level of drama, however. Most often the steps in her gardens involved minor changes in level and gradual transitions from one garden area to the next. Materials ranged from cut stone and flagstone to brick and sometimes included combinations of all three. Frequently ornamented with small-scale sculpture, and almost always framed with heavy plantings that screened the view into the area beyond, these features usually functioned as elements of a larger picture rather than main events in the visual field.

Another modest commission, though larger than Avalon, was a job that came from Mrs. Holden McGinley of Milton, Massachusetts, in 1925. A recent divorcée, McGinley was heiress to the *Cleveland Plain Dealer*

Walled garden with bronze figure by Anna Coleman Ladd, Mrs. Holden McGinley estate, Milton, Mass. Photo by Herbert W. Gleason, 1932. Cornell.

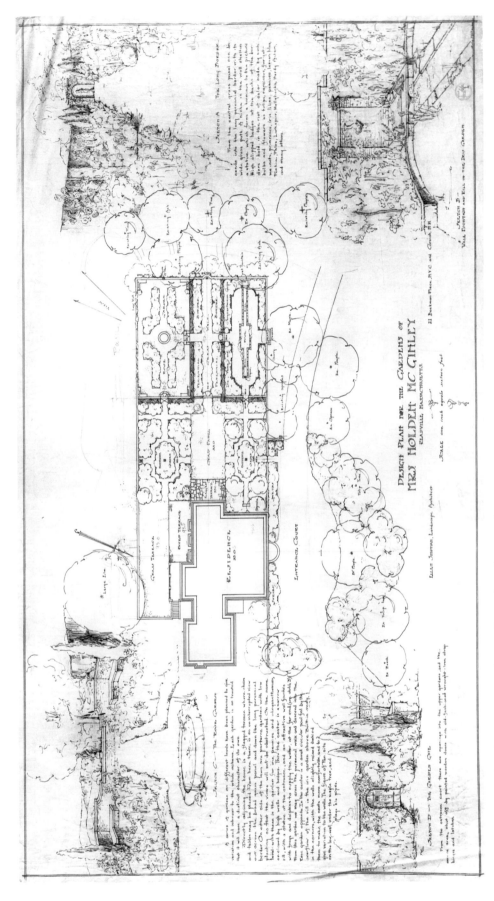

Design plan by Edith Schryver, McGinley garden, ink on linen, July 1925. Cornell.

Rill with peony, iris, and chrysanthemum beds, McGinley garden. Photo by Herbert W. Gleason, 1932. Cornell.

Edwin Lutyens and Gertrude Jekyll, Deanery Garden, Sonning-on-Thames, Berkshire, 1899. From Jekyll and Weaver, *Gardens for Small Country Houses* (London, 1912).

fortune; she may have met Shipman in Cleveland while visiting her sister, Mrs. Windsor White.[7] The site posed an interesting problem and elicited an imaginative design solution. Massive stands of trees were grouped behind and to the west of the commanding whitewashed-brick Colonial Revival house by Bigelow & Wadsworth. The property sloped gently to the south—toward open meadows and the Blue Hills. To take advantage of the view, Shipman created a two-part plan that first coaxed visitors across the lawn into the walled garden and then shifted attention ninety degrees, outward to the hills. The enclosed garden was entered through one of three gates in a brick wall; each gate opened to a different compartment. The uppermost, at the north end, was level with the house lawn; the middle garden was two steps lower; the third, at the south end, was two steps lower still. Each garden had its own character, but the three were similar enough to harmonize.

The long, narrow greensward of the middle garden was flanked by perennial borders and low walls with posts covered by climbing roses. One magazine writer recorded her impressions of the area: "Here a ver-

Pool with lotus fountain, McGinley garden. Photo by Herbert W. Gleason, 1932. Cornell.

itable tapestry was woven with tulips, shading from lightest to deepest pink, with the dark notes under double-flowering peach trees, pansies, *Phlox divaricata,* espaliered fruits, the pearlbush, and flowering almonds. Here was gay and shimmering color flung to the sun in profusion, but held within the bounds of visual harmony. Here were contrast of form and texture and irregularity of height, but here also was order, given by the carefully massed and interwoven colors and the continuing background of whitewashed brick wall."[8]

The upper garden was more simply planted. A bluestone-edged rill was set into the lawn; peony, chrysanthemum, and iris filled beds around the perimeter of the lawn. A variety of flowering shrubs and cedar added architectural heft to the composition. Again, Shipman had found design inspiration in the work Lutyens and Jekyll, who popularized the use of rills. The one in the McGinley garden strongly resembles the watercourse in the Deanery Garden, illustrated in Jekyll and Weaver's *Gardens for Small Country Houses.* Shipman's rill, however, bears only a distant spatial relationship to the main house, whereas Lutyens and Jekyll tied the two closely together.

The lower garden was given over to roses. Standard and bush roses, hybrid teas and hybrid perpetuals in shades of apricot, copper, and yellow tumbled in profusion. Golden Salmon polyanthas were clustered around the pool and lotus-leaf fountain.[9] The westward view to the hills through the opening in the wall invited the imagination into the pastoral scene beyond, the garden outside the garden.[10]

In 1928, Shipman designed a modest but charming garden at Owl's Nest, Eugene du Pont Jr.'s eighteen-acre country estate and farm complex near Wilmington, Delaware. The Tudor-style house by Harrie T. Lindberg had been built in 1915, and the grounds laid out by a local firm. Shipman proposed several gardens for the estate, but the Colonial Revival–style enclosed boxwood garden was the only one fully installed. She took into consideration the stunning views offered by Lindeberg's curved sunroom when she planned an axial garden with a small teahouse at the terminus of the vista. The focal point from the sunroom was a small circular reflecting pool and fountain, a copy of the one used in the McGinley garden several years earlier.[11] The striking fountain, which survives in the garden today, features bronze lotus flowers, leaves, and buds which spray water to float in the air before falling back into the pool. Shipman's construction drawings for the Arts and Crafts–inspired teahouse include specifications for the distinctive latches and other architectural features. The parterre garden is anchored by small flowering trees in each of the boxwood-enclosed quadrants, underplanted with Shipman's favorite peonies. In the spring, flowering crabapples, cherries, laburnums, and wisteria provided a setting for large drifts of about 170 varieties of spring bulbs, planted in masses of one to two hundred bulbs for maximum

Spring borders, Owl's Nest, Eugene du Pont estate, Greenville, Del., 1930s. Cornell.

effect.[12] The garden expresses the essentials of Shipman's design approach: enclosure, beautiful plantings, and distinctive architectural features.

During the 1920s, Shipman's client base expanded considerably beyond traditional East Coast localities. In 1928, she received an important commission in Kentucky bluegrass country, where increasing wealth was fostering new projects for many designers.[13] Alice Headley De Waal commissioned Shipman to provide plans for formal gardens to the east of her house, known as Cave Hill (sometimes called Cave Place), in Lexington. Her brother, Hal Price Headley, had purchased the historic but somewhat dilapidated property in 1925, and two years later Alice and her husband, Christian De Waal, acquired it. De Waal, whose family owned racehorses in Holland, was a successful businessman who had made his fortune in sugar plantations in the South. Envisioning genteel retirement years spent running a thoroughbred horse farm, he quickly renamed the property Clingendaal after a famous Dutch race course, and set about making improvements. He died unexpectedly in the process of restoring the property, and Alice was left to implement their ideas.[14]

The De Waal commission must have been appealing to Shipman, who rode horseback daily when living in Cornish. Her sketch for the grounds included detailed planting plans for two main areas, consisting of a formal perennial garden and a green garden tucked into the L of the house. Her design for the perennial garden was reminiscent of a formal boxwood-edged Dutch garden, which may have been her clients' wish. The intensively planted perennial garden was enclosed by low stone walls and broken into eight triangles and a network of radiating brick paths. Additional plans included tree, shrub, and seasonal bulb plantings. Construction drawings were prepared for a teahouse, stone walls, a wall fountain, and decorative latticework. Shipman also designed several gates for the property, including a Chippen-

Peonies and iris, Cave Hill, Mrs. Christian De Waal estate, Lexington, Ky. Photo by Bradley Studios, c. 1930s. Cornell.

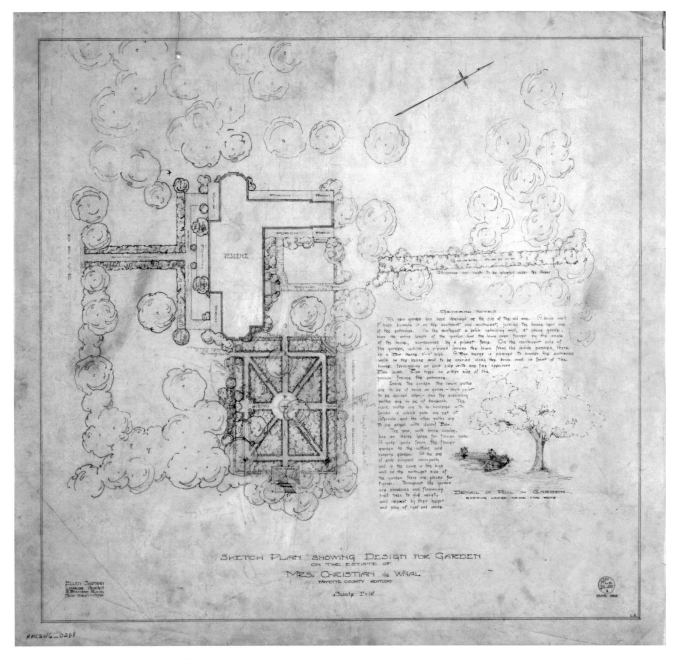

Sketch plan for garden, Cave Hill, July 1928. Cornell.

dale-style feature similar to those at the Ralph Hanes and Windsor White gardens. Period photographs show a lush and immaculately maintained garden with all of her suggested architectural elements in place.[15]

Shipman's projects caught the attention of the eminent garden writer Louisa Yeomans (Mrs. Francis) King, who praised her as a "creator of poetic and beautiful gardens all over this land." (Gertrude Jekyll seems to be the only other designer to have so captured King's enthusiasm.) One of the

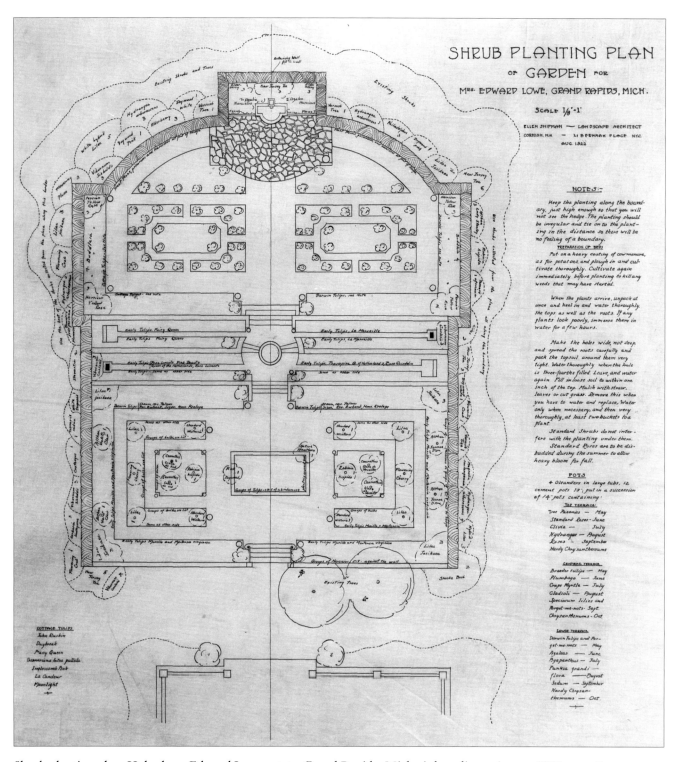

Shrub planting plan, Holmdene, Edward Lowe estate, Grand Rapids, Mich., ink on linen, August 1922. Cornell.

volumes in King's Little Garden series featured Shipman's design for the Pruyn sisters as a frontispiece, identifying it as an "illuminating example of what can be done with a small piece of ground." About 1923, Shipman gave an on-site, verbal consultation to King at the author's own Alma, Michigan, garden; her planting suggestions were happily adopted.[16]

In 1928, King wrote an article for *Country Life in America* about the garden Shipman designed for Mrs. Edward Lowe in Grand Rapids, Michigan. Reassuring her readers that "no longer do people feel that in going to the Middle West they exile themselves from all that is worth while in the arts," King revealed her sense of the hegemony of the East Coast in the garden world. One wonders whether O. C. Simonds, the prominent landscape architect who had laid out the eighty-acre estate twenty years earlier and, like King, was a Michigander, was amused. King's interpretation of Ship-

Terrace and *Mercury* pool, Holmdene. Photo by Mattie Edwards Hewitt, c. 1927. Cornell.

Rectangular pool, Holmdene. Photo by Mattie Edwards Hewitt, c. 1927. Cornell.

man's design as English—the article was titled "An English Country Place in Michigan"—reflected the widespread opinion that any sophisticated planting in America must derive from England. Shipman's innovative mix of plants and the sharp contrasts in height, texture, and shape, however, set a more idiosyncratic tone than that typical of her British colleagues. The centerpiece of Shipman's three-tiered scheme was a formal pool visible from the upper house terrace. As in her design for the Brewster pool, Shipman took advantage of the architectural form as a foil for her planting—"heucheras, sedums, statices, hostas, violas, irises, and a few stocks," according to King.[17] Hewitt's photographs for the article also record delphinium and a cluster of woodland fern where the pool was shaded by a hawthorn. The oddly stimulating juxtapositions had the authority necessary to stand up to the surrounding plantings.

August border, Holmdene. Photo by Mattie Edwards Hewitt, c. 1927. Cornell.

Fountain terrace, Overfields, George DeForest Lord estate, Syosset, N.Y. Photo by Mattie Edwards Hewitt, May 1937. Cornell.

Square pool with *Piping Pan* fountain by Louis Saint-Gaudens, Williams garden. Photo by Harry G. Healy, 1935. Cornell.

Brick walkways leading off the upper terrace were bordered more conventionally. "Alyssum, phloxes in wonderful array, ageratum, annual asters, zinnias, and statice," along with the foxglove, roses, and fruit standards fill Hewitt's midsummer photographs. The garden walk culminated in a shady flagstone terrace, leading to a raised pool and a statue of Mercury backed by one of the most ubiquitous native shrubs in the Midwest: box elder.[18]

That Shipman featured water in her designs was not unusual—her con-

Oval pool, Williams garden. Photo by Harry G. Healy, 1935. Cornell.

temporaries were also drawn to the sound, movement, and quality of light offered by pools, ponds, rills, and fountains. But Shipman's romantic treatment of water plantings was distinctive. The complexity of the plantings and the sensuousness of their arrangements made these designs recognizable as hers.

Not all of the gardens of Shipman's rich middle period were architecturally defined. In 1926, she again went to work for the Russell Algers of Grosse Pointe, for whom she had provided planting plans years before. This time she was commissioned to do a garden for the Algers' summer home in York Harbor, Maine. Shipman abandoned the close spatial relationship between garden and house and instead nestled the garden into the rocky hillside, where it was reached by a winding path. Here it provided an uninterrupted, more intimate view of the sea and remained out of view of the house—a world unto itself, innocent, spellbinding. The beds held a seed-packet summer garden of soft, small bloom, annuals and biennials mixed with hardy heather. The tiny flecks of color produced a shimmering, painterly composition. Dirt paths edged with stone connected the garden's lower edge with an overlook area bounded by a picket fence.

In spirit, the vacation garden could not have differed more sharply from its year-round counterpart in Michigan. The design typified Shipman's de-

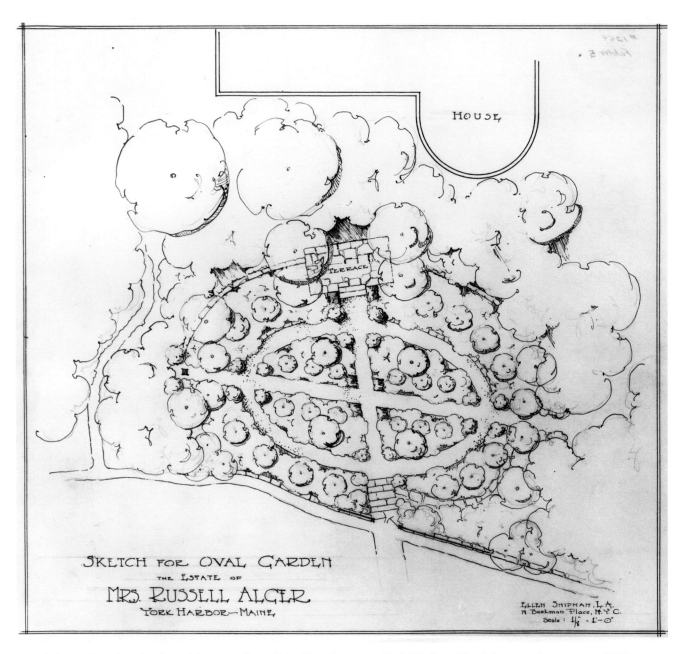

Sketch for oval garden, Starboard Cottage, Russell A. Alger Jr. estate, York Harbor, Me., ink on tracing paper, c. 1927. Cornell.

Old-fashioned flower beds, Starboard Cottage. Photo by MacLaughlass. Cornell.

parture from the world of classicism. No vestiges of the columns, fountains, and walls that defined and dominated estate designs of the period were to be found in this supple creation. Shipman's confidence was increasing. So, too, was her sense that design need not draw attention to itself to be exquisite; in fact, she was, apparently, concluding just the opposite.

Path through garden to shore, Starboard Cottage. Photo by MacLaughlass. Cornell.

Borders, Picket Farm, A. Ludlow Kramer estate, Westbury, N.Y. Photo by Mattie Edwards Hewitt, 1923. Cornell.

SEVEN

THE BORDER

Shipman used borders to spectacular effect in the majority of her garden projects, varying them according to their role in the overall design, her clients' taste in plants, staff—no garden feature was more demanding—and her own imagination. Use of the border was not, however, universal among Shipman's contemporaries, some of whom viewed them as part of an amateur tradition rather than as an artistic vehicle. Marian Coffin used them sparingly, as did Shipman's California colleagues Florence Yoch and Lucille Council, who, like Coffin, were more interested in inventing new features than in exploring the potential of old ones. Beatrix Farrand did incorporate the border effectively in many of her gardens, but it was not a central point of departure for her work. Fletcher Steele for the most part avoided the border in favor of bold experiments in color, texture, and plant mass. On those occasions when he did use herbaceous borders, he asked a female assistant to draw up the planting plans.

American homeowners of the period, on the other hand, loved borders. No feature was more common in the backyard plan, in part because it offered a simple and effective means of growing many different flowers—and flowers, of course, were the motivation for most home gardens. Shipman's genuine enthusiasm for horticulture and her respect for clients' involvement in their own gardens attracted business and put her in contact with people whose interests she shared and whose lives her design talent could enrich. "I never am quite satisfied until there is some place that I can walk between flowers," she wrote one client.[1]

Within the narrow confines of the genre, Shipman discovered extraordi-

Robert and Mildred Bliss with herbaceous borders by Beatrix Farrand, Dumbarton Oaks, Washington, D.C., c. 1936. Harvard University Archives.

Fletcher Steele, borders, Standish Backus estate, Grosse Pointe Shores, Mich., c. 1930. ESF Moon Library Archives and Special Collections, SUNY College of Environmental Science and Forestry, Syracuse, N.Y.

Double borders, Angus Smith garden, Detroit, Mich. Photo by Shipman office, 1929. Cornell.

nary variety. She used the flower border to focus and narrate the experience of a garden, and even a brief survey reveals her wide range of investigation. The textures of the Kramer garden, for example, were strong and coarse, the ephemeral plantings for Angus Smith, simple and sweet. The narrow grass path in the Murray Sales garden, where borders were the garden's main feature, was intimate and informal; a walk down it, ankle-deep in flowers, led visitors to step gingerly around an elm that grew—certainly was planted— right in the middle of it. Some designs were more interesting for the contradictions they embraced. A long formal border against the south brick wall of the McGinley terrace was edged by a dirt path, defined with broken stone, perhaps a quotation from Gertrude Jekyll's spring border at Munstead Wood.[2] Shipman's design skills, like Jekyll's, developed from practical experience: her ability to shape a garden picture in her mind evolved from years of actually digging, lifting, separating, and sinking plants in the dirt.

Shipman's intuitive understanding of the emotional importance of lush borders to her female clients—including Clara Ford, Gertrude Seiberling, Gertrude Whittemore, Elizabeth Mather, and many others—would prove crucial to her success. These women sought opportunities for intimate interaction with their gardens and looked to the domestically based activities of planning, planting, cultivating, cutting, and arranging flowers for meaningful experiences beyond aesthetic appreciation. In the case of Ford, Seiberling, Whittemore, and Mather, large residential landscapes had been designed by prominent landscape architects whose skills —and interests— fell short of border design. After years of dissatisfaction with perfunctory plantings, they summoned Ellen Shipman to create more vibrant plantings within an existing framework.

Twelve years before Shipman went to work for Henry and Clara Ford in 1927, they had hired the Chicago-based landscape architect Jens Jensen to plan a two-thousand-acre estate in Dearborn, Michigan. Jensen's mon-

Path through borders, Murray Sales garden, Grosse Pointe, Mich. Photo by George W. Hance, c. 1926. Cornell.

Double borders, Sales garden. Photo by George W. Hance, c. 1926. Cornell.

Spring border, Mrs. Holden McGinley estate, Milton, Mass. Photo by Herbert W. Gleason, 1932. Cornell.

Elizabeth Ring Mather at Gwinn, Cleveland, Ohio, late 1930s. William Gwinn Mather Papers, Gwinn Archives.

Henry and Clara Ford at Fair Lane, Dearborn, Mich., 1939. Collections of The Henry Ford.

umental and poetic design featured long, sinuous meadows and rockwork bordering the Rouge River. Formality found a place, too. The Great Meadow was to be viewed from a balustraded terrace on one end of the long house; a small terrace garden adjoining the other end was the site of a formal rose garden. Although Henry loved the landscape of Fair Lane, Clara Ford found the scarcity of flowers frustrating. Jensen's meadows offered pleasures of the most refined sort, but they did not provide the big, bold flower borders or the intimate horticultural contact that Clara wanted. In 1925, she hired Herbert J. Kellaway and the rose specialist Harriett Foote to lay out an immense rose garden—smack dab in the center of one of Jensen's meadows. Jensen exploded when he saw the results and demanded that the ASLA reprimand Kellaway for interfering with the integrity of his work. When they refused, Jensen resigned his membership. Henry and Jensen eventually reconciled, but Jensen and Clara never found the warmth of their earlier relations.

Shipman was invited to Fair Lane two years after the Kellaway blowup to design perennial plantings for Jensen's original rose garden—now that Clara Ford no longer needed it. She suggested reconfiguring the beds in the small rectangular space and adding new plantings (including herbaceous perennials, shrubs, and small trees), a teahouse, grand iron gates, and a

Shipman garden, Fair Lane. Collections of The Henry Ford.

small pool. Her planting notes for "Mrs. Ford's Garden" shed light on her sense of the garden as an entity that exists in time, the slow-motion unfolding of an art. The predominant colors of the display were blues, whites, and occasional glints of yellow, a color scheme that Shipman used extensively.

She explained her planting design technique in a letter to Clara Ford: "I usually use one main plant at a time to dominate in the garden, beginning with the bulbs, and the other plants that are used at that time are complimentary [*sic*] to the dominant one." April and May were given over to bulbs as well as other spring flowers for contrast. "The next main plant which dominates the garden," Shipman wrote, "would be the iris, beginning with the earlier varieties and running into the German iris." Under the heading "late June," Shipman wrote, "From the iris, we would run into the early and later peonies." In July: "Before the peonies have gone, the early larkspur comes, and then the larkspur completely dominates the garden." And August: "Before the larkspur is gone, the early Phlox comes." And September: "By the time the phlox is gone, the autumn garden has come and the later phlox, set off by the autumn flowers, the hardy asters (hybrid), Boltonia, the Eupatoriums, agerotoides and coledestinum, the later aconitum, anemone hupehensis, dahlias, which have been set in to take the place of the Delphiniums, that were cut back, Gladiolus, Hibiscus, Plumbago, Sedums." October: "By late autumn, the anemone japonica and the late hardy asters and chrysanthemums, and the very late aconitum and Pyrethrum. If the Nepeta and Lavendula have been cut back after the spring bloom, they will bloom again in the late autumn." Happy relations between Mrs. Shipman and Mrs. Ford extended into the 1930s, as the landscape architect returned several times to advise on planting in the area.[3]

Shipman's involvement at Stan Hywet Hall in Akron, Ohio, which began in 1928, reflected a similar wish on the part of a female client to grow beautiful flowers in a formal garden setting. In this case, however, it was the estate's original designer, Warren H. Manning, who suggested the revision of his own planting. Manning's 1911 design for Frank and Gertrude Seiberling's three-thousand-acre estate was primarily naturalistic in style and inspiration, organized around a dramatic quarry that offered unusual planting opportunities and a varied and picturesque "wilderness." The design also included several agrarian features, an English landskip–inspired front lawn, and several formal elements, most of which were worked out in consultation with the architect, Charles S. Schneider: birch and London plane tree allées, terraces, perennial borders, and the walled English Garden. A Japanese garden, designed by T. R. Otsuka, nestled between the big quarry garden and the landscape's more formal elements. Like many successful American industrialists, Frank A. Seiberling, founder of the Goodyear Tire Company, had been eager to spend lavish amounts of his newly acquired fortune in creating a country estate, but by the 1920s, his finances were in decline and large portions of the property were being subdivided. The redesign of the English Garden may have been offered to Gertrude as compensation for cutbacks elsewhere.[4]

Of all the gardens of Stan Hywet, only the English Garden offered complete privacy. According to family memory, it was Gertrude Seiberling's favorite refuge from the tensions of running her busy household. She came to the walled garden to escape—to think, to compose, and to talk privately with her children. Manning wrote to Frank Seiberling about the development of the estate's other features, but the discussion of the English Garden took place with Gertrude, whose word apparently was final. It was her suggestion to paint the trellises "verdigris green" and to site the walled garden

Gertrude Seiberling in the English Garden, Stan Hywet Hall, F. A. Seiberling estate, Akron, Ohio, c. 1920. Stan Hywet Hall Archives.

so that it would be a secret, screened by shrubbery and discovered after walking through the Japanese garden.[5]

No planting plan has survived to record the original arrangement of annuals, biennials, perennials, and vines that sounded an odd but vibrant chorus of oranges and maroons. By 1928, Gertrude, a sophisticated amateur painter, had tired of the combination and decided to do something about it, suggesting specifically a "blue, yellow, pink and white garden." Manning recommended that she call in Shipman for the revision, assuring his client that he considered "her one of the best, if not the very best, Flower Garden Maker in America."[6] The accolade may well have been repeated to other of Manning's clients, including Elizabeth and William Mather, who hired Shipman a few years later for work at Gwinn.

Irene Seiberling Harrison, the youngest of the family's seven children, remembered one of Shipman's visits to Stan Hywet in 1928. Her mother and Shipman breakfasted together as they discussed the new garden and then retired to her mother's bedroom to converse uninterrupted. Irene, who was then thirty-eight years old, remembered Shipman as "a knowledgeable person, super-educated person. . . . She was also very nice. Friendly, in a sense."[7] She also remembered Ellen Shipman's intensity about the task at hand.

Shipman drew up two planting plans in May 1929 which show the retention of Schneider's Arts and Crafts garden architecture, including the walls, niches, paths, pools, and a fountain by the sculptor Willard Paddock. She added small ornamental trees and standards to embolden the flower beds, which were designed in the pinks, blues, and yellows Gertrude had requested. Shipman's intensive planting for these borders has been likened to a "glittering mosaic of color" in contrast to the softer pastels that enlivened her designs elsewhere. More than eighty different varieties of plants were

Nancy Seiberling in the English Garden, Stan Hywet Hall, c. 1942. Stan Hywet Hall Archives.

Perennial planting plan, Stan Hywet Hall, ink on linen, 11 May 1929. Stan Hywet Hall Archives.

added. As in Clara Ford's garden, Shipman interwove bulbs, annuals, and perennials with heftier standards, shrubs, and trees "to cast shadows across the blooms in summer time."[8]

Five years before she worked on the Seiberling garden, Shipman had been called in to redesign the flower gardens at Tranquillity Farm, near Middlebury, Connecticut. The bucolic three-hundred-acre estate, a gentleman's working farm, had been laid out primarily by Warren H. Manning in the 1890s for John Howard Whittemore, a successful businessman, and his wife, Julia Spencer Whittemore.[9] Manning worked directly with Julia Whittemore on the plantings for the formal gardens near the house. In 1923, their daughter, Gertrude Whittemore, contacted Ellen Shipman (probably at the suggestion of Manning) to revitalize and expand the flower gardens near the terrace of the house. Shipman prepared a dozen planting plans for the Upper Garden, Lower Garden, Annual Garden, and a Rose Garden as well as construction drawings for walkways and other features.[10]

The circumstances of Shipman's work at Gwinn were slightly different.

She returned to the Cleveland estate in 1935 to design planting plans for the same beds she had made recommendations for two decades earlier. The Depression had forced cutbacks in general development and maintenance throughout the estate shortly after William Mather's 1929 marriage to Elizabeth Ireland, but by the mid-1930s, when the Mathers' finances had stabilized and the couple had decided to pursue a modest renovation of the grounds, Elizabeth Mather was eager to find ways to make the twenty-one-acre estate her own. It was not surprising that, as a master gardener and president of the Garden Club of Greater Cleveland, she turned her interest to the formal garden. Manning's dappled wild garden across the street offered opportunities for Thoreauvian solitude, but more of Elizabeth Mather's time would be spent amid the brilliantly flowering beds.

View through pergola, Tranquillity Farm, J. H. Whittemore estate, Middlebury, Conn. Photo by Arthur B. Eldredge.

Brick path, formal garden, Tranquillity Farm. Photo by Arthur B. Eldredge.

Shipman's recommendations for the new scheme respected the layout of Charles Platt's 1907 design but brought new complexity and spatial interest to the geometry of the walled area. As at Fair Lane, Shipman featured one type of flower to dominate each season. She retained Platt's basic color scheme of blue, white, and yellow, softening it with shades of pink and peach. Her suggestion of Japanese cherries, flowering almonds, and Japanese lilacs to surround the pool was met with some concern by the Mathers, who were accustomed to the garden's openness. But before long, the sunny geometry of Platt's layout had acquired lingering shadows and mystery; Shipman had made the walled enclosure more poetic by putting three-dimensional forms into it.

Had Shipman's client correspondence survived, her relationships with

Sundial in formal garden, Tranquillity Farm. Photo by Arthur B. Eldredge.

Formal garden, Gwinn, William G. Mather estate, Cleveland, Ohio. Photo by Walter P. Bruning, c. 1950. William Gwinn Mather Papers, Gwinn Archives.

her women clients and her role in creating settings in response to their imaginative selves would no doubt be more vivid. But there is little question that Shipman's services invariably led to garden spaces that enriched her clients' lives. At a time when women's expressiveness was not encouraged—at home or in the world generally—flower gardens provided female clients with sensuous havens and a grounding link to seasonal rhythms and cycles.

View into pergola, Gwinn. Photo by Walter P. Bruning, c. 1950. William Gwinn Mather Papers, Gwinn Archives.

Vista to pool, Penwood, Carll Tucker estate, Mount Kisco, N.Y. Photo by Harry G. Healy, late 1930s. Cornell.

EIGHT

A GRANDER SCOPE

Several commissions from the mid- to late 1920s involved more extensive architectural structures than any previous and thus catapulted Shipman to new design challenges. As the affluent traveled abroad and returned with grand cultural pretensions, American gardens were becoming increasingly exotic, and Shipman responded by incorporating a variety of architectural influences, including Italian, French, and even Spanish into her work. The aesthetic success of these more architecturally determined gardens rested on Shipman's hard-won ability to integrate large spaces and handsome detailing with her own planting style. Because Shipman's expressive style had evolved outside of these prevailing influences, it was more distinctive for not having been shaped by the European tastes that dominated so many of her colleagues' development.

The most recognizably "Shipmanesque" of these commissions was Penwood, the Carll Tucker estate in Mount Kisco, New York, not far from Wampus, the much-photographed Magee garden. Shipman worked with the Tuckers from 1926, returning at regular intervals to adjust and augment the design. The garden began at a distance from the house and was bounded on the southwest edge by a rustic Italian loggia. Thick stucco pillars supported a cedar trellis, evoking images of the sunny Tuscan campagna—associations, of course, gleaned from books since Shipman had not yet traveled to Italy. Huge slabs of fieldstone paved the loggia floor and major paths through the big flower garden, resulting in arresting contrasts as the chunky architectural forms exaggerated the delicacy of the plantings.

A parterre garden stretched in front of the loggia, adjoined by a square

Parterre garden and pergola (*top*) and pool, Penwood. Photos by Mattie Edwards Hewitt, 1927. Cornell.

September borders, Penwood. Photo by Harry G. Healy, late 1930s. Cornell.

flower garden. A pool marked the center of the square, its raised coping an ingenious, urgent afterthought—because of a mismeasurement, the feature had been plumbed about six inches too high. Shipman's assistant, Eleanor Christie, remembered the panic over the additional expense a revision would have entailed, observing: "Of course you don't just dig out a pool and redo it." She and Louise Payson solved the problem by using three levels of coping instead of the single layer originally planned; Shipman, according to Christie, "was thrilled to death" with the result.[1] So, too, apparently, were the magazine photographers who found the little pool irresistible. The design was copied in several other gardens of the period, including Shipman's own at Brook Place.

After spring tulips and narcissus faded, foxglove, delphinium, peony, columbine, and astilbe filled the garden's beds. The flower masses reached five feet, effectively swallowing spring standards of wisteria and lilacs. In September, monkshood, Japanese anemones, dahlias, hardy asters, and gladiolus succeeded the taller subjects, and the standards once again emerged from the masses, the altheas now in bloom. *House Beautiful* praised the Tucker garden for its "luxuriant growth which makes each division a self-contained unit with its own interest, but composing with the others by means of pleasant vistas."[2]

Shipman mixed lacy spring bloom with tall evergreen spires to make the transition to the greenery beyond. In one plan a sequestered wild garden and pond are indicated to the west. A more diminutive scale was explored in the tiny violets, violas, dianthus, and dwarf iris tucked amid the stones of the pool coping. Shipman returned to Penwood after a hiatus caused by World War II to revise the garden and suggested a reduced maintenance plan. More than 150 drawings and documents were generated, an indication of the seriousness with which the clients regarded their landscape.

In 1924, Shipman again stretched beyond her idiomatic approach when she was hired by Evander B. Schley in Far Hills, New Jersey, to create a series of gardens "in the Spanish mood."[3] The house by Peabody, Wilson & Brown, also of Spanish inspiration and predating her work there, was

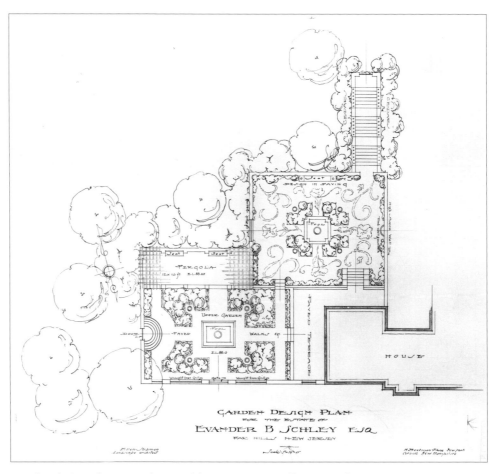

Garden design plan, Evander B. Schley estate, Far Hills, N.J., ink on tissue, c. 1924. Cornell.

Spanish-inspired steps, Schley garden. Photo by John Wallace Gilles, c. 1930. Cornell.

Tiled pool on lower terrace, Schley garden. Photo by John Wallace Gilles, c. 1930. Cornell.

perhaps the lone example of the architectural type among Shipman's client residences. The red-tiled roof and heavy stucco walls that defined Spanish Revival architecture were not common in the Northeast and Midwest, where Shipman did most of her work.

Shipman's predilection for strongly axial, walled gardens did not need much adjustment for this job, since it coincided with the traditional Spanish approach to garden making which entailed a sequence of courtyards. But the commission also offered new opportunities for experiments with exotic embellishment, and these Shipman approached with unusual relish. Elaborate paving patterns (in New England–style brick), ceramic tile work, terra-cotta pots, espaliered roses, and near-tropical plants, including *Agapanthus* (evidently overwintered indoors), summoned the unrestrained sensuality of a Spanish courtyard garden. Shipman's job notes indicate the use of large cedars and flowering trees to "simulate the cypress and fruit trees of Spain and give grateful shade." A less voluptuous upper garden organized around a central pool with four splashing jets featured enormous *tinjajones* (Spanish oil jars) at the corners of the beds.[4]

Three years earlier Shipman had been commissioned to work up an elaborate Colonial Revival garden for Chatham, a 1721 house undergoing restoration by architect Oliver H. Clarke in Fredericksburg, Virginia. The historical importance of the house—George Washington spent much of his early life at Chatham and Robert E. Lee met and married Mary Custis there—would have interested her. The charge from her clients, Colonel and Mrs. Daniel B. Devore, was to create a period garden. Shipman was apparently pleased with the result, for she later wrote, "Most people thought the garden had been there when the house was restored." In truth, the site had been a cornfield.[5]

East elevation, Chatham Manor, Col. Daniel B. and Helen Devore estate, Fredericksburg, Va. Photo by Frances Benjamin Johnston, c. 1927. Library of Congress.

Vista with sculpture, Chatham Manor. Photo by Frances Benjamin Johnston, c. 1927. Library of Congress.

Shipman was so thoroughly steeped in the forms and feeling of the Colonial Revival garden, then at the peak of its popularity, that she scarcely needed to reflect consciously on them—in this sense Chatham was simply a grander version of her usual, more modestly scaled work. In this rich design, she managed to create a believable colonial spirit and a luxuriousness not typical of such gardens. Avoiding the tight precision that so often characterized period imitation, Shipman emulated something much more elusive: the relaxed, unreflective irregularity that develops in gardens over time.

One writer recorded her impressions in 1926: "On the right of the pathway, nearest the terrace, was that part of the garden which, starting in a formal way with arches and boxwood edgings, had then abandoned the well-laid plan of the gardener and run riot, making the garden its own. And so inspirational was its plan—with its mass of apricot, rose, and white *Phlox drummondi* spreading a lovely carpet over the garden beds and reaching beyond, its miniature fruit-trees and tendriled arches growing in willful pleasure—that the fair gardener, putting beauty before order, allowed it to remain and acknowledged her defeat."[6]

Despite the writer's enthusiasm for the relaxed charm of Chatham, she failed to mention Ellen Shipman's role in its design. Years later, however, in 1938, the garden was featured on the cover of the annual garden week guidebook of the Garden Club of Virginia. Shipman's design lasted only

Perennial borders and pergola, Chatham Manor. Photo by Frances Benjamin Johnson, c. 1927. Library of Congress.

until World War II, when the landscape architect Charles Gillette simplified it for the new owner, John Lee Pratt, by replacing the labor-intensive perennials and beds of annuals with more boxwood.[7] Like most of her contemporaries, Shipman ultimately watched the majority of her landscape designs disappear, victims of changing taste and shifting fortunes.

Somewhat more focused than these historical amalgamations was Shipman's involvement with the Arts and Crafts movement. Centered in the Cotswolds, the approach was developed by a group of architects and designers who worked in a vernacular architectural style as opposed to the Tudor-derived style promoted by the formalists. The pages of *Country Life* magazine and numerous British books of the period show many examples that exhibited the two fundamental aspects of the Arts and Crafts movement: the collaboration of architect and craftsman working in regional building traditions and the close alliance of house, garden, and decorative arts.[8] In America, the Arts and Crafts garden took on regional shadings, with a strong emphasis on handcrafted decorative arts and use of local building materials and garden architecture.[9] Many eastern and midwestern estates of the period, whose surroundings resembled the gently rolling Cotswold hills, reflected this influence. Chestnut Hill, Pennsylvania, and other areas rich in local stone were particularly well suited to it. But the Cotswold style was also transplanted to unlikely settings, such as Long Island's Gold Coast, where it expressed a taste for exoticism rather than regionalism. Shipman created two particularly significant Arts and Crafts–inspired gardens there during the decade.

The first was for Rynwood, the manor house estate commissioned from Roger H. Bullard by Samuel A. Salvage in 1926. It was one of Shipman's largest and most important jobs to date. The site plan included a large courtyard, a service courtyard, a terrace, three separate formal gardens, a swimming pool, a tennis court, and several acres of surrounding fields. A photograph of a detailed model (the only surviving example in Shipman's archives) shows the architectural components and plantings of the estate.

The garden's major architectural ornaments were a round, slate-roofed dovecote, designed by Shipman in response to Bullard's Tudor-inspired architectural detailing, and a teahouse modeled after a small building at Snowshill Manor in the Cotswolds.[10] She placed the dovecote opposite the teahouse, midway down the west side of a large walled garden, where it would also serve as an anchor for a smaller garden, thereby capitalizing twice on its distinctive silhouette and old English charm. The center of the teahouse garden was marked by a circular, *Bergenia*-edged pool and shaded by an old apple tree. Fruit tree allées, boxwood-edged beds filled with masses of mixed perennials, and enormous hydrangeas followed examples from simple Cornish gardens and also contributed to the spatial

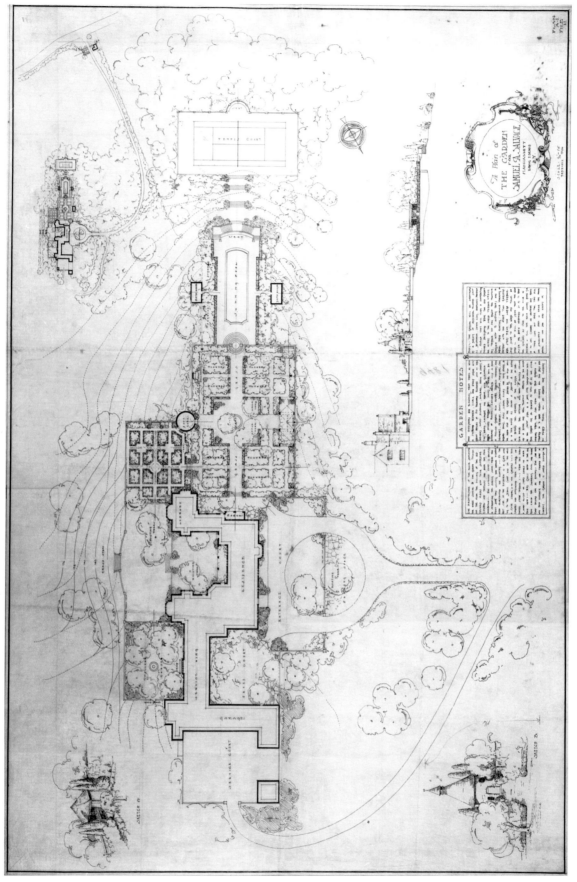

General design plan for Rynwood, Samuel A. Salvage estate, Glen Head, N.Y., ink on linen, February 1926. Cornell.

Model of Rynwood. Photo by Mattie Edwards Hewitt, c. 1926. Cornell.

Sketch for Loggia
Salvage

Sketch for teahouse, Rynwood, pencil on trace, 1926. Cornell.

Teahouse walk, Rynwood. Photo by Mattie Edwards Hewitt, May 1934. Cornell.

Dovecote, Rynwood. Photo by Harry G. Healy, 1935. Cornell.

Pool, Rynwood. Photo by Harry G. Healy, 1935. Cornell.

definition of the area.[11] The quirky eclecticism of Shipman's planting design—in this case drawn from Italian, French, and English gardens—was perhaps its single most defining "American" quality.

Shipman's garden for Mrs Ormsby Mitchell in Greenwich, Connecticut, begun three years after the Salvage estate, also expressed Arts and Crafts ideals and attracted the praise of American critics—"no Cotswold house that we know has had the advantage of such delightful gardening," wrote one of them proudly."[12] The design marked a new level of assurance in her work. Here Shipman combined a cohesive spatial plan with unusually spare plantings, most of which related strongly to the garden architecture and also recalled English prototypes—ivy-covered garden walls, for example. Yet some planting passages achieved an unexpected and original character.

Flagstone path, Rynwood. Photo by Harry G. Healy, 1935. Cornell.

A November 1929 drawing by Shipman's assistant Irma Berger shows the overall design scheme. A lawn terrace at the back of the house was flanked by perennial borders; a walled, paved terrace at the south end of the house, and sited directly on axis with it, had a small octagonal pool in the center and a dovecote-toolhouse (similar to the Salvages') placed at the intersection of this area and a formal, walled entry court. Filling the corner between the paved terrace and lawn terrace was a square rose garden, marked by two intersecting grass walks. The architect, Alfred Hopkins, used stone from the Greenwich vicinity in the Cotswold-style house and all the outbuildings.

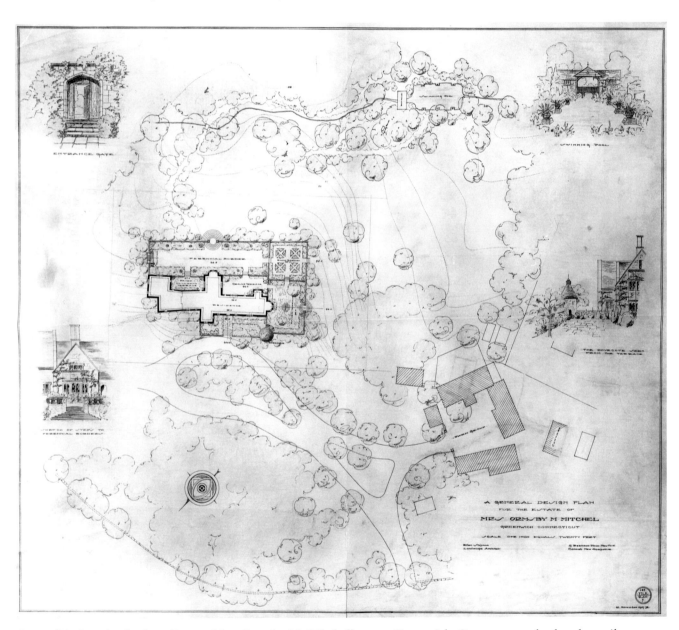

General design plan by Irma Berger, Mrs. Ormsby M. Mitchell estate, Greenwich, Conn., pen and colored pencil on trace, 12 November 1929. Cornell.

Millstone terrace, Mitchell estate. Photo by Harry G. Healy, c. 1937. Cornell.

Rose garden and terrace (*top*) and dovecote-toolhouse, Mitchell estate. Photos by Harry G. Healy, c. 1937. Cornell.

Dining room terrace and playroom, Mitchell estate. Photo by Harry G. Healy, c. 1937. Cornell.

Wisteria pool, Mitchell estate. Photo by Harry G. Healy, c. 1937. Cornell.

One of these was a small house that held a studio and open hearth fireplace. Shipman's unusually restrained plantings tied these separate structures, terraces, and paved courts together.

The sculptural proportions of the garden areas reflected the masses of the house and sounded a new note of authority in Shipman's body of work. The spatial clarity of these areas was unusually bold, a result, in part, of the strong walls and clear changes of level. Shipman's preoccupation with paths as spatial determinants was nowhere in evidence. Here she adopted a three-dimensional approach to garden making. The low-rising circular steps leading from the dovecote terrace to the lawn, modeled after traditional English garden steps, were also sculptural. The repetition of the curve in the steps, dovecote, openwork walls, and octagonal pool established a rhythm that pulled the parts into a whole.

Because each area in the Mitchell scheme had its own definitive character, transitions from one to another were distinct. Most memorable in the several vignettes captured in Harry Healy's photographs is the pairing of an old wisteria and a small pool that it shaded—and dwarfed—beneath. The unexpected match saved the scene from the generic quality that made so many landscapes of the period more perfunctory than inspired.

Waterfall in stream garden, Rippowam, Mrs. Jonathan Bulkley estate, Ridgefield, Conn. Photo by Mattie Edwards Hewitt, 1931. Cornell.

NINE

WILD GARDENS

In the several naturalistic gardens Shipman designed through the 1920s and 1930s, she may have been influenced by Warren Manning. Manning frequently coaxed his clients to set aside portions of their properties as improved woodland, for hiking, horseback riding, and the intimate experience of nature. Shipman would have seen Manning's quarry garden at Stan Hywet in the late 1920s, when she was there working on the English Garden, and the large wild garden that he laid out at Gwinn beginning in 1914. Other landscape architects promoted wild gardens as well. Certain of them, such as Jens Jensen, advocated for broad, primarily naturalistic landscape treatments of entire estates, but almost every American landscape architect involved with residential commissions found occasion to create areas of designed wildness.

A comparison between Shipman's wild gardens and those of two of her colleagues illuminates a key factor in her garden making generally. Percival Gallagher of Olmsted Brothers was typical of many designers, including Shipman, who introduced carefully crafted wildness into Beaux-Arts–influenced designs. Gallagher's heavily planted ravine garden at Oldfields, the Indianapolis estate of Hugh and Jessie Landon, was, like Shipman's gardens, essentially ornamental in inspiration. The rocky hillside setting represented an opportunity to introduce lavish plantings that also struck a spontaneous note—a type of wild garden inspired by William Robinson's book *The Wild Garden* (1870), which enjoyed a wide readership in the United States.

Manning's approach, by contrast, derived from the idea that the wild garden was embedded in nature and could, through careful pruning, be

Percival Gallagher, ravine garden, Oldfields, J. K. Lilly Jr. estate, Indianapolis, Ind., after 1932. Indianapolis Museum of Art.

Warren Manning, Wild Garden, Stan Hywet Hall, Akron, Ohio, early 1920s. Stan Hywet Hall Archives.

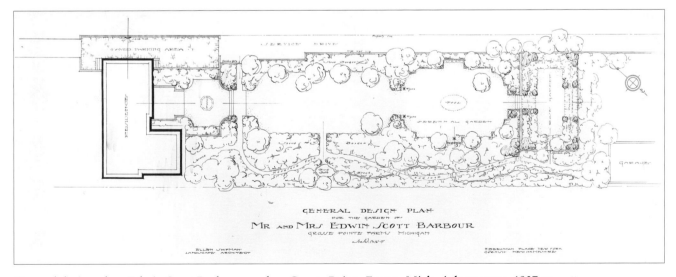

General design plan, Edwin Scott Barbour garden, Grosse Pointe Farms, Mich., ink on trace, 1927. Cornell.

extracted from it. Although Manning also recommended extensive new plantings and did not distinguish—as did his midwestern colleague Jensen—between native and nonnative species, he emphasized respect for the existing features of the site, and would have been loath to construct false features such as waterfalls and pools. While Shipman's approach more closely resembled Gallagher's, she may nevertheless have been inspired by Manning's example and his belief that the aesthetic experience of the wild garden was one that would benefit his clients. And although Shipman's

Naturalistic pool and walk, Barbour garden. Photo by Thomas Ellison, June 1936. Cornell.

wild gardens do not figure among her most compelling work, they reflect the essence of her garden making: the idea of the garden as an artistic creation, an artifice.

In addition to offering an aesthetic alternative to formality, many of Shipman's wild gardens also filled pivotal design roles. On a small suburban lot owned by the Edwin Scott Barbours in Grosse Pointe Farms, for example, she developed a shrub and birch garden as a screen to a neighboring property. Using the fieldstone path and accompanying rill and bird-bath pools as a spine, Shipman organized the plantings on either side to create a narrow stroll garden. The small-scale plantings among the irregular rockwork included alpines, bulbs, and ground-hugging thyme in seemingly haphazard, "natural" arrangement, but to knowing eyes, the lush floral display undoubtedly struck a more deliberate note.

In her 1926 design for Mrs. Henry V. Greenough in Brookline, Massachusetts, Shipman combined formal and wild gardens in an urban setting. Mrs. Greenough, Mrs. Windsor White's sister, may have met Shipman through her or one of Shipman's other Cleveland clients. The formal area reflected Shipman's prototypal layout: a rectangular space divided by walks with axial accents at both ends, a garden house and sculpture. Horticultural

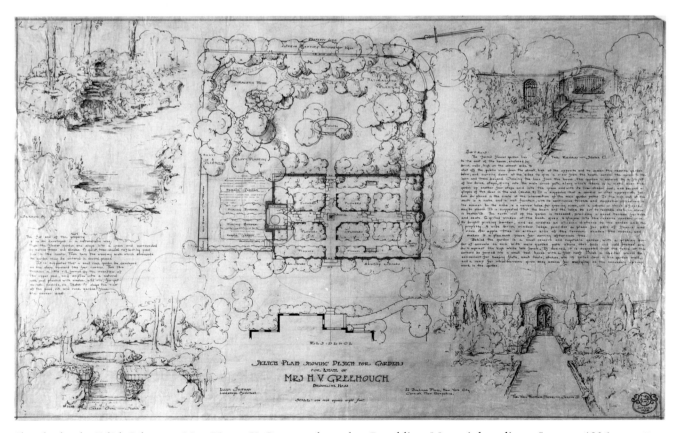

Sketch plan by Edith Schryver, Mrs. Henry V. Greenough garden, Brookline, Mass., ink on linen, January 1926. Cornell.

Naturalistic pool with native plants, Greenough garden. Photo by Dorothy Jarvis Studio, c. 1931. Cornell.

interest and color were planned for all seasons—masses of bulbs in spring, heliotrope and petunias in summer, asters and boltonia in autumn, juniper and pachysandra through winter. Beyond the formal area lay an informal lawn surrounded by trees and shrubs, and beyond this, a woodland with a pool and miniature waterfall. High brick walls surrounded the densely canopied garden. Shipman's idealized plant scheme was more exotic than anything that would have occurred naturally. The palette included a wide variety of native and nonnative species, as one writer noted: "Mountain-ash, arborvitae, hemlock, dogwood, laurel rhododendron and viburnum . . . big leaf saxifrage, calla lilies, waterlilies, iris, eupatorium, Shortia, and other native creeping wood- and water-loving plants."[1] That Shipman *intended* these gardens to seem "natural" is beyond question; but she was also aware of the complexities of the design task at hand. "You are trying to copy nature," she wrote, "her pocket has no bottom, and her lavishness is unbound, . . . her art of arrangement is the art of the Lord."[2]

The wild garden that Shipman designed for the Willard Clapp estate in a suburban setting in Cleveland Heights, Ohio, was also typical of her work in the genre. One of Shipman's 1927 construction drawings referred to a plan "supplied by Manning's offices," suggesting that he provided engineering and site-planning services for the job. Its formal counterpart, developed on axis with the large house, was typical as well; it featured a central reflecting pool and airy flower borders that recalled designs from many of Shipman's other projects. At the rear of the lawn was a naturalistic pond where irregular stones surrounding the water's edge were interplanted with a mixture of native and exotic plants, including iris, coral bells, *Bergenia*, and several

Wild garden and stone terrace, Willard M. Clapp estate, Cleveland, Ohio. Photo by Thomas Ellison. Cornell.

Reflecting pool with *Diana* by Edward McCartan, Rippowam. Photo by Mattie Edwards Hewitt, 1931, Cornell.

varieties of thyme. Rhododendron and small specimen trees created a screen planting for the little woodland.

A more elaborate wild garden was developed for Mrs. Jonathan Bulkley at Rippowam in Ridgefield, Connecticut, in the late 1920s or early 1930s. Mrs. Bulkley was a prominent member and, between 1932 and 1935, president of the Garden Club of America. In Shipman's design a dense woodland backdrop was the setting for Edward McCartan's statue of Diana and a

Stream garden, Rippowam. Photo by Mattie Edwards Hewitt, 1931. Cornell.

large swimming pool. Elsewhere on the property, a rocky waterfall composed a more deliberate "wilderness" and set up a dramatic mountain view. Masterfully engineered, the complex stonework waterfall and path were nonetheless mannered, theatrical beyond anything wind and water might have worn in the side of a mountain. The studied planting design—of ferns, dianthus, ajuga, campanula, iris, and other ornamentals—heightened the impossibly arcadian look of the hillside.[3]

In 1915, when Shipman was working with Charles Platt on a formal garden at The Causeway, the James and Alice Parmelee estate in Washington, D.C., she also drew up a planting plan for the network of bridle paths winding through the bucolic property. She returned twelve years later, in October 1927, to plan an extensive wild garden.[4] Frances Benjamin Johnston's period photographs of the woodland design suggest a different tone from most of her other wild gardens. Shipman's planting plans record a complex scheme that, as in other designs, mixed drifts of ornamental exotics with indigenous varieties. Mature trees and large clumps of rhododendron open to sun-drenched clearings. The wooded areas include a network of paths for

Woodland planting, The Causeway, James and Alice Parmelee estate, Washington, D.C.
Smithsonian Institution.

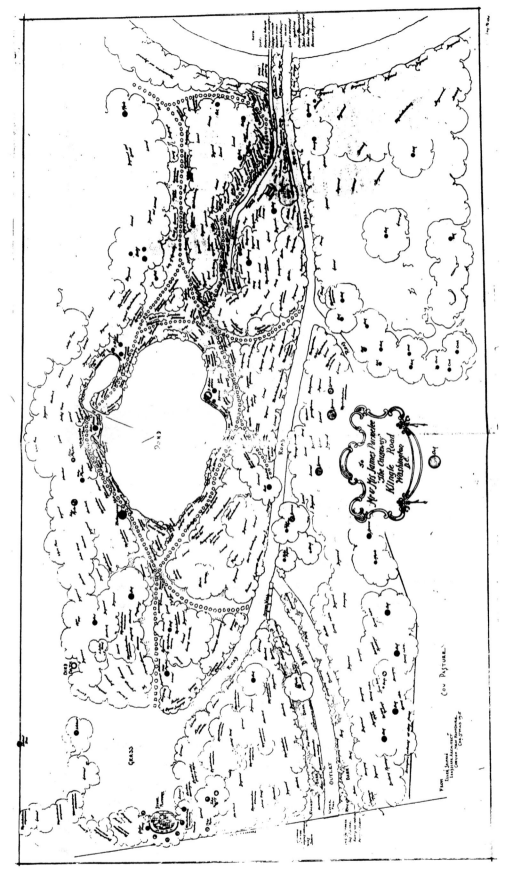

Presentation plan of pond, bridle path, and grass area, The Causeway, 1915. Cornell.

walking and riding, with rustic stone bridges and retaining walls inspired by the ancient causeway.[5] Two streams bordering the property (whose banks Shipman planted to stabilize) and a pond added to the sylvan scene.[6]

During the 1930s and 1940s, Shipman developed a wild garden for Edith Stern, a New Orleans client whose enthusiasm for native plants led her to

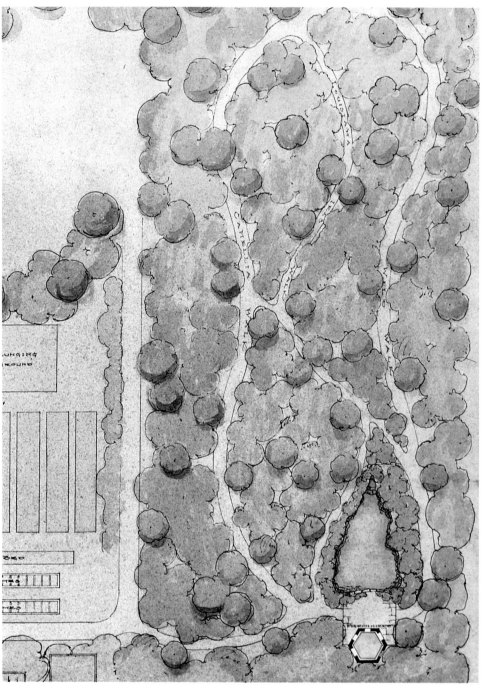

Wild garden detail, general design plan, Longue Vue, New Orleans, La., December 1942. Cornell.

ELLEN SHIPMAN AND THE AMERICAN GARDEN

Woodland garden, The Causeway. Photo by Shipman office, 1920s. Cornell.

underwrite the 1934 publication of Caroline Dormon's *Wildflowers of Louisiana*. Three paths gave the garden its structure; one was designated for camellias, the other two for Louisiana iris and wildflowers. Stern consulted primarily with Dormon about the plantings but relied on Shipman for overall design structure. John Mackenroth, Longue Vue's head gardener from 1927 to 1942, dug thousands of native plants from the woods. The iris were made to feel at home in wire-reinforced concrete beds that were periodically flooded to produce swamp conditions.[7]

Shipman designed wild gardens as discrete areas within larger residential landscapes, but she also routinely attempted to tie the formal garden to the surrounding landscape through the use of native plants in boundary areas. In a sense these transitional landscapes, whether copses, meadows, or shrubberies, were all wild gardens of a sort. As she later explained, "Each part [of the landscape] should lure you on and should become less and less formal until you reach the wild walk leading to the wild garden."[8]

Pergola garden, Ralph P. and DeWitt Hanes estate, Winston-Salem, N.C., 1929. Photo by Shipman office. Cornell.

TEN

THE GREAT DEPRESSION
AND THE LURE OF EUROPE

After Louis Shipman departed for France in 1925, he never returned to the United States. For reasons unknown, Ellen Shipman kept his study and memorabilia intact behind the secret door in the library of their Cornish home. They divorced in 1927, and the following year Louis married an actress named Lucille Watson. He died five years later, leaving a small legacy to Evan but nothing to his daughters.[1]

The stock market crash of 1929 had an immediate impact on Ellen Shipman's practice. During the Depression years that followed she earned most of her income from a few extremely wealthy clients whose large fortunes weathered the economic crisis. In response to the shrinking number of residential jobs, she began to seek institutional and interior design commissions. As had Charles Platt, Shipman used her design skills to move from the landscape into the residence. For some of her patrons, such as Ralph and DeWitt Hanes, of Winston-Salem, North Carolina, Shipman worked on both the house interiors and the garden simultaneously. These Haneses, and others in the region, eventually provided Shipman with a steady and welcome stream of business during troubled years.[2] Her working relationship with the Haneses had an inauspicious beginning, however. DeWitt later recalled, "The night we moved into this great big house was the night of the Crash, and Ralph sat up till dawn." Shipman had visited that spring while the house was still under construction, "when money was rolling." But, DeWitt pointed out, "she loved Ralph, so she kept coming when the money didn't."[3]

The small garden Shipman designed for the Haneses was reminiscent of her earliest work, an enclosed space structured by four converging paths, a central sundial, and a long Colonial Revival loggia; it was anchored at opposite corners by a brick garden house with dovecote and a white Chippendale-style gate. Beds were given three-dimensional interest with bamboo arches wreathed with the single yellow rose 'Mermaid.'[4] The Haneses affectionately referred to Shipman as "Dim," using her grandchildren's nickname for her. Ralph once said of Shipman that he had admired her work since he was a college student; she in turn had taught him the therapeutic delights of pruning. DeWitt remembered Shipman's interest in their ideas: "Before she did any work she sat down with us and said, 'Now you must both tell me your favorite flowers and what you want from a garden—because if anyone asks you who did it, I've been a complete failure.'"[5]

The same aesthetic sensibilities that served Shipman in the landscape also served her in her interior design work; her responsiveness to color, line, texture, and form guided selection of English creamware as surely as her choice of camellia varieties. Shipman bought from the period's best suppliers—Nancy McClelland, Elinor Merrell, and Scalamandré—and scouted auctions and antique shops regularly. Euphanie Mallison, an interior design specialist, joined Shipman's staff around 1938 and directed much of her work for her most enduring clients, Edgar and Edith Stern.

During the 1930s, Shipman began to lecture widely, her lively presentation and "vivid personality" beguiling audiences throughout the country.[6] Her most popular talk was "Color Combination and Perpetual Bloom," but she also spoke about the design and planting of the small garden—her specialty—illustrating the lecture with slides of the Pruyn, Warren, Daniels, Sales, and Greenough gardens, among her other works. In "The Evolution of a Garden," a lecture she first gave in October 1932 in Winston-Salem, Shipman showed one hundred of slides of her own work. In 1935, she gave a series of lectures at the Cosmopolitan Club in New York and, the same year, spoke to the Junior League of Boston.[7] In 1936, Shipman delivered a series of lectures at Lowthorpe School and returned eight years later for another series on design and construction. She commissioned Harry G. Healy, a New York–based architectural photographer, to make several hundred glass slides of her gardens for these and other lectures. (They are now lost.) Healy apparently liked Shipman's work or, at least, working for her. "I have had the most delightful time in my life visiting the several gardens on the list," he wrote. She was less effusive about his pictures and admonished the photographer for ignoring some of her suggestions for specific vantage points.[8]

The slowdown in business coupled with her considerable financial success during the previous decade may have encouraged Shipman to travel abroad for the first time in her life—at age sixty. A trip to Italy in 1929 was followed by two others to England in the early 1930s. Shipman used slides

Ailie du Chene, pencil sketch of Ellen Shipman, 1932. Nicholas Angell Collection.

from these travels in her lectures "English Wayside Gardens" and "Italian Gardens." None of her thoughts about these trips is recorded save a single mention of Europe preserved in the Garden Note Book, where Shipman remembered an evening glimpse of the garden at Ely Cathedral through a locked gate: "when the enchantment of twilight was abroad . . . the garden possessed strange mystic beauty."[9] We can only guess the influence such trips would have exerted on Shipman's style had they occurred earlier in her development, as they did for so many other designers of the period. It is ironic that the circumstances that compelled her to draw upon more internal—and, by definition, more American—resources may have led to her developing a more distinctive artistic style than she would have after an aesthetic grounding by the prototypical "grand tour."

It is equally ironic that two of Shipman's grandest private commissions, Rose Terrace in Grosse Pointe Farms, Michigan, and Longue Vue in New

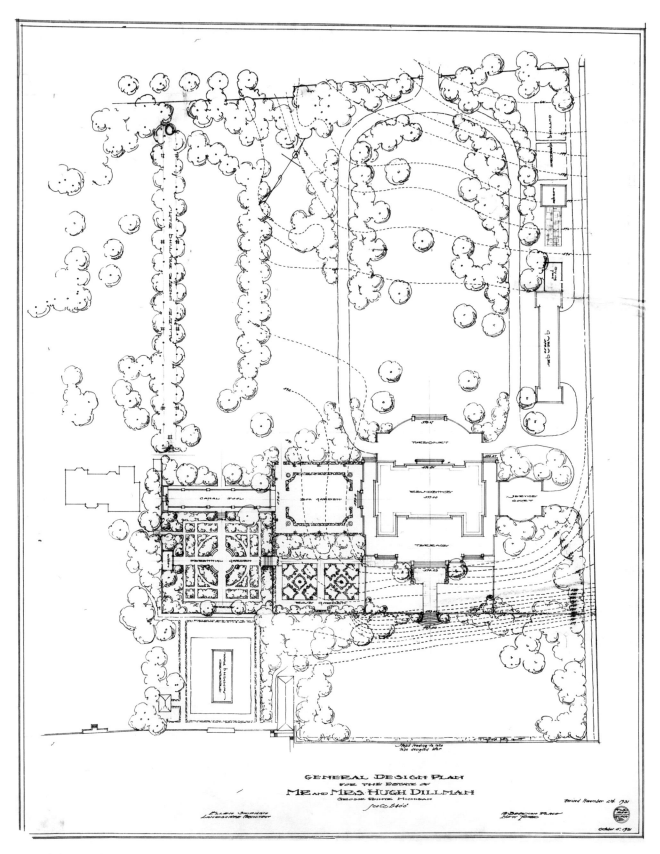

General design plan, Rose Terrace, Anna Dodge and Hugh Dillman estate, Grosse Pointe Farms, Michigan, 2 November 1931. Cornell.

Orleans—both distinctly of European influence—came to her during the worst years of the Depression. Rose Terrace, an estate on Lake St. Clair, was designed in 1930 by the Philadelphia architect Horace Trumbauer in a late-entry Gilded Age Chateau style.[10] Shipman's clients were Anna Thompson Dodge and Hugh Dillman, a retired actor Dodge had met in Palm Beach, where she owned a splendid oceanfront villa, Playa Riente, designed by the well-known architect Addison Mizner. Dodge may have met Ellen Shipman in Palm Beach, too, as Shipman sometimes overwintered there.

Beginning in 1931, Shipman's office generated nearly one hundred drawings and plans for this complex and, no doubt, lucrative project. Designed in the French style, the garden was something of an anomaly in Shipman's oeuvre. A wide velvet lawn defined by gravel walks and cushions of boxwood hedges finished in a broad, circular mirror pool. The other end of the lawn

Boxwood lawn with statues, Rose Terrace. Photo by Preston H. Sweet. Cornell.

Mirror pool (*top*), casino and swimming pool, Rose Terrace. Photos by Preston H. Sweet. Cornell.

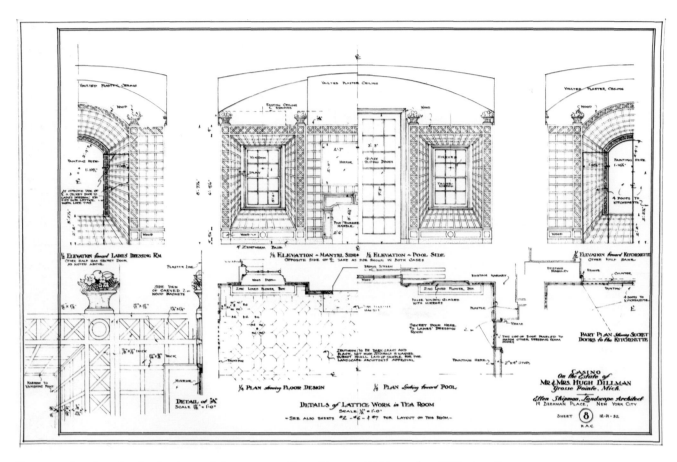

Construction drawing for latticework in tearoom, Rose Terrace, 31 December 1932. Cornell.

was bounded by a "canal pool" and latticework bathing casino. The broad proportions, wide horizontal planes, meticulously edged lawns, and delicate detailing captured the combination of intricacy and grandiosity that lay at the heart of eighteenth-century French landscape design.

Shipman's characteristic expressiveness was missing from the taut design, although the plantings that screened the boxwood garden were a typical rich mix of elm, oak, maple, and more exotic deciduous trees. In the rose garden, standards were choreographed into pristine arrangement against vine-covered arches overlooking the pool and lake beyond. The garden's architectural centerpiece was an intricately treillaged casino, a far cry from the serviceable fieldstone toolhouse Shipman had designed for the Cooper garden nearly twenty years before, although it performed a parallel role in the spatial organization of the garden. Like the toolhouse, it also was multifunctional—dressing room, tearoom, and kitchenette—and, also like the Cooper building, it repeated the style of the main house.

Several of its separate elements were exquisite, but Rose Terrace gave the overall impression that Shipman was designing with an undigested, still-unfamiliar vocabulary. The client's request for a specific stylistic treatment may have prevented her from pursuing a more intuitive scheme. The site was also was a challenge, and Shipman's spare plantings did little to disguise the banality of the flat expanse, which was characterless except for its view of the lake.

Shipman seems to have had better success with several commissions for the Knox family in East Aurora, New York, in 1931. Two years earlier she had advised on Seymour H. Knox II's winter place in Aiken, South Carolina, which no doubt led to invitations for work on his extensive country estate in East Aurora, plus another one for his sister, Marjorie Knox Campbell, who lived next door.[11] Like many of Shipman's clients, their father, Seymour Horace Knox, was a wealthy businessman and dedicated philanthropist. He had made his fortune as a founder of the F. W. Woolworth Company and from other successful business ventures. Early on he purchased several adjoining farms in East Aurora (sixteen miles southeast of Buffalo) as a summer retreat for his family, which his son (who had no interest in breeding horses) later transformed into a modern country estate. Ess Kay Farm, named in honor of his father, eventually extended to over six hundred acres.[12] Working directly with Knox's wife, Helen Northrup Knox, Shipman designed extensive gardens for the main house and guesthouse, which featured lush perennial borders against a background of white pines and hemlock. Just like the gardens at Stan Hywet Hall, clusters of iris, lupine, and poppies marked the progression of the summer months. In numerous letters to the Knoxes, Shipman shared her extensive horticultural knowledge garnered over a lifetime so that her gardens would be maintained to near perfection. In one letter, she advised feeding the large peony with bone meal and, after the ground was frozen, to cut the peonies cut back and cover with well-rotted cow manure.[13] Well into the 1940s, and as the garden matured, she continued to advise about removing overgrown hedges, covering new plantings with flower pots, the best time to plant vines, and other maintenance issues.

Concurrently, Shipman's project at Orchard House for Marjorie Knox Campbell and her husband, J. Hazard Campbell, generated almost a hundred construction drawings and plans for a pool garden, rose garden, bowling green, bird garden, roof garden, entrance plantings, paved courtyards, and more. Several plans relate to the interiors of the gracious Georgian-style house built in 1929 by Peabody, Wilson & Brown, the architects who had designed her brother's house in South Carolina. Shipman's elevations and construction drawings extended to the placement of outdoor furniture and statues on the paved terraces as well as designs for twin bathing pavilions, a stone bridge, and other landscape features which survive today. Since the house and grounds comprised 47 acres, it offered Shipman a comprehensive

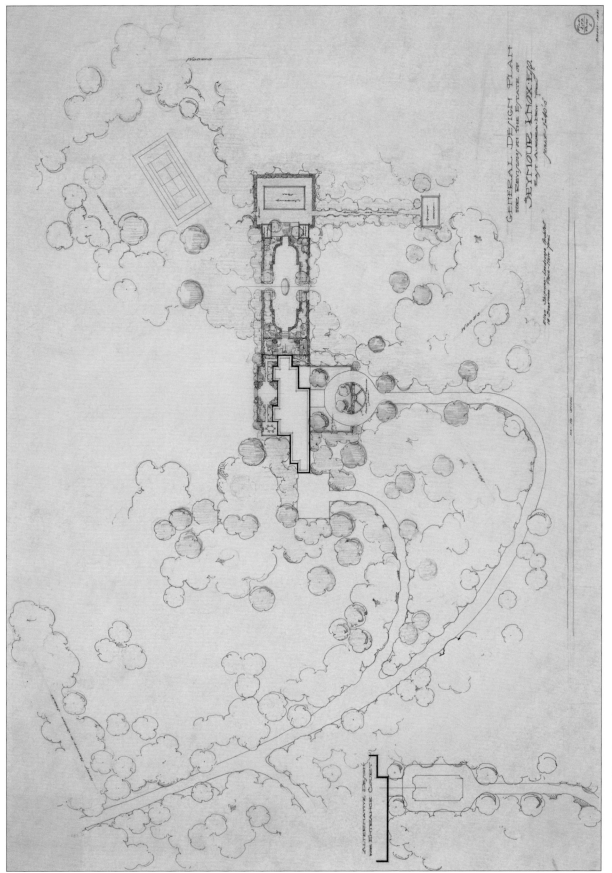

Design plan, Ess Kay Farm, Seymour H. Knox II estate, East Aurora, N.Y., August 1931. Cornell.

design opportunity that in some ways foretold her performance at Longue Vue several years later.[14]

A smaller project undertaken in 1931 involved an unusual Italian-style water garden for Arthur and Ninah Cummer that was part of a family compound of Michigan lumber barons for their home in Jacksonville, Florida. Ninah was a dedicated member of the local garden club and an avid horticulturist and devotee of azaleas. After a trip to Italy in 1931, she returned home with a large collection of Italian marble garden ornaments and ideas for a garden based on the Villa Gamberaia. The grounds of the Cummer compound had been laid out by the Michigan-based landscape architect O. C. Simonds in 1903, and in 1910, Thomas Meehan & Sons, a firm of Philadelphia nurserymen, designed Ninah's English Garden framed by a wisteria-laden pergola overlooking the St. Johns River. Ninah also commissioned the Olmsted firm for further improvements to her garden as well as the city of Jacksonville. Many landscape architects might have hesitated taking on a job with so many previous players, but Shipman ex-

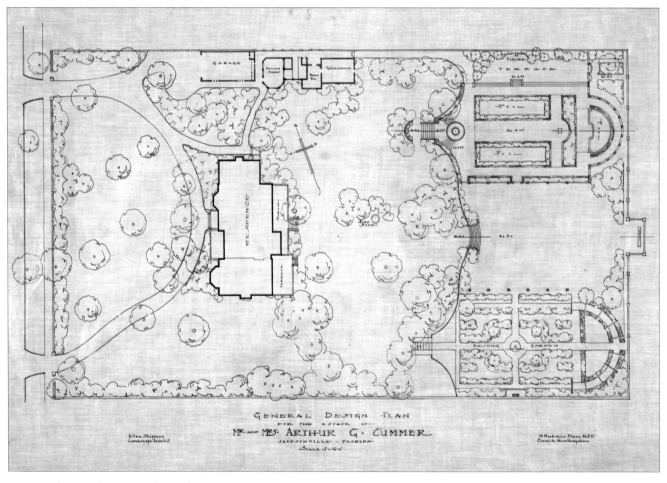

Design plan, Arthur G. and Ninah Cummer estate, Jacksonville, Fla., 1931. Cornell.

Italian Garden, 1937. Cummer.

celled at such situations.[15] What she did not anticipate was learning about
Florida plants and dealing with a strong-willed client. Nonetheless she
successfully prepared plans for a rectangular pool garden flanked by azaleas and a semicircular gloriette underplanted with a dazzling array of
annuals. The Italian Garden, built on the site of an old garage, deftly com-
plemented the existing English Garden and a putting green in between.
Not all of Shipman's recommended plantings were used (and some died),
while a number of her suggestions for paved walkways, terraces, and other
features were nixed by budget-conscious Arthur Cummer, but in the end
it was a glorious garden that is now part of the Cummer Museum of Art
& Gardens.[16]

Shipman found greater design success in her next major job, Longue

Reflecting pool, Longue Vue, Edith R. and Edgar B. Stern estate, New Orleans. Photo by Shipman office, November 1937. Longue Vue.

Vue, but here, too, her eagerness to pursue large-scale European motifs and spatial arrangements precluded her more expressive romanticism. For two decades Shipman had settled for commissions tightly circumscribed by small budgets and preexisting designs and had watched her colleagues manage much grander assignments. As her fame increased and new opportunities arose, she may have been impatient to test her talents on a more epic scale. A comment Shipman wrote on the back of a snapshot of Longue Vue captures her pride in the design: "Frank to say I'm impressed myself when I look upon this magnificence."[17]

Edith and Edgar Stern first saw Shipman's work in a neighboring garden in 1935. The following year, they hired her to design a new landscape for their own estate, whose Colonial Revival house designed by Moise Goldstein dated to 1923. Shipman's friendship with the Sterns deepened quickly. She became their trusted and much-valued arbiter of landscape, architectural, and artistic taste, precisely as Charles Platt had been for many of his clients. Edith Rosenwald Stern was energetic and wealthy, the daughter of the chief executive and principal shareholder of Sears, Roebuck Company. Her husband, a New Orleans native, was a powerful cotton broker. Both were intrepid liberals. Mr. Stern founded a southern university for African American students; Mrs. Stern founded a progressive nursery school when she judged those available to her children to be of inferior quality. In the 1930s, they flouted southern convention and hosted a dinner party for opera singer Marian Anderson. The Sterns were devoted to each other and to Longue Vue, and a memorial plaque to "the godmother of the house" attests to their devotion to Shipman.

Shipman's initial work for the Sterns was limited strictly to the garden. Her scheme for it included a boxwood parterre adjoining a house portico and beyond that, a camellia allée that traced the lines of the original garden plan and forced a dramatic vista. The camellias were transplanted at unprecedented size, all of them dug from the country outside New Orleans, where they had been "pruned" to tree shape by artistic cows.

Soon after the garden was installed, Shipman suggested a more monu-

Vista from terrace garden to south lawn, camellia allée, and tempietto. Photo by Gottscho-Schleisner, 1947. Longue Vue.

THE GREAT DEPRESSION AND THE LURE OF EUROPE   213

Portico garden and south facade. Photo by Gottscho-Schleisner, 1947. Longue Vue.

Lower hall. Photo by Gottscho-Schleisner, 1947. Longue Vue.

mental improvement: a new house. She felt that the existing structure was all wrong, since its long rear facade (where one would normally want most of the garden to be) faced east (where there was little property). Having fallen completely under Shipman's charismatic spell, the Sterns agreed to move the existing house from the property and commissioned David Adler, a well-known Chicago-based architect, to design a new residence. But Adler proved an inflexible and uncommunicative aesthetic partner and designed a house many times too large for the Sterns' needs, including upstairs and downstairs central halls that measured forty by sixty feet. Adler's plan also consumed some of the gardens Shipman had just developed. He was dismissed, and Shipman was invited to assume architectural duties. Her training had not prepared her for the complexities of the task, however, and she was stymied by a chimney that kept appearing in the center of the drawing-room plans. Aware of her limitations, Shipman introduced the Sterns to William and Geoffrey Platt, who had taken over their father's architectural practice after Charles's death in 1933. Even though the Platts designed the new house, Shipman appears to have wielded control over the general development of the design.[18]

Not surprisingly, strong emphasis was placed on the relation of the interior to the exterior and on the facades, which would furnish a lively background for the gardens. While the house exhibited many characteristics of the Classical Revival style, it also reflected an interesting variety of other influences. The east elevation was based on Shadows-on-the-Teche in New Iberia, Louisiana; the south and west elevations were similar to the Le Charpentier-Beauregard House, a raised cottage (circa 1826) in the Vieux Carré section of New Orleans. The approach view was neo-Palladian. Much more heavily fenestrated than the original, the new house presented ample garden views from every room. Most spectacular was the vista from the drawing room out to the camellia allée and tempietto. Construction on Longue Vue II began in 1939 and continued through 1942.

Shipman stepped into the role of interior designer and produced a series of floor plans and scale maquettes. Detailed letters and long telegrams kept her and her clients in near-constant contact as prospective additions to the furnishings were scouted. One such telegram from "Lady Ellen" ran: "Saw today to be sold at auction Friday most remarkable music box Plays over fifty tunes Exquisite tone About eight figures in band playing on instruments Would be wonderful in playroom May go quite high as very unique and fine Would you like me to bid on it Hope teapot arrives on time."[19]

"You see," explained Mrs. Stern in a 1977 interview, "we weren't really collectors, Mr. Stern and I, but we bought. Ellen Shipman would do all the leg work, and then we'd come up and say it was beautiful." War conditions and the size of the Sterns' fortune put them at a great advantage. "The world was our oyster," continued Edith. "Nobody else was buying. We had the whole market to ourselves."[20]

From their many shopping excursions, Edith Stern particularly remembered Shipman's sharp eye—and her gait. "Ellen Shipman was very tall. She used to walk with these long strides and, so, we went to where they had some garden furniture in the courtyard, bought our bench and, on the way back, she said, 'Did you notice the beautiful pieces of Leeds china on our left, and on our right was a hooked rug I must get for another client.' As far as I could tell, she hadn't seen anything."[21] Shipman's eclectic taste and practiced eye served her clients well. Their home evolved into a richly textured, exotic, warm environment.

Longue Vue's spare garden plan was considerably less cozy, owing to its scale and the monumentality of the major view, bilaterally symmetrical in the French tradition. Thick boundary plantings on three sides kept the eye within the designed landscape. The parterre garden near the south

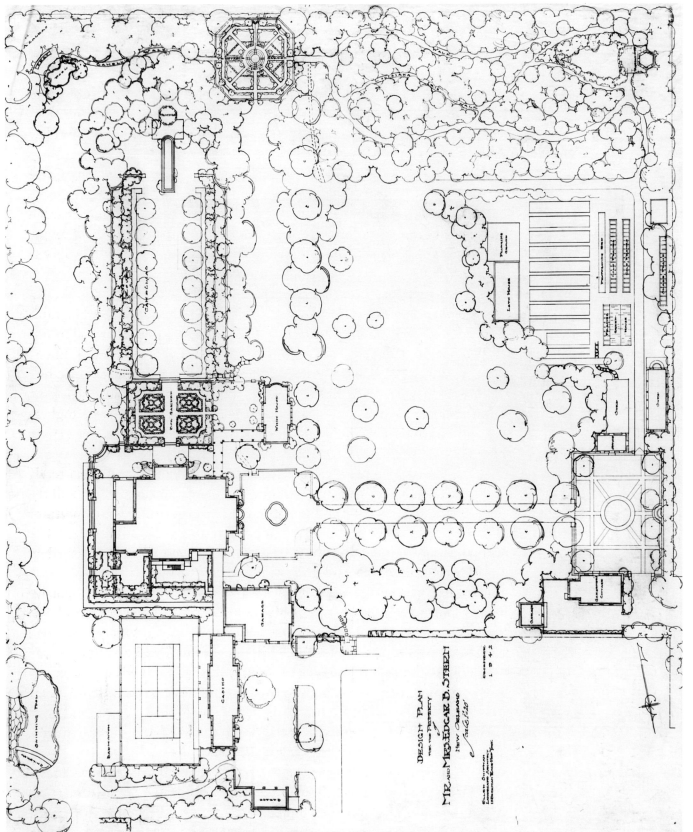

Design plan, Longue Vue II, December 1942. Cornell.

Azalea walk, Longue Vue. Photo by Gottscho-Schleisner, 1947. Longue Vue.

portico was also formal, recalling traditional French prototypes, but Shipman's planting was colorful and inventive. The garden was planted out twice: once for a spring-summer show, a second time in fall. Beyond the long vista, visitors found an informal goldfish pool and seat tucked into the southeast corner of the property and a monumental kitchen garden that combined flowers, fruits, and vegetables in meticulously ordered profusion. Three paths led through the wild garden with its collection of Louisiana iris and other native plants. North of the wild garden were several service gardens and propagating beds.

In 1942, Shipman formalized the approach to the house by creating a long, straight drive and planting a live oak allée to border it. Courtyard gardens on the north side of the house were added, as well as tennis courts. Shipman's garden survived until 1965, when Hurricane Betsy ripped through New Orleans and destroyed most of the camellia allée.[22]

Longue Vue was one of Ellen Shipman's largest commissions and one of her last residential works. She received an annual retainer of $1,200 ("extras" were carefully scrutinized, however).[23] The thrice-yearly trips she undertook to supervise maintenance and ongoing development of the gardens involved a significant amount of travel—and surely reflected a commitment that transcended pure business. The friendship she developed with Edith and Edgar lasted until she died.

Roof garden, Aetna Life and Casualty Insurance Company, Hartford, Conn. Photo by Fred Jones, 1931. Aetna.

ELEVEN

PUBLIC AND
INSTITUTIONAL PROJECTS

In several projects Shipman was able to apply her expressive, romantic
idiom to an institutional problem, translating a gardenesque response
into a design that held its own on a larger scale while retaining the delicacy and artistic complexity characteristic of her best work. Throughout
her career Shipman designed modest planting schemes for schools, libraries,
churches, town halls, private clubs, cemetery memorials, and even a railway
station.

No single community held more of her public work than Grosse Pointe
Shores, where her commissions included the Alger Museum (formerly the
Russell Alger home on which she had collaborated with Platt in 1919), a
private club, a home for nurses, and a convalescent home. In 1932, Shipman
also designed a public planting for Lake Shore Drive, which stretched five
miles along Lake St. Clair, "kept principally to evergreens [and] willows for
early light green—flowering trees and shrubs, especially flowering crabs and
plums."[1] The designer's palette represented a divergence from the generic
elm and maple street-tree plantings common during the period and may
have been influenced by the Prairie Landscape style.

One of Shipman's first recorded public works, the Women's Advisory
Council Border for the New York Botanical Garden, came to her in 1928.
She approached the design of the 254-foot border as a residential feature,
adjusting the scale of the plantings upward so that the overall proportions
and rhythms would not be overwhelmed by the expanse of lawns and big
trees nearby. Backed by a screen planting of arborvitae, the border was filled
with a mix of flowering shrubs at the rear half and perennials and standards

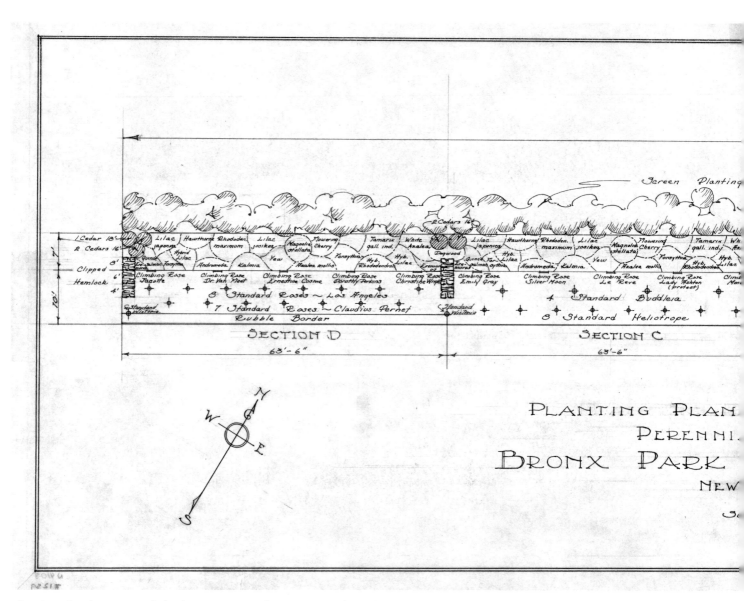

Labels within the drawing:

1 Cedar 18'
2 Cedars 16'
Clipped
Hemlock

Lilac japonica · Hawthorne · Rhododen. maximum · Lilac josikea · Magnolia stellata · Flowering Cherry · Tamarix gall. ind. · White Azalea · 2 Cedars 16' · Lilac japonica · Hawthorne · Rhododen. maximum · Lilac josikea · Magnolia stellata · Flowering Cherry · Tamarix gall. ind. · Wh.

Andromeda · Kalmia · Yew · Azalea mollis · Forsythia · Hyb. Rhododendron · Hyb. Lilac · Dogwood · Andromeda · Kalmia · Yew · Azalea mollis · Forsythia · Hyb. Lilac · Hyb. Rhododendron

Climbing Rose Jacotte · Climbing Rose Dr. Van Fleet · Climbing Rose Ernestine Cosme · Climbing Rose Dorothy Perkins · Climbing Rose Christine Wright · Climbing Rose Emily Gray · Climbing Rose Silver Moon · Climbing Rose Le Reve · Climbing Rose Lady Ashton (protect) · Climbing

8 Standard Roses ~ Los Angeles
7 Standard Roses ~ Claudius Pernet
Rubble Border
4 Standard Buddleia
8 Standard Heliotrope

SECTION D
63'-6"

SECTION C
63'-6"

N W E S (compass rose)

PLANTING PLAN
PERENNI.
BRONX PARK
NEW

Planting plan for trees and shrubs. Women's Advisory Council Border, New York Botanical Garden, Bronx, ink on trace, c. 1928. Cornell.

in the front. Shipman was called on to revamp the plantings several times, in 1931, 1935, 1938, and 1946.

During the 1930s, Shipman acquired more prominent public commissions, beginning with an important job for the Aetna Life and Casualty Insurance Company in Hartford, Connecticut, in 1930. "America's largest Colonial-style office building," designed by the Beaux-Arts architect James Gamble Rogers, required planning and planting for a twenty-two-acre site. Almost fifty plans and drawings detail Shipman's work there: wide, tree-studded lawns, formal courts, a roof garden, and decorative details such as a zodiac compass in the forecourt paving, the building cornerstone inscription, and specifications for street lamps. The company's president, Morgan B. Brainard, was also a private client.

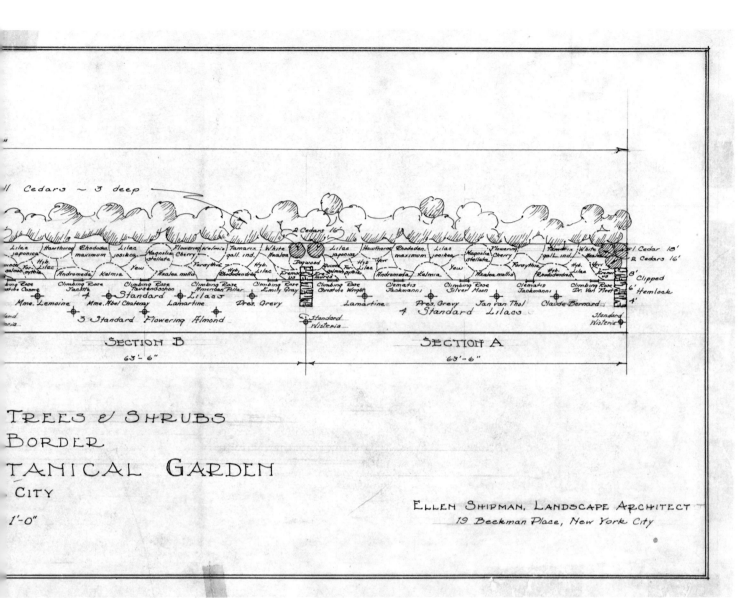

Cedars ~ 3 deep

2 Cedars 16'

2 Cedars 16'
1 Cedar 18'

8' Clipped

6' Hemlock

4'

SECTION B
63'-6"

SECTION A
63'-6"

TREES & SHRUBS
BORDER
TANICAL GARDEN
CITY
1'-0"

ELLEN SHIPMAN, LANDSCAPE ARCHITECT
19 Beekman Place, New York City

Shipman's Olmstedian plan utilized many trees already growing on the former private estates that Aetna's site comprised—one newspaper article recorded over four hundred in thirty species. In addition, twenty-eight elms were to be planted in two L-shaped groups to border the street and line the main walk, many new trees were specified for the lawn, and groups of Korean cherry and flowering crabs were to flank the two circular drives to the front entrance.

Several small gardens added color to the sprawling lawns, and two enclosed courts provided backdrops for the company's cafeterias. More original than any of these features, however, was the private eighth-floor roof garden adjacent to the president's office. Engineered with an extensive drainage system and waterproof concrete floor to hold six feet of soil, the roof

Women's Advisory Council Border, c. 1928. Cornell.

garden was surrounded by a five-foot brick wall that merged with a balustrade supporting large cast-stone urns silhouetted against the Hartford skyline. Shipman's planting included perennials, flowering shrubs, vines, and small trees, such as Korean cherry, magnolia, and plum. The intimate design was a response to the compressed scale of the roof, but it also reflected Shipman's continued interest in domesticity and privacy. Ellen Shipman had given Morgan B. Brainard a room of his own.[2]

The exact circumstances surrounding Shipman's commission for the Colorado Springs Fine Arts Center in 1935 are unclear, but it resonated with interests she developed during her formative years living in Cornish. The center, which started off in 1919 as the Broadmoor Art Academy, functioned as a flourishing art colony and an oasis of culture in a remote place at the foot of Pikes Peak. It attracted artists nationwide, but soon outgrew its facilities. A new building, designed by the well-known Southwest architect John Gaw Meen, was built in a striking Art Deco style, with decorative murals and courtyards not unlike those at Aetna Life. When the complex opened in April 1936, there were performances by Martha Graham and a new musical composition by Erik Satie, among other artists.[3]

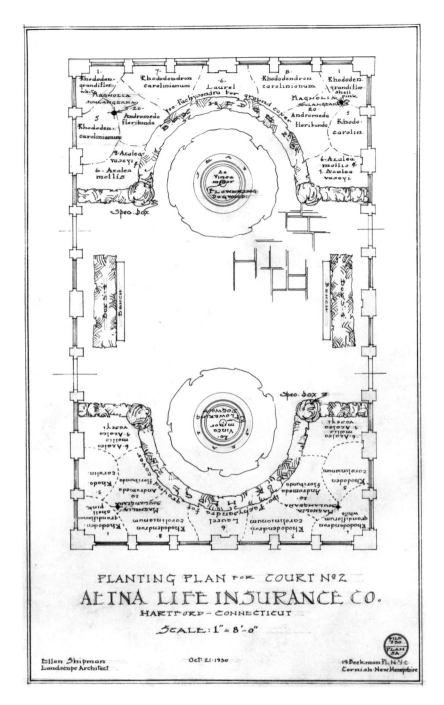

Planting plan for Court No. 2, Aetna Life, ink on trace, 21 October 1930. Cornell.

Shipman, whose name has long vanished from the institution's records, prepared several planting plans for a perennial border and tree and shrub plantings for the east court in 1936. Unlike her residential commissions, Shipman's recommendations for the center are remarkable for their restraint and practicality. It is not known whether her suggestions were ever implemented, since her tissue sketches seem not to have advanced to the

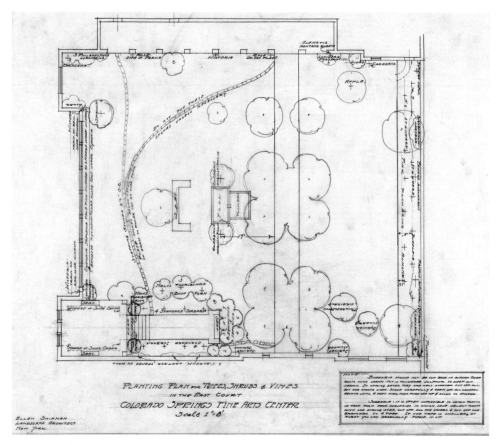

Planting plan for trees, shrubs, and vines in East Court, Colorado Springs Fine Arts Center, 1936. Cornell.

construction drawing phase. Recent expansions to the distinctive building obliterated the courtyard.

In striking contrast, Shipman's perennial planting plan for the superintendent's garden at the U.S. Military Academy at West Point, prepared in 1936 when she was working on the Colorado commission, is densely planted in a residential spirit. When Major General William D. Connor took up his post in 1932, the existing garden enclosed by a retaining wall and traditional flower beds was ripe for rejuvenation. Although Shipman was well known at the time of the commission, it is worth remembering that her father, Colonel James Biddle, attended West Point and her brother, Nicholas Biddle, was a major in the Military Intelligence Division of the U.S. Army. In Major Connor's letter to her on May 11, 1935, he exclaims that he has "heard your praises sung so loudly by my wife" and wanted to have a plan made "by someone in whose ability I have great confidence." Shipman, in turn, replied two days later that she could not imagine anything that she would rather do. She told him that she had once spent many happy weeks at West Point with her cousin, John Biddle, and thought it "one of the most heavenly places in the world."[4] And with that, he gave her the commission.

Letters went back and forth for some time with her tried-and true recommendations. In one she suggested a narrow path with flowers on either side.[5] The plan she proposed for the terrace garden was similar in concept to the residential gardens she designed in the early 1920s, with densely planted perennial borders, stone steps and walls, and sculptural figures. In a memo to the quartermaster who was assigned to work with her, Connor said, "The famous garden architect, Mrs. Ellen B. Shipman, says that she has found that crushed oyster shells in the rate of about one quart per tree is one of the best things to put around the roots of arbor vitae and second, that the very best spray for arborvitae is O.K. Plant Oil. . . . if applied upward into the tree, is sure death to the red spider and other things that mostly affect arbor vitae." In closing, he authorized a reserve of $300 for her garden plans. She had initially proposed her normal fee of $500, but would waive it if necessary. "I told her that we were not that hard up, but that I had not planned to spend more than $300 for the plans."[6] Connor's final letter, dated January 5, 1938, expresses his exasperation about a sculptural figure for the garden which she had promised but forgotten about. In the end she found a bronze figure of Silanius for $125. It is unclear to what extent her suggestions were followed, and over the years

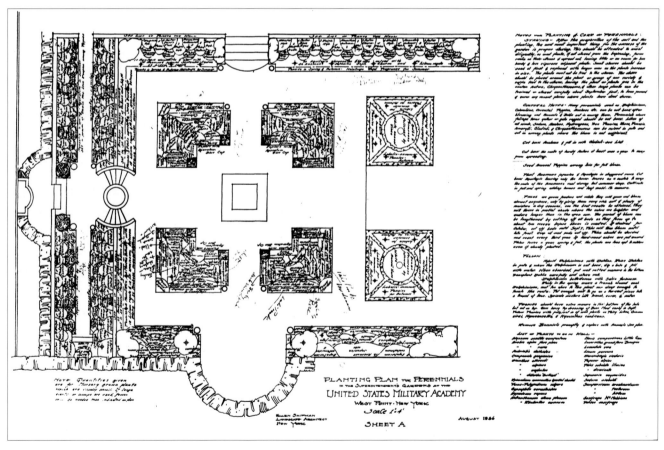

Planting plan for perennials, Superintendent's Garden, United States Military Academy, West Point, N.Y., August 1926. Cornell.

Sarah P. Duke Gardens, Durham, N.C., under construction, February 1938. Duke University Archives.

the space evolved to include new plantings to create a Garden of the States. But the outlines of the much-visited garden remain in place today.

A residential spirit also enlivened Shipman's design for a large formal garden at Duke University, originally conceived by her friend Dr. Frederick M. Hanes, an iris fancier and a member of the extended Hanes family for whom she had previously done so much work. Shipman's charge in 1936 was to revamp an ailing iris garden designed a few years before by John C. Wister, a Philadelphia landscape architect. Construction was under way by summer 1937, with costs underwritten by Mary Duke Biddle, a distant relation to Shipman by marriage and daughter of Sarah P. Duke, for whom the gardens were named. Shipman's 10 percent fee, which totaled $4,217, was modest in comparison with the $12,000 annual maintenance cost.

Shipman's new design featured seven curved terraces cradling Japanese cherries, crabapples, and perennial and shrub plantings in a lush presentation of color and texture. ("The slanting light of morning and evening still ignites the beautiful pink-tinted flagstone," wrote one appreciative visitor in 1989.)[7] The main axis extended from a wisteria-covered pergola to a pond at the bottom, the descent along the central path varied by small pools at each level.[8] Again, Shipman made the leap from private to public project without sacrificing the look and feel of a real garden.

Her success in these public jobs raises questions about why Shipman did not do more of them. She apparently did try to find similar commissions, but a variety of circumstances, including stiff competition from her professional colleagues who were also short of work, undermined her efforts. She wrote

Terraces, Sarah P. Duke Gardens, 1940. Duke University Archives.

a long letter of inquiry to the Foundation to Honor Atlanta's War Veterans about a proposed memorial in 1945, in which she cited other public commissions and all her southern references, but little seems to have come of it.[9] Shipman's landscape work would always have to be limited to those projects that did not involve large-scale site planning, grading, or natural-resource management, as her short apprenticeship with Platt had not trained her in these specialized tasks. City, campus, subdivision, and park planning, roadway design, and even large estate planning were all beyond her technical grasp. (Platt's abilities in these areas were also limited; he always collaborated with landscape architectural or engineering consultants for his public work.) In this regard Shipman differed from her female colleagues Marian Coffin, Marjorie Sewell Cautley, Beatrix Farrand, and a few others who acquired the skills and authority necessary not only to design significant public work but to supervise the male crews charged with constructing it.

View from terrace, Ease House, late 1930s or early 1940s. Streeter collection.

TWELVE

LAST YEARS

Ellen Shipman got behind the war effort by offering an intensive eight-week course for women in design and drafting skills. She also wanted to share her expertise with the U.S. Army camouflage division, but they declined her services. Not unexpectedly, she became an ardent proponent of victory gardens and proposed that the Garden Club of America use her New York office as a source of information. "Why, I even . . . conferred in Washington with the government about the best ways and means of putting across the message of victory gardens," she later wrote. In one lecture, Shipman warned her audience that "anybody who has a spot of ground suitable for raising vegetables and fails to do so is a slacker."[1]

Shipman had almost no work during the war aside from a few interior design commissions, and her business was running in the red. When the war ended, the resumption of her (or anyone else's) specialized, residential practice did not look promising. Labor and materials were in short supply; lifestyles had changed dramatically, and so had garden fashions. Shipman wrote many letters seeking new work and lining up visits to long-standing clients, but they did not yield substantial business. Her office records list twenty-three active clients in 1945, including four in Winston-Salem, four in Perrysville, Ohio, and seven in the suburban New York area. To her Brook Place caretaker, Charles Meyette, Shipman observed, "I do not believe that any other profession has been harder hit than landscape architecture."[2] She borrowed money to keep the office open and reduced her staff to four. She no longer paid herself a salary. Pressed to meet mortgage payments on the Beekman Place property, Shipman cashed in some of her stocks and bonds.

In October 1946, she reluctantly sold her New York residence, office, and furnishings to Edith and Edgar Stern's son and daughter-in-law. She had been leasing out the apartments there for several years, living instead at the Beekman Towers Hotel around the corner.

The summer after the war ended, Shipman reopened Brook Place, which had been closed since 1941. Meyette aired the house and cleaned up the garden. Shipman found a student to help in the garden, drive the car, draft, and type. The day-to-day routine was reminiscent of earlier years, but simpler. Guests were invited to lunch prepared and served by two students from the Cornell home economics school or to a light supper followed by one of Mrs. Meyette's pies. Shipman looked after the needs and expenses of her staff, and saw to it that they were treated to the movies once a week. Dona E. Caldwell, who worked for Shipman that summer, remembers that duties were light and her boss was "kind, gentle, and often protested that I should not work so hard."[3]

In 1945, another employee, Anne Bruce Haldeman, helped Shipman prepare a book outlining her design philosophies. Haldeman was a graduate of the Cambridge School and had worked in the office during the last few years.[4] The Garden Note Book, however, was never finished owing to the vagaries of the postwar market for gardening books and Shipman's increasingly ill health. William Platt's introduction, if ever realized, has never surfaced.[5] Shipman's text was aimed at the home gardener in a congenial how-to tone, suggesting that she viewed it not as a vehicle for her theoretical legacy but rather as an attempt to inspire would-be gardeners. She expressed the hope that the reader would "grow to be a great and enthusiastic gardener bringing joy and happiness to yourself, your family and your community." The impassioned prose was inspired by Shipman's own excitement for her art: "Even writing of the planning of these simple beginnings is exciting— the real experience of learning to start and grow your own plants is the thrill of a lifetime."[6]

Shipman may have planned to incorporate selections from her Blue Books into the completed publication. These well-worn loose-leaf notebooks contained a hodgepodge of *Country Life* news clippings, notes on lectures, nursery lists, client plant lists, recommended plant combinations, regional plant lists, and other horticultural information, which she shared with clients and other designers. Shipman may have imagined that a book would boost her flagging business or supplement her dwindling income, but it is likely that postwar homeowners, most of them more interested in barbecues than ornamental pools, would have found some of the ideas proposed in the text old-fashioned.

In 1946, Shipman received a letter from the architect Aymar Embury inviting her to become a member of the Institute of Arts and Letters. It would have been the only professional recognition she received during her career. She declined Embury's offer, suggesting that he look for someone younger, "to whom it might make a great difference." Shipman continued, "I know what it would have meant to me fifteen or twenty years ago, but now, soon perhaps, I shall not be working."[7] Shipman had never actively sought professional affiliation or joined her own field's professional organization, the American Society of Landscape Architects. When, after Shipman's death, her assistant Frances McCormic was asked the reason, she reported that her boss "didn't approve of it," she was "too busy," and found the people "dull."[8] All these explanations are plausible, but none speaks to the profound disparity between Shipman's goals and those of the ASLA.[9]

For its first twenty-five years, the ASLA was run almost as a men's club, not only sexist but geographically chauvinistic. "If one were not a white, male, eastern college graduate," writes the historian Diane Kostial McGuire, "the atmosphere was quite chilly."[10] Eager to secure a place for the new profession in relation to its older, well-established rivals, engineering and architecture, the organization deemphasized gardens and residential work in favor of larger, public-scale work. The vast majority of Shipman's commissions, of course, were of the former category. The network that provided Shipman with most of her clients, speaking engagements, and other professional opportunities was founded and run by women: the Garden Club of America. Their client-centered emphasis on horticulture, aesthetics, taste, community service, and the environment more clearly resembled her own.

Early in 1947, at age seventy-eight, Shipman closed her office for good. Recurring bouts of pneumonia had forced her to curtail the annual garden visits that constituted the greater part of her practice. On her doctor's advice, she reluctantly decided to refuse new work. But she had not anticipated the sense of loss she would suffer in leaving her practice. "Closing the office was much harder in *every* way than I had realized it would be," she wrote Edith Stern. "I have been through so many things in my long years—that I thought this would be nothing! But when it came to having to go through literally thousands of plans and deciding what to destroy and what to keep, and each one bringing up the past and the realization of the work that was put into them and the joys—and so many of them all gone—owing to the depression and the war." Shipman's letter continued on a happier note: she no longer had her work, but she would keep, until the end, the other source of joy in her life, her family. "I am here at Brook Place and Ellen and the children are with me for two weeks. Simply heaven. I forget the work that I must do and just rejoice in the beauty and blessed family life."[11]

With her elder daughter and her family, Shipman found a deeply satisfying domestic stability that had eluded her as a young mother. She had a close relationship with her grandchildren and her son-in-law, Montgomery

Angell, who was also her financial adviser. The Angells visited Shipman in Brook Place, Beekman Place, and at her winter home, Ease House, in Bermuda. And Shipman was a frequent visitor to their home, High House, in Garrison, New York.

Ellen Shipman on her eightieth birthday with Nicholas B. Angell and Nancy Angell Streeter, November 1949. Streeter collection.

Shipman's contacts with her two younger children were less frequent. Evan and Mary, however, were close and continued to share an interest in horses. Mary trained horses in Virginia, where her clients included the Whitneys and du Ponts; her first husband, Cary Jackson, owned a country store.[12] Evan, who struggled with alcoholism, eventually gave up writing poetry to turn his attention to a harness-racing column for the *Morning Telegraph*.

During her final years, Shipman spent more and more time in Warwick West, Bermuda, where she had purchased a piece of land from which she could see both sides of the island and designed "the nicest house in the world," with gardens down the south slope.[13] After celebrating her eightieth birthday in November 1949 with her family in New York, Shipman returned to Ease House for the winter. At the end of February 1950, she wrote excitedly to Edith Stern about an anticipated visit from her grandchildren and an upcoming Garden Club of America meeting in Grosse Pointe Shores. She expressed great pride in her designs there and a strong desire that Edith make the trip north. "I do hope [you go] because you will see more of my work in one place than in any other ten places. . . . I know of six [gardens] to be shown." Shipman said she intended to be there, too, and closed on an intimate note: "I have to limit myself to one sheet [of stationery] but that does not limit the amount of love I send you each and all."[14]

On March 27, four days before the Angells were to arrive in Bermuda, Ellen Shipman died of pneumonia at Ease House. By then, most of the six hundred gardens she had designed during her lifetime had changed beyond recognition. Many were simply gone, and her work was quickly forgotten. Ellen Shipman's talent—an extraordinary talent—had all but escaped documentation in the annals of American landscape history.

All gardens are vulnerable to the vagaries of their owners' whims and the inevitable growth and decay of plants, but Ellen Shipman's were particularly fragile in this respect. Had she pursued more monumental designs, she would have left behind a more tangible mark. Her responsiveness to place and to the wishes of her clients led her to create gardens whose sensuality and delicacy depended on an evanescence that made their eclipse almost inevitable.

EPILOGUE

Ellen Shipman's family diligently carried out her wishes regarding the disposition of her professional effects. Shipman requested that the executors "set aside such of my books, plans and photographs as seem to them to have been pertinent to my work in my profession and to give . . . [them] to one of the following institutions: (a) Vassar College; (b) Cornell University; (c) Cambridge School of Landscape Architecture; and (d) New York Public Library." Cornell University accepted the gift in 1953. Shipman left her slide collection to the Garden Club of America, although its whereabouts is unknown today. Some of her professional books were donated to the Avery Architectural Library at Columbia University, where Charles Platt's extensive archives were placed.[1] In 1946, about the time that she drew up her will, Shipman offered copies of plans for southern projects to the Department of Landscape Architecture at the University of Georgia; although the offer was enthusiastically accepted, there is no record that the gift was ever made.[2]

APPENDIX 1

CLIENT LIST

The basis for this list is an alphabetical roster of more than six hundred clients compiled by Frances McCormic in 1945, when Shipman's practice resumed after languishing during the war years. McCormic also lists twenty-three active clients for 1945, and new names were penciled in until the office closed in 1947. The lack of documentation in Shipman's archives at Cornell for some of the names on McCormic's list does not necessarily mean that those projects were not carried out. Typically, Shipman's clients would have retained their set of plans, which in some cases still exist in other archives, such as those at Longue Vue House & Gardens, the Cummer Museum of Art & Gardens, the Sarah P. Duke Gardens, and others. Not all the projects in McCormic's list were executed. Some clients may have abandoned a project before working plans were drawn up, while others may not have been able to proceed after engaging Shipman's services.

The names on McCormic's list have been cross-checked with holdings at Cornell and the University of Oregon, both of which have additional files that were not included by McCormic. Client names are arranged alphabetically by state. When available, additional information, such as property name, architect, other landscape architects, dates, and archives, has been added. Client's names and locations are cited as they appear on the plans, but they may not correspond with current names, owners, and locations. Current names where known are given in parentheses at end of entry. Missing information, such as the client's full name or the location, has been added when known. For further information on specific projects, refer to the Bibliography.

ABBREVIATIONS

a = architect

la = landscape architect

AAG = Archives of American Gardens, Smithsonian Institution

EBS Cornell = Ellen Shipman Papers, Rare and Manuscripts Collection, Cornell University Library

FBJ = Frances Benjamin Johnston Collection, Library of Congress Prints and Photographs Division

L&S Oregon = Lord & Schryver Collection, Special Collections and University Archives, University of Oregon Libraries

COLORADO
Fine Arts Center. Colorado Springs, 1935; John Gaw Meen (a), 1934. EBS Cornell. (Colorado Springs Fine Arts Center)

CONNECTICUT
Achelis, Frederick G. Greenwich, c. 1920; Harrie T. Lindeberg (a), 1919. EBS Cornell
Aetna Life and Casualty Insurance Company. Hartford, 1930; James Gamble Rogers (a), 1929. EBS Cornell
Altschul, Frank. Greenwich
Auchincloss, Edgar. Darien
Auchincloss, Mrs. Hugh D. Fairfield, 1926. L&S Oregon
Barrett, C. Reddington. Greenwich. EBS Cornell
Bartram, J. B. Greenwich
Benedict, A. N. Easton
Brainard, Morgan B. Hartford. (*See also* Aetna Life)
Brewster, Carroll. Ridgefield
Buck, John. Hartford. EBS Cornell
Bulkley, Mrs. Jonathan. Rippowam, Ridgefield, late 1920s; James L. Greenleaf (la). AAG; EBS Cornell
Cannon, Dr. A. B. New Canaan. EBS Cornell
Case, George. Norfolk
Chadbourne, T. L. Greenwich
Chase, Edith. Litchfield, 1925; Richard H. Dana (a), 1924. EBS Cornell; L&S Oregon. (Topsmead State Forest)
Chase, H. S. Madison. L&S Oregon
Clark, Cameron J. Fairfield (architect husband of Agnes Selkirk Clark)
Croft, Henry William and Augusta. Grahampton, Greenwich, 1917; Johnson & Abbott (a), 1917; James L. Greenleaf (la), c. 1921. AAG; EBS Cornell
Farrelly, C. Clifford. Westport
Forstmann, Julius. Greenwich, 1940. EBS Cornell
Godley, Mrs. George McM. Long House, Greenwich. EBS Cornell
Goldsmith, Margaret O. Bethel. EBS Cornell
Gossler, Philip G. New Canaan, 1919; Clark & Arms (a). EBS Cornell
Hale, Mrs. Robert. Darien. EBS Cornell
Hanley, William L., Jr. Greenwich; Harrie T. Lindeberg (a), 1937. EBS Cornell
Hepburn, Mrs. Alonzo Barton (Emily Eaton). Altracraig, Ridgefield
Hickox, Charles R. Litchfield. EBS Cornell
Hincks, Robert S. Bridgeport, 1923. EBS Cornell; L&S Oregon
Holt, Hamilton. Woodstock. EBS Cornell
Howe, Mrs. Ernest. Litchfield, c. 1930. AAG
Hoyt, Eva H. Stamford. EBS Cornell
Jameson, Mrs. E. C. Sharon
Kruttschnitt, Julius. New Canaan
Lane, Walcott. Old Lyme
Mahaney, David. Greenwich
Marshall, Hugh B. Greenwich, 1944. EBS Cornell
McConnell, Albert R. Greenwich. EBS Cornell
Mitchell, Mrs. Ormsby. Greenwich, 1929; Alfred Hopkins (a), 1929. EBS Cornell
Munroe, Charles. Greenwich
New Britain Normal School. New Britain

Noble, Mrs. Robert P. (Meta). Three Oaks, Greenwich, 1947; Phelps Barnum (a), c. 1930; Marian Coffin (la), 1930s. EBS Cornell

Orcutt, C. C. New Canaan, 1947. EBS Cornell

Peacock, Mrs. Sharon

Potter, Sarah. Westport

Reed, Joseph Verner. Greenwich, 1938. EBS Cornell

Rockefeller, J. Sterling. Greenwich, 1938. EBS Cornell

St. John's Parish House. Waterbury. EBS Cornell

Sanford, Anna and Ferry. Litchfield, c. 1928. EBS Cornell

Sargent, John. Greenwich

Satterlee, Herbert L. The Orchards, Greenwich, c. 1925; Frank A. Moore (a), 1909

Schutz, Robert M. Hartford; Charles A Platt (a), 1907. AAG

Stark, James H. Darien

Stranahan, Robert A. Westport

Swift, Dr. Walker. Noroton

Truesdale, Mrs. Melville D. Four Trees, Greenwich, 1945. EBS Cornell; L&S Oregon

Van Sinderen, Adrian. New Haven

Vanderbilt, Robert T. Green Farms, Westport, 1939–40; Harrie T. Lindeberg (a), 1939. EBS Cornell. (Greens Farms Academy)

Vietor, Ernest G. Greenwich

Von Ketteler, Baroness Maud Ledyard. Upper Meadow, Falls Village, 1945. EBS Cornell

Walcott, Frederick C. Norfolk and Greenwich

Weld, Mrs. Margaret W. Stamford; Richard H. Dana (a). EBS Cornell

Whittemore, Gertrude B. Tranquillity Farm, Middlebury, 1923; McKim, Mead & White (a), 1888; Charles Eliot (la), 1893; Warren H. Manning (la), 1896. EBS Cornell

Williams, Clark. Live Oak, Greenwich, 1925. EBS Cornell

Wood, Mrs. E. Allan. Greenwich; Richard H. Dana (a). EBS Cornell

Woods, Mrs. Richard A. Hillside Farm, Greenwich, 1946. EBS Cornell

Yale University, Book & Snake Club. New Haven; R. H. Robertson (a). EBS Cornell

Yandell, Lundsford P. Greenwich. EBS Cornell. (former Elkanah Mead Homestead)

DELAWARE

Callery, G. L. New Castle. EBS Cornell

du Pont. Centerville. EBS Cornell

du Pont, E. I. Wilmington, 1928. EBS Cornell

du Pont, Ernest. Wilmington. EBS Cornell

du Pont, Eugene and Ethel Pyle. Owl's Nest, Greenville, 1928; Harrie T. Lindeberg (a), 1915; J. Franklin Meehan and William Warner Harper (la). AAG; EBS Cornell. (Greenville Country Club)

Haskell, Mrs. Harry G. Hill Girt Farm, Wilmington, c. 1938; Noel Chamberlin (la). EBS Cornell

Hilles, Mrs. William. Wilmington

Willson, Reynolds. Greenville. EBS Cornell

DISTRICT OF COLUMBIA

Corbin, Henry.

Murdock, J. E. EBS Cornell

Parmelee, James and Alice. The Causeway, 1914, 1927; Charles A. Platt (a), 1912. EBS Cornell; FBJ. (Tregaron Conservancy)

Poor, E. B.

Poor, Garnet

Stewart, Alexander

Szechenyi, Count Lazlo. L&S Oregon

Townsend, Richard

Walcott, F. C.

FLORIDA

Cummer, Mrs. Arthur (Ninah). Jacksonville, 1931; Ossian Cole Simonds (la), 1903; Thomas Meehan & Sons (nursery), 1910; Olmsted Brothers (la), 1922, 1931. EBS Cornell. (Cummer Museum of Art & Gardens)

Edison, Mrs. Thomas A. (Mina Miller). Fort Myers, 1929. (Edison and Ford Winter Estates)

West, Mrs. Arthur L. Tallahassee. EBS Cornell

GEORGIA

Atkinson, Henry Morrell. Mayfair, Atlanta, 1929. EBS Cornell

Croly, Mrs. Herbert. St. Simon's Island

Goodrum, Mrs. James J. Atlanta; Philip T. Shutze (a), 1929. (Southern Center for International Studies)

McRae, Floyd W. Boxwood House, Atlanta; Philip T. Shutze (a), 1927–29

Torrey, Dr. H. N. Ossabaw Island, 1924

Williams, Joseph A. Cobb County. EBS Cornell

ILLINOIS

Armour, Lester. Lake Forest

Baird, Clay M. Evanston

Blair, William McCormick. Crab Tree Farm, Lake Bluff, 1926; David Adler (a), 1926; Arthur Huen (a). AAG; EBS Cornell

Butler, Hermon B. Winnetka

Clow, Mrs. Kent S. Lake Forest; Jens Jensen (la), 1910; Rose S. Nichols (la). EBS Cornell

Douglas, Donald B. Lake Forest, early 1930s; Howard V. D. Shaw (a), 1909; Olmsted Brothers (la), early 1930s

Gardner, Mrs. Robert A. Lake Forest; Harrie T. Lindeberg (a), 1928. EBS Cornell

Gross, Alfred H. Evanson

Lichstern, A. J. Highland Park; Jens Jensen (la), 1915

McLennan, Donald R. Lake Forest; Howard V. D. Shaw (a) 1912. AAG

Niblack, Austin. Lake Forest; Anderson & Ticknor (a), 1929; Jens Jensen (la), 1914

Reynolds, Arthur. Lake Forest; Harrie T. Lindeberg (a), 1930

Shumway, Mrs. Edward. Lake Forest. AAG

Spalding, Mrs. Vaughn G. Little Orchard, Lake Forest, 1939; Howard V. D. Shaw (a), 1896; Stanley Anderson (a), 1939

KENTUCKY

Brady, James Cox. Dixiana Farm, Lexington, 1926. EBS Cornell

De Waal, Mrs. Christian (Alice Headley), Cave Hill, Lexington, 1928. EBS Cornell

Haggin, Louis. Versailles, 1941. EBS Cornell

Speed, William S. Kanawha, Louisville, 1917; Charles A. Platt (a), 1917

LOUISIANA

Elsas, Mrs. Victor Hugo (Bertha). New Orleans

Garden Study Club. Audubon Park, New Orleans. EBS Cornell

Lemann, Monte. New Orleans, 1938. EBS Cornell

Newman, Mrs. Harold. New Orleans

Reily, W. B., Jr. New Orleans

Stern, Edgar B. and Edith R. Longue Vue, New Orleans, 1935+; Geoffrey and William Platt
  (a), 1939. EBS Cornell. (Longue Vue House & Gardens)

Williams, Mrs. Charles S. New Orleans, 1934. EBS Cornell

Williams, Mrs. Frank. New Orleans

Williams, Laurence K. New Orleans. EBS Cornell

MAINE

Alger, Mrs. Russell A., Jr. Starboard Cottage, York Harbor, 1926; William Platt (a), 1928.
  AAG; EBS Cornell

Allen, Mrs. Seabury. York Harbor, 1920s; Kittery Point, 1941. EBS Cornell

Austin, Edith. Kittery

Lewis, Mrs. Howard W. York Village, 1944; York Harbor, 1945. EBS Cornell

Mellon, Mrs. Matthews T. Mainstay, Northeast Harbor, 1945; Arthur McFarland (a), 1936.
  EBS Cornell

Parsons, Llewellyn. Kennebunk, 1914; Olmsted Brothers (la), 1910; Arthur Shurtleff (Shurcliff) (la), 1916; Fletcher Steele (la), 1945. AAG; EBS Cornell. (part of Rachel Carson National Seashore)

MARYLAND

Baker, William. Baltimore County. EBS Cornell

Conoley, Douglas. Tulip Hill, Cumberstone, 1945. EBS Cornell

Fay, Col. W. G. Leonardstown. EBS Cornell

Hale, Chandler. Upper Marlboro

Harvey, Mrs. F. B. Baltimore

Hopkins, D. Luke. Baltimore

Murdocks, Dora. Baltimore

Watts, Kate. Baltimore, c. 1930

Welles, Sumner. Oxon Hill. L&S Oregon

MASSACHUSETTS

Abbott, Gordon. Glass Head, Manchester, c. 1921

Ames, Mrs. Hobart. North Easton; Fletcher Steele (la), 1931

Ames, John. North Easton. EBS Cornell

Austin, Edith. Marion

Bemis, Frank. Beverly Farms; Boston. EBS Cornell

Bradley, Mrs. Gardner. Wellesley. EBS Cornell

Bradley, Robert. Prides Crossing

Bullock, Calvin. Royalston

Cabot, Henry B., Jr. Dover

Charles River Square, Boston; Frank A. Bourne (a), 1910

Coolidge, T. Jefferson. Magnolia

Converse, C. C. Magnolia

Crocker, Douglas. Fitchburg, 1930; Fox & Gale (a); J. D. Leland (la), 1920. EBS Cornell

Daniels, Mrs. Alanson L. Old Farm, Wenham, 1913. EBS Cornell

DeBlois, Mrs. George L. (Mary B.). Ipswich, 1918

Elliot, Dr. John. Dedham

Emmons, Mrs. Robert W. Monument Beach, 1924; J. Harleston Parker (a), 1901. EBS Cornell

Fessenden, Russell G. Concord, 1920. EBS Cornell

Frothingham, Mrs. Louis. North Easton; Herbert J. Kellaway (la). EBS Cornell

Green, Albert. Belmont

Greenough, Mrs. Henry V. Brookline, 1925. EBS Cornell

Hanna, D. R. Lenox

Harris, Mrs. Julian Hartwell. Nantucket, 1930. EBS Cornell

Harrower, Mrs. Norman (Harriet). Fitchburg, 1931

Herter, Christian A. Millis, 1935. EBS Cornell

Houghton, Arthur A. The Meadows, South Dartmouth, 1937; Chapman & Frazer (a), 1911; Warren H. Manning (la), 1910. EBS Cornell

Johnson, Wolcott H. South Hamilton

Kent, Edward L. Prides Crossing

King, Frederick P. Manchester, 1942. EBS Cornell

Leland, Lester. Manchester

Lewis, George, Jr. Sherborn. EBS Cornell

Longfellow, Alice. Cambridge, 1925; Martha B. Hutcheson (la), 1904. EBS Cornell. (Longfellow House–Washington's Headquarters National Historic Site)

Lowthorpe School. Groton, 1942. EBS Cornell

McGinley, Mrs. Holden. Milton, 1925; Winslow & Bigelow (a). EBS Cornell

Milton Bird Sanctuary. Milton

Parker, William A. North Easton. EBS Cornell

Proctor, Mrs. Rodney. Stockbridge, 1936. EBS Cornell

Putnam, Mrs. George. Manchester, 1936; Fletcher Steele (la), 1953. EBS Cornell

Sedgwick, Mrs. Ellery (Mabel Cabot). Long Hill, Beverly, 1930. EBS Cornell. (Trustees of Reservations property)

Spalding, Philip L. Milton, 1924; Fletcher Steele (la), 1928. EBS Cornell

Warren, Bayard. Prides Crossing

Warren, Mrs. Samuel D. Bohemia Manor, Mattapoisett, 1912. EBS Cornell

Warren, Sylvia. Dover. EBS Cornell

Watson, Gertrude. Pittsfield

West, Thomas. Woods Hole

Whittier, Albert R. Milton. EBS Cornell

MICHIGAN

Alger, Mrs. Frederick M. Grosse Pointe, 1928. EBS Cornell

Alger, Russell A., Jr., and Marion. The Moorings, Grosse Pointe, 1917, 1938; Charles A. Platt (a), 1908. AAG; EBS Cornell. (Alger Museum, 1937; War Memorial Association)

Alger, Mrs. Russell A. Grosse Pointe, 1930; William Platt (a). EBS Cornell

Allington, Mrs. Courtenay D. Grosse Pointe, 1930. AAG; EBS Cornell

Altland, Daniel. Grosse Pointe

Barbour, Mrs. Edwin Scott (Edith). Longue Vue, Grosse Pointe, 1927. EBS Cornell. (private memorial)

Bowen, Julian. Grosse Pointe; Wallace Frost (a), 1927

Brown, Mrs. Joseph E. Kalamazoo, 1919

Bryant, John. Grosse Pointe

Bulkley, Leavitt. Grosse Pointe

Campbell, Mrs. H. M. Detroit and Grosse Pointe. EBS Cornell

Chapin, Roy D. and Inez. Grosse Pointe, 1946; Bryant Fleming (a); Fletcher Steele (la), 1954.
    EBS Cornell

Clark, Emory W. Woodley Green, Grosse Pointe; Hugh T. Keyes (a), 1934

Corbett, Valeria. Grosse Pointe

Dillman, Hugh. (*See* Dodge)

Dodge, Anna Thompson (formerly Mrs. Horace E. Dodge) and Hugh Dillman. Rose Terrace,
    Grosse Pointe, 1931; Horace Trumbauer (a), 1930. EBS Cornell

Dyar, Mrs. John. Grosse Pointe

Edwards, Allen F. Grosse Pointe; Charles A. Platt (a), 1927

Ferry, Mrs. Dexter M. Grosse Pointe. Trowbridge & Ackerman (a), 1915. EBS Cornell

Ford, Henry and Clara. Fair Lane, Dearborn, 1927; Jens Jensen (la), 1915; Herbert J. Kellaway
    (la); Harriett Risley Foote (la). AAG; EBS Cornell. (Henry Ford Estate)

Greening Nurseries. Munroe. EBS Cornell

Grosse Pointe Club. Grosse Pointe; Robert O. Derrick (a), 1927

Grosse Pointe Nurses Home (Cottage Hospital?). Grosse Pointe. (Grosse Pointe Theater)

Harris, Julian Hartwell. Grosse Pointe; William B. Stratton (a), 1924. EBS Cornell

Harris, William. Detroit

Hudson, Judge Robert P. Sault Ste. Marie. EBS Cornell

Hull, Blanche. Kalamazoo

Jackson, Roscoe. Grosse Pointe, c. 1933

Kanzler, Ernest and Josephine Ford. Grosse Pointe, 1947; Bryant Fleming (a). EBS Cornell.
    (replaced by Edsel Ford House)

King, Mrs. Francis. Orchard House, Alma, c. 1923. EBS Cornell

Lake Shore Drive. Grosse Pointe, 1932. EBS Cornell

Lee Gate Subdivision. Grosse Pointe. EBS Cornell

Longyear, Mrs. Howard. Grosse Pointe

Lord, Herbert. Grosse Pointe

Lord, John N. Grosse Pointe. EBS Cornell

Lowe, Edward. Holmdene, Grand Rapids, 1921; Winslow & Bigelow (a), 1908; Ossian Cole
    Simonds (la). EBS Cornell. (Aquinas College)

MacCrone, Ed. Grosse Pointe

McGraw, Mrs. Arthur. Grosse Pointe; Charles A. Platt (a), 1926

McGraw, Mrs. Theodore, Jr., Grosse Pointe, 1922; Alfred Hopkins (a). EBS Cornell

McNaughton, Lynn. Grosse Pointe. EBS Cornell

Mendelsonn, Louis. Grosse Pointe. EBS Cornell

Miller, Sidney, Jr. Grosse Pointe

Mount Clemens Convalescent Home. Mount Clemens

Murphy, Blanche. Grosse Pointe

Murphy, Dr. Frederick T. (Mrs. F. M. Alger). Grosse Pointe, c. 1933. EBS Cornell

Newberry, Mrs. John Stoughton, Jr. Lone Hill Farm, Grosse Pointe, 1928; Albert Kahn (a),
    1911; A. B. Youmans (la), 1908. AAG; EBS Cornell

Newberry, Mrs. Truman H. Grosse Pointe; Trowbridge & Ackerman (a); William Pitkin (la)

O'Brien, John, Jr. Grosse Pointe

Pittman, Stuart. Grosse Pointe

Remick, Jerome. Detroit

Rust, A. M. Saginaw. EBS Cornell

Sales, Carter. Grosse Pointe

Sales, Mrs. Murray W. Grosse Pointe, 1927; Louis Kamper (a), 1917. EBS Cornell

Schlotman, Joseph B. Grosse Pointe, c. 1929; Albert H. Spahr (a), 1915. EBS Cornell

Shelden, Henry D. Grosse Pointe

Sigma Gamma Association. Grosse Pointe

Smith, Angus. Detroit, 1928. EBS Cornell

Smith, Henry B. Bay City, 1927. EBS Cornell

Smith, Howard. Grosse Pointe, 1928; Eleanor Roche (la). EBS Cornell

Smith, Hubert. Bay City. EBS Cornell

Stephens, Mrs. Henry. Grosse Pointe, 1917; Charles A. Platt (a), 1913. EBS Cornell

Stevens, William P. Grosse Pointe, 1929. EBS Cornell

Talbot, Mrs. George. Saginaw, 1937. EBS Cornell

Upton. Detroit

Webber, Oscar. Grosse Pointe, 1928. EBS Cornell

Webber, Richard. Grosse Pointe

MINNESOTA

Kalman, Paul, Jr. St. Paul

NEW HAMPSHIRE

Baynes, Ernest Harold. Memorial, Meriden, c. 1925

Drake, Joshua. EBS Cornell

Dyer, Lyman T. Orford, 1937. EBS Cornell

Goodyear, A. Conger and Mary. High Court, Cornish, 1914; Charles A. Platt (a), 1890. EBS Cornell

Griffith, Mrs. Theodore B. (Helen). Thimble Farm, Little Boar's Head, Rye, c. 1939. EBS Cornell

Hill, Albert E. Plainfield

Meriden Bird Club. Meriden

Peabody, Julian. Harlakenden House, Cornish; Charles A. Platt (a), 1899

Philip Read Memorial Library. Plainfield

Plainfield School. Plainfield, c. 1929

Saint-Gaudens Memorial. Cornish, 1928, 1940. EBS Cornell. (Saint-Gaudens National Historic Site)

Shipman, Louis and Ellen. Brook Place, Plainfield, 1903–1948. (private residence)

NEW JERSEY

Augustus, Ellsworth. Orange

Beinecke, Frederick W. Madison

Bliss, Mrs. Walter P. Wendover, Bernardsville, 1937; James L. Greenleaf (la), c. 1910. EBS Cornell. (Roxiticus Club)

Brady, James Cox. Hamilton Farm, Gladstone, 1925; Ruth Dean (la), c. 1917. EBS Cornell. (Beneficial Management Corporation)

Brown, J. Wright. Red Bank

Brown, William C. Short Hills

Castles, J. W. Convent

Colgate, Henry. Morristown

Cutting, Mrs. Charles S. (widow of James Cox Brady; *see* Brady)

Dane, William. Llewellyn Park

Duke, Mrs. James Buchanan. Somerville; James L. Greenleaf (la). (Duke Farms)

Edison, Mrs. Thomas A. (Mina Miller). Glenmont, West Orange, 1926; Ernest Bowditch (la), 1907. (Edison National Historic Site)

Farish, William.

Foster, Mrs. F. Vernon. West Orange; Edmund T. See (a), mid-1930s

Fowler, Arthur A. Glenelg, Bedminster; Mott B. Schmidt (a), 1925

Franks, Mrs. Robert A. Bonaire, Llewellyn Park, Orange, 1920s; Alexander Jackson Davis (a). AAG; EBS Cornell

Gambrill, Richard V. N. Vernon Manor, Peapack; James C. Mackenzie (a), 1927; AAG

Geddes, Susan C. Montclair

Hanks, George J. Orange, 1940. EBS Cornell

Hersloff, Nils B. Llewellyn Park, c. 1928

Hodson, Mrs. C. Orange, 1941. EBS Cornell

Hopkins, Alfred. Princeton, 1932; Alfred Hopkins (a). EBS Cornell

Kinnicutt, Mrs. G. Herman. Mayfields, Far Hills; Cross & Cross (a); Marian Coffin (la). (former residence of Sister Parrish)

Martin, Emma. Princeton, 1938. EBS Cornell

Mathews, Rev. Paul. Princeton

Metcalf, Manton B. Rumson

Mettler, John W. East Millstone

Moseley, Mrs. Frederick S., Jr. Windmill Farm, Far Hills, c. 1929. EBS Cornell

Prentice, John H. Willow Brook, Bernardsville. EBS Cornell

Ratliff, Mrs. R. Stockton, 1941. EBS Cornell

Reeves, Mrs. Richard Early. The Clearing, Summit, 1924; Calvert Vaux (la), 1889; Carl A. Pilat (la), 1924. (Reeves-Reed Arboretum)

Rutherfurd, Winthrop. Allamuchy

Schiff, Jacob. Seabright, c. 1926; James L. Greenleaf (la). EBS Cornell

Schley, Evander B. Froh Heim, Far Hills, 1924; Peabody, Wilson & Brown (a). EBS Cornell

Schley, Reeve. Ripplebrook, Far Hills; Peabody, Wilson & Brown (a). EBS Cornell

Smillie, Ralph. Essex Fells, 1943. EBS Cornell

Stillwell, Dr. Edward C. Essex Fells, 1945. EBS Cornell

Terry, Wyllys and Marie Louise Baldwin. Sarah Condict Cottage, Bernardsville, c. 1924

Vanderpool, Wynant D. Morristown

Vietor, John A. Seabright. EBS Cornell

Weston, Edward. Montclair. EBS Cornell

NEW MEXICO

Proctor, F. Santa Fe. EBS Cornell

NEW YORK

CENTRAL AND WESTERN NEW YORK STATE

Albright, Langdon. Buffalo, 1914

Angell, Dr. Edward. Rochester

Burden, Henry. Cazenovia

Campbell, J. Hazard and Marjorie Knox. Orchard House, East Aurora, 1931; Peabody, Wilson & Brown (a), 1929. EBS Cornell

Case, Theodore W. Auburn. EBS Cornell

Clarke, Mrs. C. S. Angola. EBS Cornell

Clark, Mrs. Stephen C. Cooperstown

Clement, Stephen. East Aurora

Cooper, Dr. Henry and Katherine. Heathcote, Cooperstown, 1920s

Cooper, James Fenimore, Jr. Fynmere, Cooperstown, 1912; Charles A. Platt (la), 1911. EBS Cornell

Fairchild, Mrs. Charles S. (Helen). Lorenzo, Cazenovia, 1914 (Lorenzo State Historic Site)

Finucane, Bernard. Rochester

Forman, G. M. G. Buffalo

Gaylord, Bradley. Buffalo. EBS Cornell

Hees, J. Ledlie. Sacandaga

Houghton, Amory B. The Knoll, Corning, 1946. EBS Cornell

Houghton. Cemetery plot, Corning. EBS Cornell

Hyde, L. F. Glens Falls

Kellogg, Spencer. Lochevan, Derby, early 1930s. AAG

Knox, Seymour H., II. Ess Kay Farm, East Aurora, 1932. EBS Cornell. (Knox Farm State Park)

Larkin, John, Jr. Windover, Derby. AAG

Mann, Stuart. Derby

Martin, Mrs. Darwin D. (Isabelle). Graycliff, Derby, 1930; Frank Lloyd Wright (a), 1926. EBS
    Cornell. (Graycliff Estate: Isabelle R. Martin House)

McGraw, F. Sears. East Aurora

Noyes, Mrs. E. H. Dansville

Pettee, Harry E. Saratoga Springs, 1921; Alfred Hopkins (a)

Pratt, Francis C. Governor Yates House, Schenectady; Harris & Richards (a). EBS Cornell

Prince, David and Winifred. Schenectady, 1942. EBS, Cornell

Schoelkopf, Dr. J. F. Buffalo

Schoelkopf, Al. Buffalo

Schoelkopf, W. Buffalo

Spaulding, S. S. Springfield. EBS Cornell

LONG ISLAND: NASSAU COUNTY

Bacon, Mrs. Robert Low. Old Acres, Old Westbury, 1920s; John Russell Pope (a). FBJ

Belmont, August. Syosset

Burchard, Anson. Locust Valley

Bushnell, Leslie. Oyster Bay

Clark, J. Averell. Westbury, 1927; Peabody, Wilson & Brown (a), 1920. EBS Cornell

Cushman, Paul. Syosset. L&S Oregon

Davis, Arthur Vining. Oyster Bay, 1922; Guy Lowell (a); Vitale, Brinckerhoff & Geiffert (la)

Davis, John W. Locust Valley

Dyer, George R. The Orchards, Brookville; Charles A. Platt (a), 1909

Emmet, Richard S. High Elms, Glen Cove, c. 1929; Peabody, Wilson & Brown (a)

Gossler, Philip. Topsfield, Wheatley Hills, 1925; John Russell Pope (a), 1917. AAG; EBS Cor-
    nell. (C. W. Post College)

Gould, Mrs. Edwin. Oyster Bay, 1945. EBS Cornell

Guest, Frederick E. Roslyn

Handy, Parker. Glen Cove

Harriman, Henry. Jericho

Hepburn, F. T. Locust Valley

Hutton, Edward F. Westbury, 1942; Wheatley Hills; Charles M. Hart (a). EBS Cornell

Iselin, Charles Oliver. Wolver Hollow, Brookville, 1917; Hoppin & Koen (a), c. 1914; Beatrix
    Farrand (la); Olmsted Brothers (la). EBS Cornell

Jennings, B. B. Glen Head

Kane, John P. Locust Valley; William H. Beers (a), c. 1923; Louise Payson (la)

Kramer, A. Ludlow. Picket Farm, Westbury, 1920; Peabody, Wilson & Brown (a); Olmsted
    Brothers (la). EBS Cornell

Langley, William C. Westbury, c. 1924

Ledyard, Lewis Cass, Jr. Syosset, 1917; Charles A. Platt (a), 1914

Loening, Rudolph. Glen Cove

Lord, Franklin B. Cottsleigh, Syosset, c. 1929; William H. Beers (a), 1927. EBS Cornell

Lord, George DeForest. Overfields, Syosset, c. 1930; William H. Beers (a), 1927. EBS Cornell

Maynard, Mrs. Walter E. Haut Bois, Jericho, c. 1930; Ogden Codman, Jr. (a), 1916; Jacques Grebier (la)

Morris, John B. Roslyn

Murray, Hugh A. Wheatley Hills

Peabody, Julian. Pond Hollow Farm, Old Westbury, 1924; Julian Peabody (a), 1910. EBS Cornell

Pratt, Herbert L. The Braes, Glen Cove; James Brite (a), 1912; James L. Greenleaf (la). EBS Cornell. (Webb Institute of Naval Architecture)

Preston, William P. T. Longfields, Jericho; Peabody, Wilson & Brown (a), 1924. EBS Cornell

Richmond, L. M. Sunninghill, Glen Head

Roosevelt, Kermit. Oyster Bay

Salvage, Sir Samuel Agar. Rynwood, Glen Head, 1926; Roger H. Bullard (a), 1926. AAG; EBS Cornell. (Villa Banfi)

Schmidlapp, Carl J. Mill Neck, mid-1920s; Peabody, Wilson & Brown (a). L&S Oregon

Smith, R. Penn. East Williston

Smithers, F. S. Glen Cove. EBS Cornell

Stewart, Glenn. Locust Valley. EBS Cornell

Taliaferro, Mrs. Eugene. Oyster Bay. EBS Cornell

White, A. M. Oyster Bay

Whitehouse, Norman. Brookville

LONG ISLAND: SUFFOLK COUNTY

Ferguson, Helen. Fisher's Island

Fish, Julia. Greenport, 1916. EBS Cornell

Hare, Mrs. Meredith. Pidgeon Hill, Huntington; Charles A. Platt (a), 1916

Hegeman, Miss A. M. Southampton, c. 1917

Jackson, W. H. West Hills, 1941. EBS Cornell

James, Ellery S. Southampton, Roger H. Bullard (a), 1926

Maidstone Club. East Hampton; Roger H. Bullard (a), 1922

Matheson, William J. Lloyd Neck, 1916. L&S Oregon

Peabody, Julian, Jr. Huntington, 1945. EBS Cornell

Peters, Henry T. Islip. EBS Cornell

Plumb, Mrs. E. J. Dering Harbor, Shelter Island, 1937. EBS Cornell

Poor, Charles Lane. Dering Harbor, Shelter Island

Pruyn, Mary and Neltje. East Hampton, 1919. AAG; EBS Cornell

Reed, Lansing F. Windy Hill, Lloyd Harbor, 1925; Charles A. Platt (a), 1924. EBS Cornell

Ruxton, Philip. East Hampton

Swayne, Eleanor. Red House, Shinnecock Hills; Grosvenor Atterbury (a). EBS Cornell

Towle, Florence M. Dering Harbor, Shelter Island. EBS Cornell

Weld, Francis M. Lloyd Harbor; Charles A. Platt (a), 1911

Wood, Mrs. Willis Delano. Fort Hill House, Lloyd Neck, c. 1938; Olmsted Brothers (la). AAG; EBS Cornell

NEW YORK CITY

Angell, Montgomery B. Manhattan

Arnold. Memorial, The Woodlawn Cemetery, Bronx

Astor, Vincent. Astor Court, Manhattan; Charles A. Platt (a), 1916

Bell, Gordon. Manhattan

Benkard, Henry H. Manhattan

Booker, Mrs. Neville. Manhattan

Clarke, J. W. Manhattan Beach, Brooklyn. L&S Oregon

Cutting, Robert Fulton. L&S Oregon

Erdmann, Mrs. John

Fernandez, Raoul

Forrestal, Mrs. James V. Manhattan. EBS Cornell

Gordon, Mrs. Thurlow

Hackett (James K.). Memorial, The Woodlawn Cemetery, Bronx, 1928; Sir Edwin Lutyens
(a), 1927

Humbert. Memorial, Trinity Church, Manhattan. EBS Cornell

International Garden Club. Pelham Bay Park, Bronx, 1931; Delano & Aldrich (a), 1914. EBS
Cornell. (Bartow-Pell Mansion Museum)

Iselin, Ernest.

Kelly, Thomas Smith. 1943. EBS Cornell

La Montagne, Mrs. Far Rockaway

Lancashire, J. Henry. Manhattan

Merlesmith, Van J. Manhattan

Murphy, Charles B. G.

New York Botanical Garden. Women's Advisory Council Border, Bronx, 1928. EBS Cornell

Newall, Joseph. EBS Cornell

Rockefeller. Manhattan; Sloan & Robertson (a), 1930. EBS Cornell

Spreckels, Geraldine. 1945. EBS Cornell

Strauss, Herbert. Memorial, The Woodlawn Cemetery, Bronx

Wightman, Dr. Orrin. Manhattan. EBS Cornell

SUBURBAN NEW YORK

Allen, J. Roy. Rye. EBS Cornell. L&S Oregon

Angell, Montgomery B. High House, Garrison; William Platt (a). EBS Cornell

Baldwin, Mrs. Alexander. Bedford Hills. EBS Cornell

Benkard, J. Philip. Boulder Rock, Tuxedo Park; Bruce Price (a), 1888

Berkshire Industrial School. Canaan

Biddle, Nicholas. South Salem

Blum, Henry. Scarsdale. EBS Cornell

Brewster, Mrs. Robert S., Jr. Avalon, Mount Kisco, early 1920s; Delano & Aldrich (a), 1912.
AAG; EBS Cornell. (College of Rabbis)

Cahn, A. L. Hartsdale

Canfield, George T. Peekskill

Chapman, John Jay. Sylvania, Barrytown; Charles A. Platt (a), 1904

Cook, Henry A. Greenburgh

Cottier, A. E. Scarsdale

Cotton, Mrs. Joseph. Mount Kisco

Edison, Mrs. Thomas A. (Mina Miller). Lewis Miller Cottage, Chautauqua, 1922

Emmet, Grenville T. Katonah

Ewing, Charles. Rye

Ewing, William. Bedford Hills

Fahnestock, William F. Girdle Ridge, Katonah, c. 1912; Charles A. Platt (a), 1909; Olmsted
Brothers (la), 1911–12. EBS Cornell

Frazier, Isobel. Garrison. EBS Cornell

Frost, Blanche. South Nyack

Gaige, Crosby. Harmon

Goodrich, David M. Mount Kisco; Charles A. Platt (a), 1912

Hammond, John Henry. Dellwood, Mount Kisco; Charles A. Platt (a), 1915; Nellie B. Allen (la), 1930s

Hanes, Mrs. John. Millbrook

Harris, Mrs. Basil. Sunny Lodge, Rye, 1942. EBS Cornell

Hart, Charles. Pelham Manor

Hart, Ed. Pleasantville

Hartsonne, Douglas. Rye

Hogan, Arthur and Jefferson. Rye

Holter, E. O. Mount Kisco

Howard, Graeme. Mamaroneck. EBS Cornell

King, Frederick P. Uplands, Irvington-on-Hudson, 1933; Marian Coffin (la), 1922. AAG; EBS Cornell

Lakin, Herbert. Scarsdale. AAG; EBS Cornell

Lawrence, Mrs. Arthur. Mount Kisco. EBS Cornell

Magee, John. Wampus, Mount Kisco, 1916. AAG; EBS Cornell

Malone, Halsey. Mount Kisco

Matney, Margaret. Little Knoll, Brewster, 1944. EBS Cornell

Melen, Mrs. N. McM. Hudson

Meyer, Eugene and Agnes. Seven Springs Farm, Mount Kisco; Charles A. Platt (a), 1915. EBS Cornell

Mitchell, Ormsby. Rye; Mott B. Schmidt (a), 1920

Morgan, William Fellowes. Mount Kisco

Naumberg, George W. Groton

Osborn, Frederick Henry and Mary. Cat Rock, Garrison, 1924; Hall Pleasants Pennington (a), 1919

Perkins, Thomas L. Rye, 1945. EBS Cornell

Petrasch, C. S. Mount Kisco

Platt, Geoffrey. Mount Kisco. EBS Cornell

Preston, Lewis B. Mount Kisco

Pruyn, Robert D. Apple Orchard, Mount Kisco; Charles A. Platt (a), 1911

Quimby, John. Brewster

Reese, Mrs. William W. Obercreek, Hughsonville, 1936; Mary Rutherfurd Jay (la). EBS Cornell

Ryle, Julia. Mount Kisco, 1916. EBS Cornell

Scribner, Arthur. Mount Kisco

Strauss, Percy P. White Plains

Thomas, Mrs. James A. White Plains, c. 1936. EBS Cornell

Towne, John. Mount Kisco; Arthur Shurcliff (la), pre-1921; Fletcher Steele (a), 1921

Tucker, Carll. Penwood, Mount Kisco, 1926; Walker & Gillette (a), 1925; Olmsted Brothers (la), 1920. EBS Cornell; L&S Oregon

Tweedy, R. B. Goshen

U.S. Military Academy. Superintendent's Garden, West Point, 1936. EBS Cornell

Wallerstein, Leo. Harrison

Warburg, Felix. White Plains

NORTH CAROLINA

Chatham, Mrs. Hugh. Winston-Salem. EBS Cornell

Chatham, Mrs. Thurmond (Martha). Middleton House, Winston-Salem, 1930, 1945. EBS Cornell

Craig, Mrs. S. D. Winston-Salem. EBS Cornell

Duke, James B. Durham

Duke University. Sarah P. Duke Gardens, Durham, 1937; John Wister (la), 1932. EBS Cornell

Eagle, Dr. Watt. Durham. EBS Cornell

Gray, Bowman. Roaring Gap, 1949. EBS Cornell

Gray, Gordon. Winston-Salem, 1945. EBS Cornell

Hanes, Dr. Frederick. Durham. EBS Cornell

Hanes, Gordon. Winston-Salem, 1946. EBS Cornell

Hanes, James G., III, and Mary Ruffin. Winston-Salem, 1929. EBS Cornell. (Southeast Center for Contemporary Art)

Hanes, P. Hubert. Winston-Salem, 1945. EBS Cornell

Hanes, Philip. Winston-Salem

Hanes, Ralph P. and DeWitt. Winston-Salem, 1929; Haldeman & Leland (la). EBS Cornell. (President's House, Wake Forest University)

Hanes, Robert. Roaring Gap. EBS Cornell

Hill, George Watts. Durham

Moore, Mrs. Thomas O. Winston-Salem. EBS Cornell

Mountcastle, Kenneth. Winston-Salem. EBS Cornell

Penn, Mrs. Jefferson. Reidsville

Phillips, Earl N. High Point. EBS Cornell

Reed, Joseph Verner

Shands, Dr. Alfred R. Durham, 1937. EBS Cornell

Wade, Madison. Charlotte

OHIO

Ashley, Meredith. Perrysburg, 1945

Bicknell, Warren. Willoughby; Olmsted Brothers (la), 1916. EBS Cornell

Bishop, Dr. Robert H. Chagrin Falls; Warren H. Manning (la), 1916. EBS Cornell

Bonnerwitz, Lee R. Van Wert

Burke, E. S., Jr. Hillbrook, Chagrin Falls, 1931; Meade & Hamilton (a); Warren H. Manning (la), 1919. AAG; EBS Cornell

Burns, James A. Columbus. EBS Cornell

Burton, Courtney. Gates Mills

Burton, R. C. Zanesville

Chatfield, William Hayden. Hunt's End, Madeira, c. 1928

Clapp, Willard M. Cleveland Heights, 1926; Meade & Hamilton (a), 1926; Warren H. Manning (la), 1922. AAG; EBS Cornell

Corning, Mrs. Henry. Bratenahl. EBS Cornell

Dodge, Henry M. Perrysburg, 1945. EBS Cornell

Garfield, James R. Lawnfield, West Mentor; J. Wilkinson Elliott (la). (James A. Garfield National Historic Site)

Halstead, Mrs. John. Perrysburg. EBS Cornell

Hanna, Mrs. Howard. Kirtland. EBS Cornell

Herrick, Parmeley. Chagrin Falls

Hoffman, Clare J. Washington Township, 1945. EBS Cornell

Humphrey, George M. Holiday Hill Farm, Mentor, 1946. EBS Cornell

Huntington, F. R. Columbus, c. 1927. EBS Cornell

Hunting Valley Town Hall. EBS Cornell

Ingalls, David S. Chagrin Falls, 1937; Carl Rowley (a). EBS Cornell

Ireland, Mrs. James D. Bratenahl

MacNichol, Goerge P. Perrysburg, 1944. EBS Cornell

Mather, Amasa S. Chagrin Falls; Warren H. Manning (la), 1916

Mather, William Gwinn and Elizabeth. Gwinn, Bratenahl, 1914; Charles A. Platt (a), 1907; Warren H. Manning (la), 1906

Meade, George H. Dayton

Newell, John. Mentor

Ormond, M. G. Perrysburg. EBS Cornell

Parmelee, Mrs. James. Parmelee Farm, Painesville, 1915. EBS Cornell

Perkins, Jacob B. Mentor

Robinson, Jefferson. Toledo. EBS Cornell

Secor, George Barnes. Perrysburg, 1944. EBS Cornell

Seiberling, Frank A. and Gertrude. Stan Hywet Hall, Akron, 1928; Charles S. Schneider (a); Warren H. Manning (la), 1911. (Stan Hywet Hall & Gardens)

Stranahan, Duane and Virginia. Perrysburg, 1945; Alfred Hopkins (a). AAG; EBS Cornell

Stranahan, Frank. Toledo. EBS Cornell

Stranahan, Robert A. Stranleigh, Toledo, 1936. EBS Cornell. (Metroparks Toledo)

Sullivan, Mrs. Corliss. Gates Miles; Warren H. Manning (la). EBS Cornell

Vail, Herman L. Bratenahl

White, Holden. Chagrin Falls. EBS Cornell

White, Thomas. Chagrin Falls and Cleveland. EBS Cornell

Wilbur, Rollin A. Cleveland. EBS Cornell

White, Windsor T. Halfred Farms, Chagrin Falls, 1919; Bryant Fleming (a); Warren H. Manning (la), 1919. AAG; EBS Cornell

Wick, Myron A. Chagrin Falls; Warren H. Manning (la)

PENNSYLVANIA

Andrews, Schofield. Philadelphia

Barklies, Archibald. Inver House, St. Davids; Wilson Eyre (a), 1913

Belin, D'Andelot. Waverly

Biddle, Craig. Laurento, St. Davids; Peabody & Stearns (a), 1901

Brock, Henry G. Muncy

Case, Theodore W. White Mills. EBS Cornell

Curry, Mrs. Henry M., Jr. (Elizabeth). Elm Cottage, Sewickley Heights, 1945. EBS Cornell

Foerderer, Mrs. Percival. Bryn Mawr. EBS Cornell

Gibson, Mary K. Philadelphia. EBS Cornell

Gilpin, John C. Sugar Loaf Orchard, Chestnut Hill; AAG

Goodyear, C. W. Lewistown

Hanks, George J. Bradford

Heinz, Howard. Pittsburgh. EBS Cornell

Ingersoll, Frank B. Pittsburgh, 1931; Janssen & Cocken (a). EBS Cornell

Laughlin, George, Jr. Pittsburgh

Liversidge, T. K. Narberth, 1943. EBS Cornell

Lloyd, Horatio. Haverford

Lucas, Maitland B. Bucks County, 1941. EBS Cornell

McClintic, H. H. Pittsburgh

Mellon, Richard. Pittsburgh

Milligan, Robert F. Sewickley

Mills, Paul. Saint Davids

Morgan, Randal and Frances. Wyndmoor, Chestnut Hill; F. L. & J. C. Olmsted (la), 1897; Marian Coffin (la), 1934; Fletcher Steele (la), 1935. (Morgan Towers)

Morris, I. Wistar. Chestnut Hill; L&S Oregon

Morris, Samuel. Edgehill, Chestnut Hill, 1922. AAG; EBS Cornell

Paul, A. J. Drexel and Isabel Biddle. Box Hill, Radnor; Charles A. Platt (a), 1914. AAG; EBS
    Cornell
Pinchot, Mrs. Gifford (Cornelia Bryce). Grey Towers, Milford, 1918; Rose S. Nichols (la), 1937
Richards, Mrs. Ralph S. Cemetery plot, Sewickley, 1946. EBS Cornell
Riley, Edward. Lumberville, 1939. EBS Cornell
Rivinis, E. F. Chestnut Hill
Robertson, N. G. Waverly. EBS Cornell
Rolling Rock Club. Ligonier
Scranton, W. W. Scranton
Smith, W. Hinckle. Timberline, Bryn Mawr; Charles A. Platt (a), 1907; Olmsted Brothers (la),
    1907
Smith, William Watson. Pittsburgh, 1924; Laughlintown, 1929, Janesse & Cocken (a), 1929;
    Ligonier, 1937. EBS Cornell
Starr, Isaac Tatnall. Laverock Hill, Chestnut Hill, 1915; Charles A. Platt (a), 1915. AAG; EBS
    Cornell
Steel, A. G. B. Chestnut Hill
Strubing, Philip. Chestnut Hill, c. 1940; Warren H. Manning (la), 1917
Suydam, Fred D. White Mills, 1941. EBS Cornell
Thomson, Anne. Bryn Mawr
Thomson, Frank. Devon
Tyler, George. Elkins Park
Van Voorhes, H. W. Sewickley
Warden, William Gray. Philadelphia
Warren, Edward. Waverly. EBS Cornell

RHODE ISLAND
Allen, Mrs. Frederick H. The Mount, Newport, 1932. EBS Cornell
Lihme, C. Bai. Watch Hill
Thacher, T. D. Watch Hill

SOUTH CAROLINA
Craig, William. Mocksville
Keane, Jerome. Aiken
Kenefick, T. S. Aiken. EBS Cornell
Knox, Seymour H. II. The Balcony, Aiken, 1929; Julian Peabody (a). EBS Cornell
Legendre, Sidney. Berkeley County and Mount Holly
William, Clark. Camden, 1925. EBS Cornell

TENNESSEE
Ewing, Mrs. Henry O. Lookout Mountain. EBS Cornell
Martin, C. G. Chattanooga. EBS Cornell
Patten, Mrs. George. Riverview. EBS Cornell

TEXAS
Brown, Lutcher. Oak Court, San Antonio. EBS Cornell
Dickson, Mrs. J. F. Houston. EBS Cornell
Farish, Stephen Power. Ravenna, Houston; John F. Staub (a), 1934. EBS Cornell

Green, John E. Houston; McKenzie & Briscoe (a); Louis Frothingham (la). EBS Cornell

Hill, Mrs. George A. River Oaks, 1938; Ruth London (la)

Hogg, Ima. Bayou Bend, Houston; John F. Staub (a), 1926; Ruth London (la)

Neff, Mrs. Richard Wayne. Houston; Birdshall Briscoe (a), c. 1938. EBS Cornell

Paddock, W. A. Houston, 1936. EBS Cornell

Sharp, Mrs. W. B. Houston. EBS Cornell

Stewart, Graham. Graham, c. 1934. EBS Cornell

Weiss, Mrs. Harry C. Houston; John F. Staub (a), 1930; Harrie T. Lindeberg (a); W. W. Watkin (a); Ruth London (la). EBS Cornell

Winston, James O., Jr. Houston, 1939; John F. Staub (a), 1938; Harrie T. Lindeberg (a). EBS Cornell

Wrightsman, Mrs. Stafford. Houston. EBS Cornell

VERMONT

Bennington Library. Bennington

Billings, Frederick, Julia, and Elizabeth. Woodstock, 1912; Robert Morris Copeland (la), 1869; Charles A. Platt (la), 1899; Martha Brookes Hutcheson (la), 1902. EBS Cornell. (Marsh-Billings-Rockefeller National Historical Park)

Brooks, Henry. Woodstock

Brown, Horace. North Mowing, Springfield, 1914, 1928. EBS Cornell

Brown, J. Russell. Malletts Bay

Burgess, Mrs. F. V. Burlington. EBS Cornell

Davis, Gilbert. Windsor

Field, William. Rutland, 1947. EBS Cornell

Jennings, Philip B. Bennington, 1914; Albro & Lindeberg (a), 1912. EBS Cornell. (Four Chimneys Inn)

Johnson, Guy B. Bennington

Judd, Mrs. Edith. Redding

Matney, Margaret. Sheddsville

McCullough, J. G. North Bennington

Mead, Taylor. Windsor, 1943. EBS Cornell

Parmelee, Robert M. Old Bennington, 1926. EBS Cornell

Proctor, Redfield. Proctor, 1935. EBS Cornell

Shoemaker, Mrs. M. M. Old Bennington. EBS Cornell

Squiers, Charles B. Bennington

Webb, Capt. J. Watson. Brick House, Shelburne, 1919. (Shelburne Museum)

Willson, Mrs. E. V. K. Rutland, 1931. EBS Cornell

Woodstock Congregational Church. Woodstock

Woodstock Railway Station. Woodstock, 1915

VIRGINIA

Davis, T. B. Middleburg, 1933. EBS Cornell

Devore, Col. Daniel B. and Helen. Chatham Manor, Fredericksburg, 1924. EBS Cornell; FBJ. (Fredericksburg and Spotsylvania Memorial National Military Park)

Gildersleeve, Mrs. Alfred. Charlottesville, 1940. EBS Cornell

Grayson, Cary Travers. Blue Ridge Farm, Upperville; Waddy B. Wood (a), 1933. L&S Oregon

Greenhalgh, George P. Springsbury Farm, Berryville, 1945; Percy, Shaw & Hepburn (a), 1937. EBS Cornell. (Casey Trees)

Jackson, Mrs. Cary. Keswick and Orange, 1942. EBS Cornell

Jenkins, Edward. Millwood, 1936. EBS Cornell
Lloyd, Mrs. Stacy (Rachel Lambert Lloyd, later Mrs. Paul Mellon). Apple Hill, Millwood. EBS
    Cornell
Pratt, John Lee. Chatham Manor, Fredericksburg, 1931; Charles Gillette (la), 1955. EBS Cor-
    nell. (*See also* Devore)
Reed, William. Sabot, 1937. EBS Cornell
Ruddock, A. B. Richmond
Warburg, Frederick. Middleburg. EBS Cornell

WASHINGTON STATE
Merrill, Richard D. Seattle, 1915; Charles A. Platt (a), 1909; Lord & Schryver (la), 1929;
    Thomas D. Church (la), 1960s

WEST VIRGINIA
Goldthrope, Mrs. Edward C. Charleston, 1938. EBS Cornell
Ketcham, Mrs. D. A. Charleston. EBS Cornell

WISCONSIN
Ingram, Erskine B. Eau Claire; Charles A. Platt (a), 1921

OTHER LOCATIONS
Dubuc, J. E. Chicoutimi, Quebec
Truesdale, M. D. Bermuda

UNIDENTIFIED LOCATIONS
Black, Durel. EBS Cornell (photographs)
Hayes
Hill, Francis Powell. EBS Cornell (photographs)
Jander
Miller, George and Rachel
Nugent
Sanders Memorial. EBS Cornell (photographs)

GARDENS TO VISIT

Chatham Manor
Fredericksburg and Spotsylvania National Military Park
(former Col. Daniel B. and Helen Devore residence)
120 Chatham Lane
Fredericksburg, Va.
nps.gov/frsp

Crab Tree Farm
(former William McCormick Blair residence)
Lake Bluff, Ill.
(limited openings through The Garden Conservancy's Open Days Program)
gardenconservancy.org

Cummer Museum of Art & Gardens
(former Arthur and Ninah Cummer residence)
Italian Garden
829 Riverside Avenue
Jacksonville, Fla.
cummermuseum.org

Sarah P. Duke Gardens
Terrace Gardens
Duke University
420 Anderson Street
Durham, N.C.
gardens.duke.edu

Edison & Ford Winter Estates
Mina Edison's Moonlight Garden
2350 McGregor Blvd.

Fort Myers, Fla.
edisonfordwinterestates.org

Fair Lane / Henry Ford Estate
(former Henry and Clara Ford residence)
4901 Evergreen Road
Dearborn, Mich.
henryfordestate.org

Gaiety Hollow
(former Edith Schryver residence)
545 Mission Street SE
Salem, Ore.
lordandschryverconservancy.org

Graycliff Estate and Conservancy
(former Darwin D. and Isabelle Martin residence)
6472 Old Lake Shore Road
Derby, N.Y.
graycliffestate.org

Longfellow House – Washington's Headquarters National Historic Site
105 Brattle Street
Cambridge, Mass.
nps.gov/long

Longue Vue House & Gardens
(former Edgar B. and Edith R. Stern residence)
7 Bamboo Road
New Orleans, La.
longuevue.com

Marsh-Billings-Rockefeller National Historical Park
(former Frederick Billings residence)
54 Elm Street
Woodstock, Vt.
nps.gov/mabi

The Meadows
(former Arthur A. Houghton residence)
South Dartmouth, Mass.
(limited openings through The Garden Conservancy's Open Days Program)
gardenconservancy.org

Saint-Gaudens National Historic Site
(former Augustus Saint-Gaudens residence)
139 Saint Gaudens Road
Cornish, N.H.
nps.gov/saga

Shapiro/Bloomberg Garden
(former Mrs. Holden McGinley residence)
Milton, Mass.
(limited openings through The Garden Conservancy's Open Days Program)
gardenconservancy.org

Southeast Center for Contemporary Art
(former James G. and Mary Hanes residence)
750 Marguerite Drive
Winston-Salem, N.C.
secca.org

Stan Hywet Hall & Gardens
(former Frank A. and Gertrude Seiberling residence)
English Garden
714 North Portage Path
Akron, Ohio
stanhywet.org

Topsmead State Forest
(former Edith Chase residence)
P.O. Box 1081
Litchfield, Conn.
ct.gov/deep/topsmead

Tregaron Conservancy
(former James and Alice Parmelee residence)
3100 Macomb Street NW
Washington, D.C.
tregaronconservancy.org

The War Memorial
(former Russell A. and Marion Alger residence)
32 Lake Shore Drive
Grosse Pointe Farms, Mich.
warmemorial.org

ARCHIVES AND RESOURCES

MAIN REPOSITORIES

Cornell University, Ithaca, N.Y. Ellen McGowan Biddle Shipman Papers, file no. 1259, Division of Rare and Manuscript Collections, Cornell University Library. Approximately four thousand plans and drawings, five hundred photographs, correspondence, clippings, and other material. The collection represents nearly three hundred projects. A catalog is available. (Cornell)

Nancy Angell Streeter Family Collection. Private collection of correspondence, photographs, and memorabilia. (Streeter collection)

Judith B. Tankard Collection. Private collection of correspondence, research files, photographs, Shipman notebooks, and memorabilia.

Archives of American Gardens, Smithsonian Institution, Capital Gallery, Suite 3300, MRC 506, Washington, D.C. Collection of glass lantern slides and other resources.

Library of Congress Prints and Photographs Division, Washington, D.C. Frances Benjamin Johnston Collection: Lantern Slides for Garden & Historic House Lectures. Glass lantern slides, most hand colored. Collection is digitized and available online.

Long Island Studies Institute, Nassau County Museum, Hempstead, N.Y. Collection of Mattie Edwards Hewitt photographs of Long Island commissions.

Society for the Preservation of Long Island Antiquities, 93 North Country Road, Setauket, N.Y. Information on Long Island commissions.

University of Oregon, Special Collections and University Archives, Knight Library. Lord & Schryver architectural records, 1929–1970, no. 98, files 87–89. Plans only; twenty-five projects associated with Edith Schryver.

OTHER REPOSITORIES

Local libraries and historical societies (Greenwich, Conn., and Grosse Pointe, Mich., for instance) have additional information. Private owners of extant Shipman gardens occasionally have plans, photographs, and correspondence. In addition, the following institutions have information on Shipman commissions or related material.

Cummer Museum of Art & Gardens, Jacksonville, Fla. Landscape plans, photographs, correspondence, and plant lists in archives. (Cummer)

Dartmouth College, Hanover, N.H. Special Collections, Baker Library. Diaries, photographs, memorabilia relating to the Cornish Colony.

Duke University, Durham, N.C. University Archives holds photographs, reports, and correspondence.

Fredericksburg and Spotsylvania National Military Park, 120 Chatham Lane, Fredericksburg, Va. Plans and photographs, small exhibition on view.

Gwinn Estate, 12407 Lake Shore Boulevard, Bratenahl, Ohio. Plans, photographs, and correspondence.

Henry Ford Museum and Research Center, 20900 Oakwood Blvd., Dearborn, Mich. Correspondence, blueprints, and photographs in Fair Lane Papers.

Longue Vue House & Gardens, 7 Bamboo Road, New Orleans, La. Extensive archives including plans, correspondence, and photographs. (Longue Vue)

Philip Read Memorial Library, Plainfield, N.H. Plan for Plainfield School.

Plainfield Historical Society, Plainfield, N.H. Photographs of Brook Place, memorabilia, and hand-colored glass slides from annual garden contests.

Saint-Gaudens National Historic Site, Cornish, N.H. Artwork and photographs relating to the Cornish Colony; Garden Note Book (partial copy).

Stan Hywet Hall & Gardens, 714 North Portage Path, Akron, Ohio. Plans, photographs, and correspondence in archives. (Stan Hywet)

OTHER RESOURCES

Library of American Landscape History, P.O. Box 1323, Amherst, MA 01004, lalh.org. Publications, annual magazine *VIEW,* and website provide information and research on American landscape architects and design history.

The Cultural Landscape Foundation, 1711 Connecticut Avenue NW, Suite 200, Washington D.C. 20009, tclf.org. Maintains an extensive database, What's Out There, which can be searched by creator and property. Numerous Shipman properties are included.

The Garden Conservancy, P.O. Box 219, Cold Spring, N.Y. 10516, sponsors an Open Days program that occasionally includes private Shipman gardens.

NOTES

1. EARLY YEARS

1. "House & Garden's Own Hall of Fame," *House & Garden*, June 1933, 50; "Mrs. Ellen Shipman, Landscape Designer," obituary, *New York Times*, 29 March 1950. The term "good taste" has a variety of sources, including Mariana van Rensselaer's *Art Out-of-Doors, Hints on Good Taste in Gardening* (1893) and Elsie de Wolfe's *The House in Good Taste* (1913).

2. Working steadily for thirty-five years (1912–47) at the average rate of fifteen to twenty projects per year, Shipman would have completed approximately six hundred.

3. Shipman quoted in Anne Petersen, "Women Take the Lead in Landscape Art," *New York Times*, 13 March 1938.

4. Preface, Garden Note Book, 1 (partial contents in box 10, folder 15, Cornell; hereafter, GNB).

5. Shipman quoted in Peterson, "Women Take the Lead."

6. Foreword, GNB, 3.

7. The date of Shipman's birth is cited in a letter of 27 June 1944 from her to her executors (Streeter collection). The location of her birth is based on information from Streeter and other sources.

8. Ellen McGowan Biddle, *Reminiscences of a Soldier's Wife* (Philadelphia: J. B. Lippincott, 1907), 154.

9. Foreword, GNB, 2.

10. Biddle, *Reminiscences*, 136.

11. Ibid., 188–89.

12. Ellen McGowan Biddle, *Recollections* (Boston: Small, Maynard, 1920), 3; foreword, GNB, 11–12.

13. Foreword, GNB, 3.

14. Biddle, *Reminiscences*, 220.

15. Deborah E. Van Buren, "Landscape Architecture and Gardens in the Cornish Colony: The Careers of Rose Nichols, Ellen Shipman, and Frances Duncan," *Women's Studies* 14 (September 1988): 367–88; Frances McCormic, letter to Van Buren, 13 August 1985, author's collection.

16. The Harvard Annex, located on Appian Way, Cambridge, was established in 1879 "to

provide women with access to a Harvard education." During Shipman's term the school was the Society for the Collegiate Instruction of Women.

17. Nicholas B. Angell, interview by the author, 19 January 1994; Angell, interview by Deborah E. Van Buren, August 1985, in "Women and Landscape Architecture: Rose Nichols and Ellen Shipman in the Cornish Colony," paper presented at the annual meeting of the American Studies Association, San Diego, 1985, n. 48.

18. Mary Lucy Wilkins Rogers, undated typescript (Annie Ware Winsor Allen Papers, Radcliffe College Archives, Schlesinger Library, Radcliffe College, Cambridge, Mass.).

19. *National Cyclopaedia of American Biography* (New York: James T. White, 1962), 45:396–97.

20. Harvard University Directory (1910) lists Louis Shipman as c. 1892–93, but the trail ends in *Special Students* (1894–95) grade reports, which note his withdrawal on 12 April 1893, two months after his roommate Herbert Croly temporarily withdrew from classes.

21. The Biddles, it seems, may not have approved of the match. Angell-author interview; also Angell–Van Buren interview, n. 17.

2. LIFE IN THE CORNISH COLONY

1. The date of this trip is uncertain; an early draft of the Garden Note Book, written fifty years after the event, states that Shipman's first visit was August 1894, but subsequent versions state 1895.

2. For more on the Cornish Colony, see Deborah Kay Meador, "The Making of a Landscape Architect: Ellen Biddle Shipman and Her Years at the Cornish Art Colony" (M.L.A. thesis, Cornell University, 1989), 40–46, and Alma M. Gilbert and Judith B. Tankard, *A Place of Beauty: The Artists and Gardens of the Cornish Colony* (Berkeley: Ten Speed Press, 2000).

3. Foreword, GNB, 1.

4. The script was written by Louis Shipman and Percy MacKaye, with music by the composer Arthur Whiting performed by the Boston Symphony Orchestra. John H. Dryfhout et al., *A Circle of Friends: Art Colonies of Cornish and Dublin* (Durham, N.H.: University Art Galleries, 1985), 52, 110.

5. Frances Grimes, "Reminiscences," undated typescript (Dartmouth College Library, Hanover, N.H.), 1; *New York Daily Tribune,* 11 August 1907, quoted in Dryfhout et al., *Circle of Friends,* 40.

6. Virginia Colby, private collection, Cornish, N.H. See "Ellen Biddle Shipman—Landscape Architect: 1869–1950," *Windsor (Vt.) Chronicle,* 23 January 1987. In a letter she wrote to Lawrence W. Rittenoure, 15 June 1944 (Cornell), Shipman states that Poins House was theirs for ten years; they leased it using the money from Louis's story "The Curious Courtship of Kate Poins." However, the Shipmans' ten-year lease of the house began in 1895, six years before the publication of Louis's story.

7. Grimes, "Reminiscences," 1.

8. One of the only published views of this garden is in Frances Duncan, "The Gardens of Cornish," *Century Magazine,* May 1906, 8.

9. Mary Caroline Crawford, "Homes and Gardens of Cornish," *House Beautiful,* April 1906, 12–14.

10. Foreword, GNB, 2; design chapter, GNB, 35–36.

11. Rose Standish Nichols, "A Hilltop Garden in New Hampshire," *House Beautiful,* March 1924, 237; Duncan, "Gardens of Cornish," 18. For further information on Duncan, who was a summer resident of Cornish and a prolific writer, see Virginia Lopez Begg, "Frances Duncan: The 'New Woman' in the Garden," *Journal of the New England Garden History Society* 2 (1992): 29–35.

12. Foreword, GNB, 2.

13. Alan Crawford, "New Life for an Artists' Village," *Country Life*, 24 January 1980, 252–54.

14. See Judith B. Tankard, "William Robinson and the Art of the Book," *Hortus* 27 (Autumn 1993): 21–30, and Tankard, *Gardens of the Arts and Crafts Movement* (New York: Harry N. Abrams, 2004).

15. Helena Rutherfurd Ely, *A Woman's Hardy Garden* (New York: Macmillan, 1903), and Alice Morse Earle, *Old Time Gardens* (New York: Macmillan, 1902). See Beverly Seaton, "Gardening Books for the Commuter's Wife, 1900–1937," *Landscape* 28 (1985): 41–47. See also Virginia Tuttle Clayton, "Reminiscence and Revival: The Old-Fashioned Garden, 1890–1910," *Magazine Antiques,* April 1990, 892–905; May Brawley Hill, "Grandmother's Garden," *Magazine Antiques,* November 1992, 726–35.

16. David W. Levy, *Herbert Croly of "The New Republic"* (Princeton, N.J.: Princeton University Press, 1985), 77–79. The Crolys are buried next to Shipman in Gilkey Cemetery, adjacent to Brook Place, in Plainfield, N.H.

17. See John H. Dryfhout, "The Gardens of Augustus Saint-Gaudens," *House & Garden,* December 1985, 144–48, 199; Marion Pressley and Cynthia Zaitzevsky, *Cultural Landscape Report for Saint-Gaudens National Historic Site* (Boston: National Park Service, 1993).

18. Mary Wilkinson Mount, "The Gardens of Cornish," *Suburban Life,* March 1914, 133. For further information on Parrish's garden diaries and an excellent study of the making of the garden at Northcote, see William Noble, "Northcote: An Artist's New Hampshire Garden," *Journal of the New England Garden History Society* 2 (1992): 1–9.

19. Dryfhout et al., *Circle of Friends,* 50; Grimes, "Reminiscences," 1; Meador, "Making of a Landscape Architect," 45.

20. Louis wrote for several publications, including *Leslie's Weekly* during 1895–96, and occasionally collaborated with fellow Cornishites, including Churchill and Remington, rewriting their works for the stage. His first published book, *Urban Dialogues* (1896), is a witty spoof on urban life, but his romantic comedy *D'Arcy of the Guards* gave his reputation a needed boost; it was dedicated to Shipman's brother Nicholas Biddle.

21. Margaret Homer Nichols Shurcliff, *Lively Days* (Taipei: Literature House, 1965), 35, as quoted in Virginia Colby, "Plainfield and the Cornish Colony through Biographies," in *Choice White Pines and Good Land: A History of Plainfield and Meriden, New Hampshire,* ed. Nancy Norwalk and Harold Zea (Portsmouth, N.H.: Peter E. Randall, 1991), 366; Harry B. Fuller, letter to Shipman, 29 August 1906 (Dartmouth).

22. Foreword, GNB, 3.

23. Property agreement (box 8, folder 12, Cornell) refers to John Gilkey's deeds to Ellen Shipman dated 18 April 1903 (Sullivan County Record of Deeds, vol. 156, 309) and 16 October 1906 (vol. 166, 196). Plainfield tax records indicate that the Shipmans were first taxed for 182 acres on the Gilkey farm in 1904 (Plainfield Historical Society). They probably moved to Brook Place in 1906 after their ten-year lease on Poins House was up. Hugh Mason Wade, in *A Brief History of Cornish, 1763–1974* (Hanover, N.H.: University Press of New England, 1976), states that the Shipmans acquired the farm in 1902 (69–70); John H. Dryfhout (letter to Catherine Zusy, 24 September 1984) maintains that the Shipmans lived at Poins House from 1897 until 1907, rather than from 1895 to 1905; foreword, GNB, 4.

24. The addition is dated 1911 (William Macdonald, McLaughry Associates, Realtors, West Lebanon, N.H.). Platt's biographer Keith N. Morgan doubts that Platt had anything to do with its design (telephone interview by the author, 7 July 1994).

25. Design chapter, GNB, 1.

26. G. H. Edgell, *The American Architecture of To-Day* (New York: Charles Scribner's Sons, 1928), 125.

27. Hewitt's photographs were published in "A New Hampshire House and Garden," *House & Garden,* March 1924, 75–77.

28. Foreword, GNB, 4.

29. These articles include Herbert C. Wise, "A Day at Northcote, A House and Garden in New Hampshire," *House & Garden,* June 1902, 244, 249; Crawford, "Homes and Gardens of Cornish"; Duncan, "Gardens of Cornish"; Duncan, "An Artist's New Hampshire Garden," *Country Life in America,* March 1907, 516–20, 554–58; "A Cornish House and Garden," *Architectural Record,* October 1907, 288–98; Duncan, "A Cornish Garden," *Country Life in America,* March 1908, 507–8; Mount, "Gardens of Cornish," 133–36, 184; Rose Standish Nichols, "A Hilltop Garden in New Hampshire," *House Beautiful,* March 1924, 237–39, 290. Quotation from Crawford, "Homes and Gardens," 12–14.

30. Frederick Law Olmsted to William Platt, 1 February 1892, quoted from Laura Wood Roper, *FLO: A Biography of Frederick Law Olmsted* (Baltimore: Johns Hopkins University Press, 1973), 433.

31. Nichols, "Hilltop Garden," 237. Platt's *Italian Gardens* was published in a new edition, with additional plates and an overview by Keith N. Morgan, by Sagapress/Timber Press (Portland, OR) in 1993.

32. Royal Cortissoz, introduction to *Monograph of the Work of Charles A. Platt* (New York: Architectural Book Publishing, 1913), v–vi.

33. Lazarus sold High Court in 1900 to Norman Hapgood, editor of *Collier's Weekly* (a magazine to which Louis Shipman contributed), who in turn sold it to A. Conger Goodyear and his wife in 1912. Shipman designed a planting plan, dated September 1914, for Mrs. Goodyear. James Farley, letter to Deborah Van Buren, 20 August 1985.

34. Wilhelm Miller, "An 'Italian Garden' That Is Full of Flowers," *Country Life in America,* March 1905, 485.

35. Richard G. Kenworthy, "Bringing the World to Brookline: The Gardens of Larz and Isabel Anderson," *Journal of Garden History* 11 (1991): 228; E.T., "The Garden of 'Weld,'" *House & Garden,* March 1904, 106.

36. George Taloumis, "Rose Standish Nichols," *Boston Sunday Globe,* 16 September 1956. After taking design lessons from Platt around 1889, Nichols apprenticed with the New York architect Thomas Hastings and then studied at the École de Beaux-Arts in Paris and with H. Inigo Triggs, author of *Formal Gardens in England and Scotland* (1902). For more information on Nichols, see Judith B. Tankard, introduction to Rose Standish Nichols, *English Pleasure Gardens* (Boston: David R. Godine, 2003).

37. "Going to School," in Norwalk and Zea, *Choice White Pines,* 289; Shipman, "How I Teach My Own Children," *Ladies' Home Journal,* September 1911, 60.

38. Candace Wheeler, "Home Weaving in Country Homes," *Country Life in America,* July 1903, 198–200; see also Beatrice Clark, "Mothers' and Daughters' Club and Mothers' and Daughters' Rug Industry, "in Norwalk and Zea, *Choice White Pines,* 201–9.

39. The absence of her personal papers has obscured many details of her emotional life.

40. Shipman, letter to Gertrude Eisendrath Kuh, c. 1942, quoted in Mary Elizabeth Fitzsimons, "Outdoor Architecture for the Midwest: The Modern Residential Landscapes of Gertrude Eisendrath Kuh, 1935–1977" (M.L.A. thesis, University of Minnesota, January 1994), 18.

41. Nancy Streeter, interview by the author, 2 September 1994. Amy Cogswell, who became director of the Lowthorpe School in Groton, Mass., in 1916, may have worked briefly as a tutor and nanny for the Shipman children during a summer break while she was a student at Lowthorpe. Frances McCormic, interview by Deborah E. Van Buren, 2 August 1985, transcript, author's collection.

3. COLLABORATION WITH CHARLES PLATT

1. Foreword, GNB, 4.

2. Shipman's correspondence with the Moravian Pottery and Tile Works regarding her work

at Fynmere, generally regarded as her earliest work, dates between 17 March and 22 July 1913. See Catherine Zusy, "A Unity of Design in the American Spirit: James Fenimore Cooper II's 'Fynmere,'" paper written for Cooperstown History Museum Studies Program, 1984.

3. Shipman, letter to Mrs. Roy Chapin, Detroit, Mich., 25 May 1946 (box 9, folder 5, Cornell).

4. Gertrude Jekyll, *Colour in the Flower Garden* (London: Country Life, 1908), vi. See also Judith B. Tankard, "The Influence of British Garden Literature on American Garden Design during the Country Place Era," in *Proceedings, Masters of American Garden Design III*, ed. Robin Karson (New York: Garden Conservancy, 1995).

5. Keith N. Morgan, *Charles A. Platt: The Artist as Architect* (New York: Architectural History Foundation; Cambridge, Mass.: MIT Press, 1985), 251. Two articles confirm Shipman's role as the garden designer. There are five letters about the job; all are on Shipman's Cornish letterhead.

6. Shipman, "Design and Construction," transcript of lecture given for the St. Paul (Minn.) Garden Club, 5 February 1935, 27, 30 (Streeter collection).

7. Henry S. F. Cooper, letter to Keith Morgan, 6 January 1977.

8. Shipman was not identified by name in "Looking over the Garden Wall," *Country Life in America*, March 1917, 68–69, but was in *House & Garden's Book of Gardens* (New York: Condé Nast, 1921), 81.

9. Plans date from May 1914 to 1919. Six photographs of the project were shown in the Architectural League of New York annual exhibition in 1924.

10. Shipman did not return to Gwinn until the early 1930s, when she consulted with Mather's wife, Elizabeth Ring Mather. See Robin Karson, *The Muses of Gwinn: Art and Nature in a Garden Designed by Warren H. Manning, Charles A. Platt, and Ellen Biddle Shipman* (Sagaponack, N.Y.: Sagapress/Abrams in association with Library of American Landscape History, 1995), 135–37; Karson, "Gwinn: A Collaborative Design by Charles A. Platt and Warren H. Manning," *Journal of the New England Garden History Society* 3 (1993): 29.

11. Morgan, *Charles A. Platt*, 248. See illustrations of Platt's garden in *Monograph on the Work of Charles A. Platt* (1913) and additional illustrations in "Four Views of the Garden at the Estate of William Fahnestock, Esq., Katonah, New York," *Journal of the International Garden Club* 2 (September 1918): 360–64.

12. In 1929, Shipman handed over responsibility for the garden to the new Oregon firm of Elizabeth Lord and Edith Schryver; Schryver had been her employee in New York.

13. Design chapter, GNB, 18.

14. Robin Karson, "A Woman's Place: Ellen Shipman's Gardens Frame a Divided World," *Garden Design,* February–March 1997, 46–48; Judith B. Tankard, "Defining Their Turf: Pioneer Women Landscape Designers," *Studies in the Decorative Arts* 8 (2000–2001): 31.

15. Samuel Howe, *American Country Houses of To-Day* (New York: Architectural Book Publishing, 1915), 6.

16. After Marion Alger gave the property to the Detroit Institute of Arts, Shipman redesigned one of the areas as a knot garden in 1936.

17. Design chapter, GNB, 38.

18. In his project list for Platt, Morgan cites jobs for the following clients as showing evidence of Shipman's involvement: Russell Alger, James F. Cooper, William Fahnestock, James Parmelee, A. J. Drexel Paul, the Misses Pruyn, William Speed, Isaac Starr, Henry Stephens, and Clark Williams (*Charles A. Platt,* 239–62).

19. Shipman, letter to Ernest Kanzler, Detroit, Mich., 3 June 1946 (box 9, folder 9, Cornell); Edith Stern, interview by Pamela Bardo, 3 July 1997, typescript, 1–2 (Longue Vue). Shipman later claimed that she never designed plantings unless she did the entire design. Letter to Mrs. Roy D. Chapin, Detroit, Mich., 25 May 1946 (box 9, folder 5, Cornell).

4. A STYLE OF HER OWN

1. Design chapter, GNB, 1; "Mrs. Ellen Shipman, Famous Landscape Architect, Thrills Hearers," *Winston-Salem Journal,* 8 October 1932.
2. Design chapter, GNB, 6.
3. Shipman, letter to Mrs. Roy Chapin, Detroit, Mich., 17 June 1946 (box 9, folder 5, Cornell); Shipman, letter to Mrs. Willis G. Wilmot, Hermitage, Tenn., 28 June 1945 (box 8, folder 35, Cornell).
4. Robin Karson, *The Muses of Gwinn: Art and Nature in a Garden Designed by Warren H. Manning, Charles A. Platt, and Ellen Biddle Shipman* (Sagaponack, N.Y.: Sagapress/ Abrams in association with Library of American Landscape History, 1995), 81, 83.
5. Shipman quoted in Helen Grant Wilson, "Good Counsel for Gardeners: Hosta or Funkia Stages Comeback in Gardens," *Cleveland Plain Dealer,* 7 May 1942.
6. Preface no. 1, GNB, 2.
7. Design chapter, GNB, 2, 7.
8. Shipman's notation appears on the reverse of the plan: "The first plan I ever made for a garden—Dora Murdocks, Baltimore" (Streeter collection).
9. Other Lindeberg clients for whom Shipman is known to have done garden plans are Eugene du Pont, Greenville, Del., 1917; Mrs. Frederick G. Achelis, Greenwich, Conn., 1919; and R. T. Vanderbilt, Greens Farms, Conn., 1939. She may also have carried out commissions for Laurance Armour, Lake Forest, Ill., and William L. Hanley Jr., Greenwich, Conn.
10. Elizabeth Leonard Strang, a 1910 graduate of Cornell College of Agriculture, remained with Shipman for only about a year before she moved to Leominster, Mass., when she began teaching at the Lowthorpe School (where Shipman would also maintain close professional ties). Strang's formal training would eventually far exceed Shipman's—she later apprenticed with three influential practitioners: Ferruccio Vitale, Carl Pilat, and John Nolen. See Daniel W. Krall, "Ellen Biddle Shipman: Dean of Women Landscape Architects," undated manuscript, 113, and "Elizabeth Leonard Strang: Teacher and Advocate for Landscape Architecture," undated manuscript (both, Department of Landscape Architecture, Cornell University).
11. Lucinda Brockway, interview by the author, 24 August 1994.
12. Two articles that chronicle the inclusion of the garden in the 1923 Architectural League of New York annual exhibition give varying credit: the caption to an illustration that appears in both credits Shipman in one (*Garden Magazine,* June 1924, 279) and Greenleaf in the other (*House & Garden,* June 1924, 54).
13. Design chapter, GNB, 38.
14. Shipman quoted in Lamar Sparks, "A Landscape Architect Discusses Gardens," *Better Homes & Gardens,* November 1930, 20.
15. "A House in New Canaan, Connecticut," *House Beautiful,* January 1924, 41; on the Gossler garden, see also *Garden Magazine and Home Builder,* October 1924, 91.
16. No plan for the garden has been found, but drawings for the pergola and other ornamental details survive. Shipman's pencil sketch of the fountain terrace is dated March 1916.
17. Jekyll's book was first published in 1908 as *Colour in the Flower Garden* (London: Country Life). Shipman owned the third edition, published in 1914.
18. Fletcher Steele, ed., *House Beautiful Gardening Manual* (Boston: Atlantic Monthly, 1926), 10.

5. THE NEW YORK OFFICE

1. Mary Shipman briefly attended Ethel Walker's School but harbored more interest in horses and riding than books. Evan, Ellen's son, had left the Groton School in 1917 at age thirteen after a poor academic performance and entered the Salisbury School in July 1919,

which he left without explanation in 1922. Hoping that Evan would attend Harvard, the Shipmans sent him to Europe for tutoring, but he soon drifted into the Paris-based "lost generation." Mary and Evan's older sister, Ellen, who attended St. Timothy's in Maryland, was married in 1918. Nancy Streeter, interview by the author, 21 June 1994; Herbert Channick, memoir on Evan Shipman, privately published on the occasion of the fiftieth reunion of Evan's class at Groton School.

2. Shipman, letter to John N. Wheeler, New York City, 15 June 1945 (box 8, folder 38, Cornell); Robert A. M. Stern, Gregory Gilmartin, and Thomas Mellins, *New York 1930: Architecture and Urbanism between Two World Wars* (New York: Rizzoli, 1987), 433 n. 324. In 2013, 21 Beekman Place sold for $35 million (it was offered at $48.5 million). See Christopher Gray, "Streetscapes: 19–21 Beekman Place," *New York Times,* 30 August 2009, for the history of the property.

3. "A House on Beekman Place, New York," *House Beautiful,* November 1927, 513–16, 568–69.

4. Among women who had landscape businesses in New York City in the early 1920s were Nellie B. Allen; Ruth Bramley Dean; Agnes Selkirk Clark, who briefly worked for Shipman before opening her own office in 1922; Marian Cruger Coffin, who worked in the city from 1910 until 1927; Beatrix Farrand, who came in 1900; Annette Hoyt Flanders, who worked there sporadically from 1914 to 1942; Martha Brookes Hutcheson; Mary Deputy Lamson; Louise Payson; and Isabella Pendleton.

5. Shipman quoted in "Professional Opinions," *Lowthorpe School Catalogue,* 1926–27, Groton, Mass. Curiously, one source lists Shipman's name among the alumnae. See Richard A. Schneider, "Lowthorpe" (thesis, Rhode Island School of Design, 1988), 86.

6. Shipman quoted in *Lowthorpe School Catalogue,* 1925, 4.

7. Frances McCormic, telephone interview by Daniel Krall, 10 January 1990.

8. Schryver was an excellent draftsman and worked on many important jobs in both the Cornish and the New York office until 1929, when she opened her own practice in partnership with Elizabeth Lord in Salem, Oregon. Their office was the first on the West Coast to be run entirely by women. Among their archives at the University of Oregon are documents from two dozen projects that Schryver worked on while in Shipman's office. Kenneth I. Helphand, "Lord and Schryver," in *Pioneers of American Landscape Design*, ed. Charles A. Birnbaum and Robin Karson (New York: McGraw-Hill, 2000), 227–30. The Lord & Schryver Conservancy maintains Gaiety Hollow, the former home and garden of Lord and Schryver, in Salem, Ore.

   Agnes Selkirk Clark's husband, Cameron Clark, was associated with the architectural firm of Clark & Arms, which worked with Shipman on several commissions, including the Philip Gossler residence in New Canaan, Conn., in 1919.

   Louise Payson and Eleanor Christie roomed together while working in the Cornish office during their summer breaks from Lowthorpe. Upon graduation, Christie returned to Ohio and opened her own office in Cincinnati in 1928.

   Less well known employees were Louise Jocelyn, Carol Farley, Irmgard Berger Graham, Virginia Prince, Eleanor Roche, Mary Louise Speed, and Florence Stroh. Draftsmen were Louanne Eggleston, Shirley Harris, Helen Kippax, Louise Leland, Katherine Rogers, and Doris Turnball. These names have been culled from Shipman's office correspondence, notations in her notebooks, news articles, and references by Knight, Krall, Meador, McCormic, and Van Buren.

9. McCormic-Krall interview; Frances McCormic attended Oberlin College and, subsequently, the University of Wisconsin, where she heard about the Lowthorpe School. Frances McCormic, interview by Deborah E. Van Buren, 2 August 1985.

10. Shipman, letter to Mrs. Willis G. Wilmot, Hermitage, Tenn., 28 June 1945 (box 8, folder 35, Cornell).

11. McCormic, memo to Daniel Krall, August 1989 (Streeter collection); Eleanor Christie, interview by Noel Dorsey Vernon, 29 July 1985, transcript, 2.

12. Shipman, invoice to Mrs. Douglas Conoley, Cumberstone, Md., 15 May 1946 (box 9, folder 5, Cornell).

13. Irene Seiberling Harrison, interview by Robin Karson, Stan Hywet Hall, Akron, Ohio, 18 February 1991.

14. Nancy Streeter, interview by the author, 21 June 1994.

15. Anne Bruce Haldeman, introduction, GNB.

16. Shipman, letter to Mrs. Carll Tucker, Mt. Kisco, N.Y., 14 June 1946 (box 9, folder 1, Cornell).

17. Shipman, letter to Mr. and Mrs. William G. Mather, Cleveland, Ohio, 15 November 1945 (box 8, folder 54, Cornell).

18. Viscountess Wolseley, *In a College Garden* (London: John Murray, 1916), 104.

19. Shipman will, 9 November 1948, Probate Records, Newport, N.H. According to the terms, Meyette was to receive a sum of $1,500 plus $3,800 for 38 years of service, a substantial remembrance.

20. Streeter-author interview, 21 June 1994.

21. Clark, "Mothers' and Daughters' Club," 208 and ill. 333. The Plainfield Historical Society has a collection of hand-colored glass slides of these gardens.

22. Matthew Josephson, "Evan Shipman: Poet and Horse-Player," *Southern Review* 9 (October 1973): 828–56.

23. "To Remind You of July," *House & Garden*, December 1923, 51; "A New Hampshire House and Garden," *House & Garden*, March 1924, 75–77.

24. Shipman, "List of Annual Seeds for Autumn Planting for Brook Place," in Blue Book, summer 1930 (Streeter collection).

6. ARTISTIC MATURITY

1. *Garden Magazine*, July 1923, 319, and June 1924, 268; *House & Garden*, October 1923, 65; *House Beautiful*, March 1924, 256.

2. About one hundred titles from Shipman's library were donated in 1974 to the Avery Architectural Library, Columbia University, New York.

3. According to Dan Kiley, who worked for Warren Manning from 1932 to 1938, Shipman and Manning were friends. He remembered seeing her in Manning's office more than once. Dan Kiley, telephone interview by Robin Karson, 15 June 1995.

4. Shipman, letter to Mrs. Windsor T. White, 11 February 1942 (box 8, folder 35, Cornell); Marie Daerr, "Arts and Flowers," *Cleveland Press*, 18 April 1941; "Ellen Shipman Coming to Discuss Group of Different Gardens," *Your Garden and Home* (Cleveland), March 1941, 11, 20–21; Mac Griswold and Eleanor Weller, *The Golden Age of American Gardens* (New York: Harry N. Abrams / Garden Club of America, 1991), 283.

5. Griswold and Weller, *Golden Age*, 78.

6. Sparks, "Landscape Architect Discusses Gardens," 20, 70–71.

7. Another sister, Mrs. Henry Greenough, was also a Shipman client.

8. Ethel B. Power, "A Blue-Ribbon Garden: The Garden of Mrs. Holden McGinley," *House Beautiful*, March 1933, 88.

9. The same fountain was also used in the Eugene du Pont garden in Wilmington, Del.; its price was $1,500.

10. Many of the features of the garden, such as the pool, walls, and terraces, still exist. The essential views to the middle and far distance, however, are now occluded by trees and other vegetation. The recent replanting gives a nod to Shipman's expertise.

11. There is another example of the lotus fountain at nearby Longwood Gardens. The foun-

tain was manufactured by Kim Manufacturing Company, a West Coast firm specializing in Japanese-related decorations. Sam Watters, correspondence with author, 16 November 2013.

12. In 1961, the property was sold to the Greenville Country Club, a private organization which has preserved key aspects of the grounds, including the boxwood garden. The site is now listed on the National Register of Historic Places.

13. Shipman's work in Kentucky included Dixiana Farm in Lexington for her New Jersey client James Cox Brady; Louis Haggin in Versailles; and Kanawha, in Louisville, in collaboration with Charles Platt. Her colleague Marian Coffin had designed a large plantation garden in Louisville for the Bullitt family, and in 1911, Jens Jensen began an extensive Prairie-style landscape at Airdrie in Lexington for W. E. Simms. See Griswold and Weller, *Golden Age,* 195–200.

14. See Elizabeth Murphey Simpson, *Bluegrass Houses and Their Traditions* (Lexington, Ky.: Transylvania Press, 1932), 71–81.

15. Since the 1930s, there have been several subsequent owners of Cave Hill, including most famously Governor John Y. Brown, who prepared a National Register of Historic Places application in 1980 based in part on the historic slave quarters as well as the house and grounds. The present owners are restoring the gardens, which include the original teahouse and other features.

16. Mrs. Francis King, *From a New Garden* (New York: Alfred A. Knopf, 1928), 12–13. I am indebted to Virginia Lopez Begg for this reference.

17. Mrs. Francis King, "An English Country Place in Michigan," *Country Life in America,* April 1928, 59.

18. Holmdene, the former Edward Lowe estate, is now Aquinas College, where features, such as the pool, still exist.

7. THE BORDER

1. Shipman, letter to Major General William D. Conner, 12 June 1936 (U.S. Military Academy, West Point, archives).

2. See Judith B. Tankard and Martin Wood, *Gertrude Jekyll at Munstead Wood* (London: Pimpernel Press, 2015), 30–32, for detailed discussion of Jekyll's spring garden borders.

3. Shipman, letter to Clara Ford, Dearborn, Mich., 3 June 1930 (box 37, Fair Lane Papers). The Fords may have recommended Shipman to Thomas A. Edison, in Lewellyn Park, N.J., for whom she also did a garden, but the design and dates of her work there escaped documentation. Fair Lane, the Henry Ford Estate, is a National Historic Landmark and the grounds are currently undergoing restoration.

4. Robin Karson, *A Genius for Place: American Landscapes of the Country Place Era* (Amherst: University of Massachusetts Press/Library of American Landscape History, 2013), 113–14.

5. Manning, letter to Gertrude Seiberling, Akron, Ohio, 19 January 1916; Manning, letter to Frank Seiberling, Akron, Ohio, 7 March 1916 (Stan Hywet).

6. Manning, letter to Frank Seiberling, Akron, Ohio, 20 July 1917; Manning report, 20 April 1928; Manning, "Report on the Estate of Mr. Frank A. Seiberling, Akron, Ohio," typescript, 7 November 1928 (Stan Hywet).

7. Irene Seiberling Harrison, interview by Robin Karson, Stan Hywet Hall, Akron, Ohio, 18 February 1991.

8. M. Christine Doell and Gerald Doell, "Restoration of the English Garden Plantings at Stan Hywet Hall," report, January 1991, 9 (Stan Hywet); Shipman, letter to Clara Ford, Dearborn, Mich., 3 June 1930 (box 37, Fair Lane).

9. Charles Eliot and later John Charles Olmsted provided the original layout for the land-

scape, but by 1896, Warren Manning, who had worked for Olmsted, Olmsted & Eliot and had recently opened his own office, was solely in charge of the project.

10. The original mansion, designed by McKim, Mead & White in 1893, is no longer on the site, but Manning's landscape and Shipman's gardens have been partially restored by the present owners.

8. A GRANDER SCOPE

1. Eleanor Christie, interview by Noel Dorsey Vernon, 29 July 1985, transcript, 2.
2. "The Garden in Good Taste: The Garden of Carll Tucker, Esq.," *House Beautiful*, October 1928, 388–91.
3. "To Link the Lawns and Garden," *House & Garden*, August 1930, 49, 55–57.
4. The Alhambra-inspired gardens at the former Schley estate (now known as Froh Heim) were restored and replanted for New Jersey's annual Mansion in May fundraiser in 2008.
5. Shipman, letter to Mrs. R. F. Willingham, Atlanta, Ga., 23 April 1945 (box 8, folder 27, Cornell).
6. Adaline D. Piper, "The Charm of Chatham," *House Beautiful,* April 1926, 437–38.
7. Now part of the Fredericksburg and Spotsylvania National Military Park, the garden at Chatham Manor underwent preservation treatment by the National Park Service in the 1980s which focused on stabilizing Shipman's garden walls and structures and restoring the parterre. In 2016, the National Park Service commissioned a Cultural Landscape Report to explore possibilities of bringing back Shipman's famous borders.
8. In a rare bit of British publicity, Shipman was hailed by London *Garden Design* as "one of the best known landscape architects in the United States, . . . noted for her use of the formal garden, when closely related to the house, as well as her naturalistic development of the whole place." Alice Bourquin and Jessie Bourquin, "The Formal in American Gardens," *Garden Design* (London) 17 (1934): 104. For more information on the Arts and Crafts movement, see Judith B. Tankard, *Gardens of the Arts and Crafts Movement* (New York: Harry N. Abrams, 2004).
9. For more on the topic, see Harold Donaldson Eberlein, "The Cotswold Influence in America," *Country Life in America*, June 1921, 58–60.
10. Notation on reverse of small snapshot of Snowshill included in Salvage file (box 5, envelope 32, Cornell).
11. The dovecote, teahouse, and other built structures (but not the plantings) are still intact. The property is the American headquarters of Villa Banfi.
12. Giles Edgerton, "Cotswold Again Influences American Architecture," *Arts and Decoration,* June 1937, 20.

9. WILD GARDENS

1. "Variety of Form and Abundance of Bloom within a Small Area: The Garden of Mrs. Henry V. Greenough, Brookline, Massachusetts," *House Beautiful*, March 1931, 62.
2. Design chapter, GNB, 50.
3. Shipman's notation on the reverse of a snapshot taken at the Clapp project—"brook from which we got the stone"—offers proof of her willingness to "reinvent" nature (box 1, envelope 40, Cornell).
4. A 26 June 1955 article in the *Washington Post* cited an invoice for $25,000 for the "florist architect" that had been recently discovered (Kirstina Larson, *Tregaron: A Magical Place* [Signature Books, 2002], 20).
5. Robinson & Associates, *Tregaron: Landscape Documentation and Evaluation* (Washington, D.C.: Friends of Tregaron, 1999), 23.

6. Over the years, subsequent owners, including Marjorie Merriweather Post, made changes to the property, which is now divided into two segments. The woodland gardens at Tregaron, the only surviving example of a wild garden designed by Ellen Shipman, are currently being rehabilitated by the Tregaron Conservancy. Once completed, it will rival Beatrix Farrand's Dumbarton Oaks Park in nearby Georgetown, which is managed by the National Park Service in collaboration with the Dumbarton Oaks Park Conservancy. The Tregaron Conservancy, which was formed in 2006 after a years-long effort by a developer to build houses on the property, entails thirteen acres that are preserved in perpetuity. Tregaron is listed on the National Register of Historic Places.

7. Melanie Fleischmann, "Long Live Longue Vue," *House Beautiful,* July 1994, 34–38.

8. Design chapter, GNB, 50.

10. THE GREAT DEPRESSION AND THE LURE OF EUROPE

1. Louis E. Shipman obituary, *New York Times,* 3 August 1933.

2. At various points Shipman worked for the Gordon, James, P. Huber, Ralph, and Robert Haneses, as well as the Chatham and Knox families, who were related by marriage.

3. DeWitt Hanes quoted in Mac Griswold, "Carolina Grown," *House & Garden,* September 1988, 181.

4. The Ralph and DeWitt Hanes house and garden now serves as the president's house at Wake Forest University. The gardens and features, such as the dovecote and gates, have been restored.

5. *Winston-Salem Journal,* 8 October 1932; Griswold, "Carolina Grown."

6. Lois Byrd, "Landscaper, at 72, Takes a New Job," *Louisville (Ky.) Courier-Journal,* 5 November 1942.

7. *Boston Herald,* 27 October 1935 (Virginia Colby, private collection, Cornish, N.H.).

8. Harry G. Healy, letter to Shipman, 15 July 1935; Shipman, letter to Healy, 22 July 1935 (box 10, folder 7, Cornell).

9. Design chapter, GNB, 56.

10. The interior of the Michigan house featured one of the country's outstanding private collections of eighteenth-century art, assembled by Joseph Duveen. See Hawkins Ferry, "Mansions of Grosse Pointe: A Suburb in Good Taste," *Michigan Society of Architects Journal,* March 1956.

11. Shipman began working on plans for The Balcony, Aiken, S.C., in 1928; the Knox family lived here until the 1990s, and the property is now privately owned.

12. The main house had been built by Knox's other sister, Dorothy Knox Goodyear, in 1916, but she sold the estate to her brother in 1929. Ess Kay Farm is now Knox Farm State Park, East Aurora, N.Y. For a detailed family history, consult Gerald L. Halligan and Renee M. Oubre, *Knox Farm State Park* (Charleston, S.C.: Arcadia Publishing, 2013).

13. Ibid., 49.

14. By the early 1980s, the labor-intensive grounds had fallen into disrepair. A new owner rebuilt the entire infrastructure, including walkways, balustrades, walls, and gates, keeping in mind the original integrity and footprint. James Prise, correspondence with author, 18 November 2016.

15. It is unclear why Ninah selected Shipman rather than a local firm, but it is possible she was recommended by Ninah's friend Mina Edison, for whom Shipman had recently completed a garden in Fort Myers. There may have been some family rivalry also, since Ninah's sister-in-law simultaneously hired William Lyman Phillips to design her garden next door.

16. Judith B Tankard, *A Legacy in Bloom: Celebrating a Century of Gardens at The Cummer* (Jacksonville: Cummer Museum, 2008).

17. Notation on reverse of photograph (box 6, envelope 11, Cornell).
18. Edith Stern, interview by Pamela Bardo, 3 July 1977, typescript, 1–2 (Longue Vue).
19. Shipman, telegram to Mrs. Edgar Stern, 3 July 1946 (Longue Vue).
20. Stern-Bardo interview, 6.
21. Ibid., 3.
22. Edith Stern took the opportunity to transform the classical French vista into a Spanish court, having recently visited the Generalife garden of the Alhambra. William Platt assisted with the new design. In August 2005, Hurricane Katrina all but destroyed the grounds at Longue Vue, but reconstruction began almost immediately. See "Devastated Garden Treasures of New Orleans Get Helping Hands from the Garden Conservancy," *Newsletter of the Garden Conservancy,* Winter 2006, 1–3.
23. Edgar B. Stern, letter to Shipman, 27 February 1945 (box 8, folder 22, Cornell).

11. PUBLIC AND INSTITUTIONAL PROJECTS

1. Shipman, letter to Mrs. R. F. Willingham, 23 April 1945 (box 8, folder 9, Cornell).
2. The grounds were severely damaged by the hurricane of 1938; later additions to the building and the encroachment of I-84 reduced the acreage. The roof garden and pavilion, however, still exist today. For a description of the roof garden, see "Flowers Look Down on Tallest Trees from Aetna's Wonderland in the Air," *Hartford Courant,* 1 June 1952.
3. David G. Turner, "The Beginnings of the Fine Arts Center for Colorado Springs," *Modern Deco: An Architectural Guidebook for the Colorado Springs Fine Arts Center* (1996), 6.
4. William D. Connor, Major General, Superintendent, letter to Ellen Shipman, 11 May 1936, and Ellen Shipman, letter to Major General William D. Connor, 13 May 1936, courtesy Lt. Col. Rudy T. Veit, Director of Operations, Plans, and Security, United States Military Academy, West Point, N.Y. United States Military Academy Archives.
5. Ellen Shipman, letter to Major General William D. Connor, 12 June 1936. USMAA.
6. William D. Connor, memo for the quartermaster, 18 May 1936. USMAA.
7. Marcus Embry, "Watching the Gardens Grow: The Sarah P. Duke Gardens: A Botanical Birthday," *Duke Magazine,* July–August 1989, 8.
8. After the war, when the gardens needed rejuvenation, Shipman was asked to advise but noted that the new gardener was loath to follow her suggestions and complained, "It is like leaving a baby on a doorstep—I just can't let one of my gardens go without developing it as it should be." Shipman, letter to T. L. Perkins, New York City, 12 April 1946 (box 9, folder 11, Cornell).
9. Shipman, letter to Willingham.

12. LAST YEARS

1. Byrd, "Landscaper, at 72, Takes a New Job"; "Drive That Nail," *Laurel (Miss.) Leader-Call,* undated clipping (box 10, folder 7, Cornell).
2. Shipman, letter to Charles Meyette, Plainfield, N.H., 18 September 1945 (box 8, folder 12, Cornell).
3. Dona E. Caldwell, interview by the author, 6 September 1994; Shipman, correspondence with Charles Meyette and others, 1945–46 (box 8, folder 12, Cornell); Caldwell, letter to author, 29 December 1993.
4. Anne Bruce Haldeman, letter to John H. Dryfhout, 12 September 1984 (Saint-Gaudens National Historic Site Archives).
5. Haldeman worked on the book as late as 1958. Introductory pages from the manuscript resurfaced in 1984, when Catherine Zusy received the outline and prefaces from Haldeman and sent copies of this material to Saint-Gaudens National Historic Site, where they

can be examined today. The remainder of the manuscript and Shipman's working notes were located by the author in September 1994.

6. Preface no. 2, GNB, 1.
7. Shipman, letter to Aymar Embury II, New York City, 6 May 1946 (box 9, folder 7, Cornell).
8. Frances McCormic, interview by Deborah E. Van Buren, 2 August 1985, transcript, author's collection.
9. Nearly all of Shipman's female contemporaries, such as Beatrix Farrand, Marian Coffin, Martha Brookes Hutcheson, and Annette Hoyt Flanders, were active members of the ASLA, serving on committees and submitting examples of their work for the ASLA's annual yearbooks. Some of her office staff, notably Eleanor Roche, were also members.
10. Diana Kostial McGuire, letter to Robin Karson, Amherst, Mass., 18 November 1994.
11. Shipman, letter to Henry S. Walker, Evansville, Ind., 20 December 1946 (box 9, folder 14, Cornell); Shipman, letter to Edith Stern, 11 July 1947 (box 8, folder 58, Cornell).
12. Barbara Johnstone, letter to author, 5 November 1994.
13. Shipman, letter to Gertrude Kuh, 4 March 1946 (courtesy of Betsy Fitzsimmons).
14. Shipman, letter to Edith Stern, 26 February 1950 (box 8, folder 58, Cornell).

EPILOGUE
1. Will, 9 November 1948, Newport Probate Office, Newport, N.H.
2. Correspondence between Shipman's office and Hubert B. Owens, Head, Department of Landscape Architecture, University of Georgia, Athens, 22 April to 2 May 1946 (box 9, folder 11, Cornell).

BIBLIOGRAPHY

Following is a selection of references to Ellen Shipman's work as well as noteworthy general studies on the Country Place era. Known regional publications and newspaper references have been cited. Mattie Edwards Hewitt supplied photographs of architecture, gardens, and interiors to *McCalls, Town & Country, Vogue,* and other popular periodicals, which may provide additional sources of information. The name of the relevant client is given in brackets.

Adams, Denise Wiles. *Restoring American Gardens, 1640–1940.* Portland, Ore.: Timber Press, 2004.

Anner, Rosemarie T. "The Golden Age of Landscaping: Digging Up the Past." *Greenwich* 47 (May 1994): 56–76. [Croft, Mitchell]

Baker, John Cordes, ed. *American Country Houses and Their Gardens.* Philadelphia: John C. Winston/House & Garden, 1906.

Barensfeld, Wendy. "Colour and Compromise: Ellen Shipman's Design for the Gardens at Elm Cottage." *Studies in the History of Gardens and Designed Landscapes* 26 (October– December 2000): 309–27. [Curry]

Barnstone, Howard. *The Architecture of John F. Staub: Houston and the South.* Austin: University of Texas Press, 1979. [Farish, Hogg]

Beagan, Christopher, and Eliot Foulds. *Cultural Landscape Report for Chatham, Fredericksburg and Spotsylvania National Military Park.* Boston: National Park Service, Olmsted Center for Landscape Preservation, 2017. [Devore]

———, Margie Coffin Brown, Jan Haenraets. *Cultural Landscape Report for Saint-Gaudens National Historic Site. Vol. 3: Treatment and Record of Treatment.* Boston: National Park Service, Olmsted Center for Landscape Preservation, 2013.

Bedford, Stephen, and Richard Guy Wilson. *The Long Island Country House, 1870–1930.* Exh. cat. Southampton, N.Y.: Parrish Art Museum, 1988.

Berg, Shary Page. *Cultural Landscape Report for Longfellow National Historic Site. Vol. 2: Analysis of Significance and Integrity.* Boston: National Park Service, Olmsted Center for Landscape Preservation, 1999.

Biddle, Ellen McGowan. *Recollections.* Boston: Small, Maynard, 1920.

———. *Reminiscences of a Soldier's Wife.* Philadelphia: J. B. Lippincott, 1907.

Birnbaum, Charles A., and Stephanie S. Foell, eds. *Shaping the American Landscape*. Charlottesville: University of Virginia Press, 2009.

Birnbaum, Charles A., and Robin Karson, eds. *Pioneers of American Landscape Design*. New York: McGraw-Hill, 2000.

Bourquin, Alice, and Jessie Bourquin. "The Formal in American Gardens." *Garden Design* (London) 17 (1934): 104–6. [Newberry, Sales]

Briggs, Martha, et al. *Long Island Estate Gardens*. Exh. cat. Greenvale, N.Y.: Long Island University, 1985. [Kramer, Lord, Salvage]

Brower, Carol Ann. "Tregaron: Form and Transformation of an American Villa." M.L.A. thesis, Cornell University, 1986. [Parmelee]

Brown, Catherine R. "Women and the Land: A Biographical Survey of Women Who Have Contributed to the Development of Landscape Architecture in the United States." Morgan State University Built Environment Studies, Baltimore, 1979.

Bullard, Roger H. "A House Especially Designed for the Dunes of East Hampton." *Arts & Decoration*, October 1929, 68–69, 112, 170. [James]

Bush-Brown, Louise, and James Bush-Brown. "Laverock Hill: The Garden of Mr. and Mrs. Issac T. Starr at Chestnut Hill," in *Portraits of Philadelphia Gardens*. Philadelphia: Dorrance, 1929.

Byrd, Lois. "Landscaper, at 72, Takes a New Job." *Louisville (Ky.) Courier-Journal*, 5 November 1942.

Cane, Percy, ed. *Modern Gardens British and Foreign*. London: The Studio/Special Winter Number, 1926–27, 102. [Croft]

Caparn, Harold A. "Garden Paths and How to Make Them." *Arts & Decoration*, April 1937, 29. [Bulkley]

Carbonara, Mary Jane. "The Evolution of the Sarah P. Duke Gardens at Duke University: The Growth of an Aesthetic Institution." Paper submitted to Department of Landscape Architecture, Duke University, 1978.

Carley, Rachel. *Building Greenwich: Architecture and Design, 1640 to the Present*. Greenwich, Conn.: Historical Society of the Town of Greenwich, 2005.

Close, Leslie Rose. "Ellen Biddle Shipman." In *American Landscape Architecture: Designers and Places*. Edited by William Tishler. Washington, D.C.: Preservation Press, 1989.

———. *Portrait of an Era in Landscape Architecture: The Photographs of Mattie Edwards Hewitt*. Exh. cat. Bronx, N.Y.: Wave Hill, 1983.

"A Connecticut House with a Southern Accent." *House & Garden*, July 1949, 70–71.

Cortissoz, Royal. "Charles Adams Platt, 1861–1933, An Appreciation." *Architecture* 68 (November 1922): 271.

———. *Domestic Architecture of H. T. Lindeberg*. New York: William Helburn, 1940.

Crawford, Mary Caroline. "Homes and Gardens of Cornish." *House Beautiful*, April 1906, 12–14.

Croly, Herbert D. "The Architectural Work of Charles A. Platt." *Architectural Record* 15 (March 1904): 181–242.

———. "English Renaissance at Its Best. The House of James Parmelee at Washington, D.C., Charles A. Platt, Architect." *Architectural Record* 36 (August 1914): 81–97.

———. "A Waterfront Villa. The House of Russell A. Alger, Jr." *Architectural Record* 36 (December 1914): 481–86.

Cummin, Hazel E. "What Constitutes a Good Garden? The Garden of Mr. and Mrs. George Meade in Dayton, Ohio, Answers This Question." *House Beautiful*, March 1931, 241–45.

Cunningham, Mary P. "Design in Planting." *House Beautiful*, October 1924, 320, 323, 324. [Kramer]

———. "Notes from Some Virginia Gardens." *House Beautiful*, August 1930, 164, 179–80. [Devore]

Daerr, Marie. "Arts and Flowers." *Cleveland Press,* 18 April 1941, 29.

Davey, Charles, and Carol McMichael Reese. *Longue Vue House and Gardens.* New York: Rizzoli, 2015.

"Design in a Michigan Garden." *House & Garden,* September 1926, 108–9. [McGraw]

Dryfhout, John H. "The Gardens of Augustus Saint-Gaudens." *House & Garden,* December 1985, 144–48, 199.

———, et al. *A Circle of Friends: Art Colonies of Cornish and Dublin.* Exh. cat. Durham, N.H.: University Art Galleries, 1985.

Dubrow, Gail Lee, and Jennifer B. Goodman. *Restoring Women's History through Historic Preservation.* Baltimore: Johns Hopkins University Press, 2003.

Duncan, Frances. "The Gardens of Cornish." *Century Magazine,* May 1906, 3–19. [Poins House]

Eberlein, Harold Donaldson. "The Cotswold Influence in America." *Country Life in America,* June 1921, 58–60.

Edgell, G. H. *The American Architecture of To-Day.* New York: Charles Scribner's Sons, 1928. [Brook Place]

Edgerton, Giles. "Cotswold Again Influences American Architecture." *Arts & Decoration,* June 1937, 20–22. [Mitchell]

"The Edging Plant in Herbaceous Gardens." *House Beautiful,* July 1925, 34, 73. [Croft]

"Ellen Shipman Coming to Discuss Group of Different Gardens." *Your Garden and Home* (Cleveland), March 1941, 11, 20–21.

Elwood, P. H., Jr., ed. *American Landscape Architecture.* New York: Architectural Book Publishing, 1924. [Brewster, Croft, Parmelee, Smith]

Embry, Marcus. "Watching the Gardens Grow: The Sarah P. Duke Gardens: A Botanical Birthday." *Duke Magazine,* July–August 1989, 6–11.

Embury, Aymar, II. "Charles A. Platt—His Work." *Architecture* 26 (August 1912): 130–62.

Evans, Catherine. *Cultural Landscape Report for Longfellow National Historic Site. Vol. 1: Site History and Existing Conditions.* Boston: National Park Service, North Atlantic Region Cultural Landscape Program, 1993.

Famous Gardens Selected from Country Life. New York: Country Life / American Home Corporation, 1937. [Bacon, Salvage]

Fenelon, Eunice. "Open House in the Gardens of Greater Cleveland." *Your Garden and Home* (Cleveland), June 1934, 13, 20. [White]

Ferry, Hawkins. "Mansions of Grosse Pointe: A Suburb in Good Taste." *Michigan Society of Architects Journal,* March 1956.

Fitch, James M., and F. F. Rockwell. *Treasury of American Gardens.* New York: Harper and Brothers, 1956. [Kanzler, Mather]

Fleischmann, Melanie. "Long Live Longue Vue." *House Beautiful,* July 1994, 34–38. [Stern]

"Flower Time in Two Gardens at Grosse Pointe." *Garden & Home Builder,* April 1928, 165. [Brewster]

"A Focal Point for the Garden." *House & Garden,* January 1927, 69. [White]

"Four Views of the Garden at Estate of William Fahnestock, Esq., Katonah, New York." *Journal of the International Garden Club* 2 (September 1918): 361–64.

Frary, I. T. "Residence of Mr. and Mrs. Willard M. Clapp, Cleveland Heights, Ohio." *Architectural Record* 62 (October 1927): 273–80.

"Fynmere, the Garden of Mr. James Fenimore Cooper, Cooperstown, N.Y." *Country Life in America,* undated tearsheet, courtesy Catherine Zusy.

"Fynmere, the House of James Fenimore Cooper, Esq., Frank P. Whiting, Architect." *Architectural Record* 30 (October 1911): 360–68.

"A Garden by the Sea." *House Beautiful,* March 1930, 290–91. [Alger]

"The Garden in Good Taste." *House Beautiful,* August 1923, 132. [Croft]

"The Garden in Good Taste: The Garden of Carll Tucker, Esq." *House Beautiful*, October 1928, 388–91.

"The Garden in Good Taste: The Garden of Miss Mary Pruyn, East Hampton, Long Island." *House Beautiful*, March 1924, 236, 253–56.

"The Garden of A. L. Kramer, Esq., Westbury, Long Island." *House Beautiful*, March 1924, 255.

"The Garden of James Fenimore Cooper at Cooperstown, New York." *House Beautiful*, July 1924, 30–31.

"The Garden of Mr. and Mrs. Edwin Scott Barbour." *House Beautiful*, June 1930, 738–40.

"The Garden of Mrs. A. L. Kramer at Westbury, L.I." *Garden Magazine*, April 1924, 128–29.

"The Garden of Mrs. C. Suydam Cutting at Gladstone, N.J." *Country Life in America*, June 1933, 42–43.

"The Garden of Mrs. Robert A. Franks, Orange, New Jersey." *House Beautiful*, August 1926, 166–67.

"The Garden of Samuel Morris, Esq., in Chestnut Hill, Pennsylvania." *House Beautiful*, July 1927, 30–31.

Garden Magazine, April 1923, 101 [Croft]; June 1923, 238 [Croft]; July 1923, 319 [Magee]; August 1923, 361 [Croft]; October 1923, 71, 73, 75, 92–93 [Pruyn, Kramer, Brewster]; June 1924, 268, 269, 279 [Brewster, Croft, Magee].

Garden Magazine and Home Builder, September 1924, 11 [Morris]; October 1924, 91 [Gossler]; February 1926, 433 [Starr]; March 1926, 25 [Starr]; September 1926, 29, 41 [Starr]; November 1926, 204 [Starr]; July 1927, 486 [Reeves]; September 1927, 44 [Starr].

"A Garden Which Looks Well All Year." *House & Garden*, December 1949, 140–41. [Spalding]

"The Gardener's Calendar for July." *House & Garden*, July 1923, 76.

Gardens and Gardening 1939. London: The Studio, 1939, 45. [Tucker]

Gardens and Gardening 1940. London: The Studio, 1940. [de Waal, McGinley, Tucker]

"The Gardens of H. W. Croft, Greenwich, Ct." *House & Garden*, March 1923, 54–55, 57.

Gilbert, Alma M., and Judith B. Tankard. *A Place of Beauty: The Artists and Gardens of the Cornish Colony*. Berkeley, Calif.: Ten Speed Press, 2000.

Griswold, Mac. "Carolina Grown." *House & Garden*, September 1988, 176–83. [Hanes]

———, and Eleanor Weller. *The Golden Age of American Gardens: Proud Owners, Private Estates, 1890–1940*. New York: Harry N. Abrams/Garden Club of America, 1991. [Alger, Brewster, Brown, Devore, Franks, Kellogg, Neff, Parmelee, Schley, Starr, Stern, White]

Haldeman, Anne Bruce, and Louise Leland. "In Vermont Hills, Mr. and Mrs. Horace Brown." *House Beautiful*, June 1934, 40–43, 79.

Halligan, Gerald L., Renee M. Oubre, and Seymour Knox IV. *Knox Farm State Park*. Charleston, S.C.: Arcadia Publishing, 2015.

Hefner, Robert J., Clay Lancaster, and Robert A. M. Stern. *East Hampton's Heritage: An Illustrated Architectural Record*. New York: W. W. Norton, 1982. [James, Maidstone Club]

Henke, Ellen. "Garden Destinations: Longue Vue Gardens." *Flower & Garden*, December 1992/January 1993, 18–23. [Stern]

Hewitt, Mark Alan. *The Architect and the American Country House, 1890–1940*. New Haven, Conn.: Yale University Press, 1990.

Hildreth, Chris, ed. *The Sarah P. Duke Gardens: A Wonderful Wander*. Durham, N.C.: Duke University Press, 2006.

"An Historic House Regains Its Youth." *House & Garden*, May 1934, 55–57. [F. Pratt]

Hopkins, Alfred. "An Architect Turns Client." *House & Garden*, November 1933, 24, 62.

"House & Garden's Own Hall of Fame." *House & Garden*, June 1933, 50.

"A House in New Canaan, Connecticut." *House Beautiful*, January 1924, 41. [Gossler]

"House of Alfred Hopkins, Architect, Princeton, New Jersey." *Architecture* 68 (November 1933): 273–82.

"House of Philip Gossler, Wheatley Hills, Long Island." *Architecture* 54 (December 1926): 383–88.

"House of Samuel A. Salvage, Glen Head, Long Island." *Architecture* 59 (June 1929): 359–66.

Howe, Samuel. *American Country Houses of To-Day*. New York: Architectural Book Publishing, 1915. [Alger, Brewster, Jennings, Parmelee]

Hull, Sam. "A Legacy of Garden Design." *Duke Magazine*, January–February 1998, 40–43 [Duke]

"In a Long Island Garden." *House & Garden*, October 1926, 129. [Schmidlapp]

"In a Michigan Garden." *House & Garden*, March 1927, 88–91. [Sales]

"In Memoriam." *Garden Club of America Bulletin*, July 1950, 1.

Jacques, Kiley. "Whole Again." *Clem Labine's Period Homes* 18, no. 3 (May 2017): 8–15. [Hepburn]

Karr, Gerald. *Historic Structure Report [for] Chatham*. Denver, Colo.: U.S. Department of the Interior, 1984. [Devore]

Karson, Robin. *A Genius for Place: American Landscapes of the Country Place Era*. Amherst: University of Massachusetts Press/Library of American Landscape History, 2007.

———. *The Muses of Gwinn: Art and Nature in a Garden Designed by Warren H. Manning, Charles A. Platt, and Ellen Biddle Shipman*. New York: Sagapress/Library of American Landscape History, 1995.

———. "A Woman's Place: Ellen Shipman's Gardens Frame a Divided World." *Garden Design*, February–March 1997, 46–48.

———, Jane Roy Brown, and Sarah Allaback, eds. *Warren H. Manning, Landscape Architect and Environmental Planner*. Athens: University of Georgia Press/Library of American Landscape History, 2017.

Keefe, Charles S., ed. *The American House*. New York: U. P. C. Book, 1922. [Mitchell]

Kenworthy, Richard. *The Italian Garden Transplanted: Renaissance Revival Landscape Design in America, 1850–1939*. Exh. cat. Troy, Ala.: Troy State University, 1988.

King, Mrs. Francis. "An English Country Place in Michigan." *Country Life in America,* April 1928, 58–60. [Lowe]

Knight, Jane A. "An Examination of the History of the Lowthorpe School of Landscape Architecture for Women." M.L.A. thesis, Cornell University, 1986.

Krall, Daniel W. "Early Women Designers and Their Work in Public Places." In *Proceedings for Landscapes and Gardens: Women Who Made a Difference*. Edited by Miriam Easton Rutz. East Lansing: Michigan State University, June 1987.

———. "Ellen Biddle Shipman and Her Design for Longue Vue Gardens." *CELA 89: Proceedings*. Gainesville, Fla.: Council of Educators in Landscape Architecture, 1989.

———. "Ellen Biddle Shipman: Dean of Women Landscape Architects." Paper presented at Masters of American Garden Design symposium, PaineWebber and American Horticultural Society, New York, January 1990.

———. "Ellen Biddle Shipman: Dean of Women Landscape Architects." Undated manuscript, Department of Landscape Architecture, Cornell University.

———. "A Half Century of Garden Design: The Drawings of Landscape Architect Ellen Shipman." Exh. notes. Ithaca, N.Y., Hartell Gallery, Cornell University, April 1986.

Krider, Karen. "Ellen Biddle Shipman." In *Pioneers of American Landscape Design*. Edited by Charles Birnbaum and Lisa Crowder. Washington, D.C.: National Park Service, Preservation Assistance Division, 1993.

———. "Ellen Biddle Shipman's Planting Design Focusing on Stan Hywet Gardens." M.L.A. thesis, University of Oregon, 1995. [Seiberling]

Kummen, Merle, S. Zimmerman, and R. Pawlowski. *Hartford Architecture*. Vol 3. Hartford, Conn.: Hartford Architectural Conservancy, 1980. [Aetna]

Larsen, Kirstina. *Tregaron: A Magical Place*. Washington, D.C.: privately printed, 2002. [Parmelee]

Lay, Charles Downing. "An Interview with Charles A. Platt." *Landscape Architecture* 2 (April 1912): 127–31.

Leong, William B. S. "University Gardens: A Development Plan." *Landscape Architecture* 50 (Autumn 1959): 35–44. [Duke]

Levy, David W. *Herbert Croly of "The New Republic": The Life and Thought of an American Progressive*. Princeton, N.J.: Princeton University Press, 1985.

Lidz, Maggie. *The du Ponts: Houses and Gardens in the Brandywine, 1900–1951*. New York: Acanthus Press, 2009.

Lockwood, Alice G. B., ed. *Gardens of Colony and State*. New York: Charles Scribner's Sons/Garden Club of America, 1931, 1934. [Grosse Pointe gardens]

"Long Island Shows a Varied Garden." *House & Garden*, October 1936, 89. [Salvage]

"Looking over the Garden Wall." *Country Life in America*, March 1917, 68–69. [Parmelee]

Lowell, Guy, ed. *American Gardens*. Boston: Bates and Guild, 1902. [Cornish gardens]

McCormick, Kathleen. "In the Path of the Setting Sun: The Gardens at Henry Ford's Fair Lane." *Historic Preservation*, May–June 1995, 86–91, 125.

———. "On a Clear Day: Akron's Stan Hywet Restores Its American-Style Landscape." *Historic Preservation*, July–August 1994, 68–69, 99–103. [Seiberling]

Mackay, Robert B., Anthony K. Baker, and Carol Traynor, eds. *Long Island Country Houses and Their Architects, 1860–1940*. New York: W. W. Norton/SPLIA, 1997.

"Magnificently Done in Chagrin Falls: The Ohio Estate of Mr. and Mrs. E. S. Burke, Jr." *Country Life in America*, March 1937, 65–66.

Malley, Anna O. *Artist's Gardens: American Impressionism and the Garden Movement*. Philadelphia: University of Pennsylvania Press, 2015.

Mateyunas, Paul J. *North Shore Long Island Country House, 1890–1950*. New York: Acanthus Press, 2007.

Meador, Deborah Kay. "The Making of a Landscape Architect: Ellen Biddle Shipman and Her Years at the Cornish Art Colony." M.L.A. thesis, Cornell University, 1989.

Miller, Wilhelm. "An 'Italian Garden' That Is Full of Flowers." *Country Life in America*, March 1905, 485.

Mitchell, Evelyn Scott. "Longue Vue: A Short History of the Gardens." Manuscript, Longue Vue House & Gardens, New Orleans. [Stern]

"A Modernist Garden Appears in America." *House & Garden*, November 1929, 105. [Clapp]

Monograph on the Work of Charles A. Platt. Introduction by Royal Cortissoz. New York: Architectural Book Publishing, 1913.

Montgomery, Gladys. "The House in Its Gardens." *Old-House Interiors*, June 2008, 74–81. [Cooper]

Morgan, Keith N. *Charles A. Platt: The Artist as Architect*. Cambridge and New York: MIT Press/Architectural History Foundation, 1985.

———. "Charles A. Platt's Houses and Gardens in Cornish, New Hampshire." *Antiques*, July 1982, 117–29.

———. *Shaping an American Landscape: The Art and Architecture of Charles A. Platt*. Hanover, N.H.: University Press of New England, 1995.

Mortimer, Senga. "The Romance of the Rose: Ellen Shipman's Garden for a Historic Virginia House." *House & Garden*, April 1997, 150–57. [Devore]

"Mrs. Ellen Shipman, Famous Landscape Architect, Thrills Hearers." *Winston-Salem Journal*, 8 October 1932.

"Mrs. Ellen Shipman, Landscape Designer." Obituary. *New York Times*, 29 March 1950.

"Mrs. Robert Brewster's Garden at Mt. Kisco, New York." *Garden Magazine*, October 1923, 75, 92–93.

Mozingo, Louise A., and Linda Jewell, eds. *Women in Landscape Architecture: Essays on History and Practice*. Jefferson, N.C.: McFarland, 2012.

Murray, Pauline. *Planning and Planting the Home Garden*. New York: Orange Judd Publishing, 1932. [Pruyn]

Nevins, Deborah. "The Triumph of Flora: Women and the American Landscape, 1890–1935." *Antiques*, April 1985, 904–22.

"A New Hampshire House and Garden." *House & Garden*, March 1924, 75–77. [Brook Place]

"New Jersey Follows Spain in a Garden within Patio Walls." *House & Garden*, August 1930, 49, 55–57. [Schley]

Nichols, Rose Standish. "A Hilltop Garden in New Hampshire." *House Beautiful*, March 1934, 237–39, 290.

Noble, William. "Northcote: An Artist's New Hampshire Garden." *Journal of the New England Garden History Society* 2 (1992): 1–9.

Norwalk, Nancy, and Harold Zea, eds. *Choice White Pines and Good Land: A History of Plainfield and Meriden, New Hampshire*. Portsmouth, N.H.: Peter E. Randall, 1991.

Nowak, Lisa. *Cultural Landscape Report for Saint-Gaudens National Historic Site. Vol. 2: Recent History, Existing Conditions, and Analysis*. Boston: National Park Service, Olmsted Center for Landscape Preservation, 2009.

O'Donnell, Patricia M. *Tregaron Cultural Landscape Assessment*. Charlotte, Vt.: Heritage Landscapes, 2005.

———. *Tregaron Cultural Landscape Report*. Charlotte, Vt.: Heritage Landscapes, 2007.

O'Donnell, Patricia M., Gregory Wade De Vries, and Sarah LeVaun Graulty. *The Cummer Cultural Landscape Report and Management Plan*. Charlotte, Vt.: Heritage Landscapes, 2011.

O'Donnell, Patricia M., Gregory Wade De Vries, and Tamara Orlow. *Graycliff Cultural Landscape Report and Treatment Plan*. Charlotte, Vt.: Heritage Landscapes, 2008.

O'Donnell, Patricia M., and Robin Karson. *Longue Vue House and Gardens Historic Landscape Report*. Charlotte, Vt.: Heritage Landscapes, 1997.

O'Donnell, Patricia M., and Carrie Mardorf. *Longue Vue House and Gardens Landscape Renewal Plan*. Charlotte, Vt.: Heritage Landscapes, 2007.

O'Donnell, Patricia M., Lori Tolliver, and Roselyn Romberg. *Obercreek Estate Historic Landscape Feasibility Study: Confidential Report*. Charlotte, Vt.: Heritage Landscapes, 2000.

"Old English Magnificiently Done in Chagrin Falls." *Country Life in America*, March 1937, 64–69. [Burke]

Patterson, Augusta Owen. *American Homes of To-Day, Their Architectural Style, Their Environment, Their Characteristics*. New York: Macmillan, 1924. [Brewster, Lord]

———. "Mrs. Robert Bacon's Westbury Garden." *Town & Country*, August 1926, 44–47.

"Paved Pools Add the Final Terrace Touch." *House & Garden*, May 1933, 44. [Godley]

Perrett, Antoinette. "A Rose and Purple Garden in July." *House Beautiful*, July 1922, 21, 72. [Abbott]

Petersen, Anne. "Women Take the Lead in Landscape Art." *New York Times*, 13 March 1938.

Piper, Adaline D. "The Charm of Chatham." *House Beautiful*, April 1926, 437–41. [Devore]

"Planting That Reflects the Natural Surroundings: The Estate of Mr. and Mrs. Allan Wood." *House Beautiful*, August 1931, 130–32.

Platt, Charles A. *Italian Gardens*. 1894. Reprint, with an overview by Keith N. Morgan. New York: Sagapress/Timber Press, 1993.

"A Pool for Every Garden." *House & Garden*, June 1920, 26. [Mitchell]

Power, Ethel B. "A Blue-Ribbon Garden: The Garden of Mrs. Holden McGinley." *House Beautiful*, March 1933, 86–89, 118–19.

Pratt, Richard H. "Gardens Adorned and Negligée." *House & Garden*, June 1924, 54–55. [Croft]

Pressley, Marion, and Cynthia Zaitzevsky. *Cultural Landscape Report for Saint-Gaudens National Historic Site. Vol. 1: Site History and Existing Conditions*. Boston: National Park Service, North Atlantic Region Cultural Landscape Program, 1993.

Randall, Monica. *The Mansions of Long Island's Gold Coast*. New York: Rizzoli, 1987. [Kramer]

Rehmann, Elsa. *Garden-Making*. Boston: Houghton Mifflin, 1926. [Abbott, Magee, Mitchell]

"Residence of Grenville T. Emmet, New York." *Architectural Record* 46 (November 1919): 476–83.

Russell, Elizabeth H. "A House on Beekman Place." *House Beautiful*, November 1927, 512–16, 568–69. [Shipman]

"Rynwood, House of Samuel A. Salvage, Esq." *Architectural Forum* 53 (July 1930): 51–85.

Sale, Edith Tunis. *Historic Gardens of Virginia*. Revised edition. Richmond, Va.: James River Garden Club, 1930. [Devore]

Sclare, Lisa, and Donald Sclare. *Beaux-Arts Estates: A Guide to the Architecture of Long Island*. New York: Viking Press, 1980. [Gossler, Hutton]

Sexton, R. W. "A House and Garden in Suburban New Jersey." *Arts & Decoration*, February 1937, 14–15, 49. [Foster]

Shelton, Louise. *Beautiful Gardens in America*. New York: Charles Scribner's Sons, 1915. [Merrill]

———. *Beautiful Gardens in America*. Revised edition. New York: Charles Scribner's Sons, 1924. [Abbott, Brewster, Croft, Morris, Smith, Starr]

Shinn, Meghan. "Dazzling Duke." *Horticulture*, January 2014, 29–33.

Shipman, Ellen. "How I Teach My Own Children." *Ladies' Home Journal*, September 1911, 60.

———. "Rhymes of Bermuda." *Garden Club of America Bulletin*, March 1933, 54.

———. "The Saint-Gaudens Memorial Gardens." *Garden Club of America Bulletin*, May 1948, 61–65.

———. "Window Gardens for Little Money." *Ladies' Home Journal*, September 1911, 30.

"Some Garden Pictures." *House Beautiful*, July 1923, 45. [Croft]

"Some Philadelphia and Wilmington Gardens." *Landscape Architecture* 28 (April 1938): 123. [Starr]

"Southern Colonial." *Country Life in America*, January 1937, 30. [Stern]

Sparks, Lamar. "A Landscape Architect Discusses Gardens." *Better Homes & Gardens*, November 1930, 20, 70–71.

Steele, Fletcher, ed. *House Beautiful Gardening Manual*. Boston: Atlantic Monthly, 1926. [Brewster, Cooper, Daniels, Franks, Pruyn]

Stern, Robert A. M., Gregory Gilmartin, and Thomas Mellins. *New York 1930: Architecture and Urbanism between Two World Wars*. New York: Rizzoli, 1987. [Beekman Place]

Stone, Doris M. "Longue Vue." *American Horticulturist*, June 1987, 28–31.

Tankard, Judith B. "The Artistry of Ellen Shipman." *Horticulture*, January 1997, 72–75. [Seiberling]

———. *Beatrix Farrand: Private Gardens, Public Landscapes*. New York: Monacelli Press, 2009.

———. "Defining Their Turf: Pioneer Women Landscape Designers." *Studies in the Decorative Arts* (Bard Graduate Center) 8 (Fall–Winter 2000–2001): 31–53.

———. "Ellen Shipman's New England Gardens." *Arnoldia*, Spring 1997, 1–11.

———. "The History of the Gardens at the Cummer Museum of Art & Gardens." Unpublished report, 2001. [Cummer]

———. "Landscape: Jacksonville's Long Lost Gardens, *Garden Design*, March 2010, 32–34. [Cummer]

———. *A Legacy in Bloom: Celebrating a Century of Gardens at the Cummer*. Jacksonville, Fla.: Cummer Museum of Art & Gardens, 2008.

———. "Shipman in Seattle." *Pacific Horticulture*, Summer 1997, 30–37. [Merrill]

———. "Splendor Restored." *Horticulture*, April 2003, 50–55. [Cummer]

———. "Women Pioneers in Landscape Design." *Radcliffe Quarterly* 79 (March 1993): 8–11.

Taylor, Curtice, and Caroline Seebohm. *Rescuing Eden: Preserving America's Historic Gardens*. New York: Monacelli Press, 2015. [Cummer, Saint-Gaudens]

Thomas, Elizabeth Patterson. *Old Kentucky Homes & Gardens*. Louisville, Ky.: Standard Printing Company, 1939. [de Waal]

"Three Pages of Charming Gardens." *House & Garden*, October 1923, 65. [Magee]

"Three Pennsylvania Gardens, *Garden & Home Builder*, September 1924, 11. [Morris]

"To Link the Lawns and Garden." *House & Garden*, August 1930, 49, 55–57. [Schley]

"To Remind You of July." *House & Garden*, December 1923, 51. [Brook Place]

Town & Country, 1 February 1927, 47–51. [Gossler]

Turpin, John K., and W. Barry Thompson. *New Jersey Country Houses: The Somerset Hills*. 2 vols. Far Hills, N.J.: Mountain Colony Press, 2004.

"Two Gardens at Mount Kisco, New York." *House Beautiful*, March 1924, 256. [Brewster, Magee]

"Use Pattern in a Vista." *House & Garden*, March 1951, 167. [Kanzler]

Van Buren, Deborah E. "The Cornish Colony: Expressions of Attachment to Place, 1885–1915." Ph.D. diss., George Washington University, May 1987.

———. "Landscape Architecture and Gardens in the Cornish Colony: The Careers of Rose Nichols, Ellen Shipman, and Frances Duncan." *Women's Studies* 14 (September 1988): 367–88.

———. "Women and Landscape Architecture: Rose Nichols and Ellen Shipman in the Cornish Colony." Paper presented at the annual meeting of the American Studies Association, San Diego, October 1985.

Van Horn, Henry. "Mr. A. L. Kramer's Residence at Westbury." *Town & Country*, 1 May 1920, 53–56.

"Variety of Form and Abundance of Bloom within a Small Area: The Garden of Mrs. Henry V. Greenough, Brookline, Massachusetts." *House Beautiful*, March 1931, 259–62.

Wade, Hugh Mason. *A Brief History of Cornish, 1763–1974*. Hanover, N.H.: University Press of New England, 1976.

Warren, Bonnie. "Longue Vue: A Tribute to Classical Tradition in New Orleans." *Southern Accents*, September–October 1985, 72, 79. [Stern]

Warren, Dale. "The Garden as a Frame for the House." *House Beautiful*, October 1926, 426–27. [Brook Place]

Watters, Sam. *American Gardens, 1890–1930*. New York: Acanthus Press, 2006.

———. *Gardens for a Beautiful America, 1895–1935: Photographs by Frances Benjamin Johnston*. New York: Acanthus Press, 2012.

Way, Thaisa. *Unbounded Practice: Women and Landscape Architecture in the Early Twentieth Century*. Charlottesville: University of Virginia Press, 2009.

"Weeping Cherry for Spring Enchantment." *House & Garden*, March 1941, 16. [Williams].

"When It's Spring in an Ohio Garden." *House & Garden*, May 1929, 111–13. [Clapp]

White, Edward, "Garden Design." *Journal of the International Garden Club* 1 (August 1917): 45. [Hegeman]

Wilson, Richard Guy, Shaun Eyring, and Kenny Marotta, eds. *Re-Creating the American Past: Essays on the Colonial Revival*. Charlottesville: University of Virginia Press, 2006.

Wright, Cornelia B., ed. *The Influence of Women on the Southern Landscape*. Winston-Salem, N.C.: Old Salem, 1996.

Wright, Richardson, ed. *House & Garden's Book of Gardens*. New York: Condé Nast, 1921. [Abbott, Mitchell, Parmelee]

———. *House & Garden's Second Book of Gardens*. New York: Condé Nast, 1927. [Croft, Sales, White]

Yearbook of the Architectural League of New York, 1923. [Croft, Magee]

Yearbook of the Architectural League of New York, 1929. [Salvage]

Zaitzevsky, Cynthia. *Long Island Landscapes and the Women Who Designed Them*. New York: W. W. Norton/SPLIA, 2009.

Zusy, Catherine. "A Unity of Design in the American Spirit: James Fenimore Cooper II's 'Fynmere.'" Paper prepared for the Cooperstown [N.Y.] History Museum Studies Program, 1984.

AUTHOR'S ACKNOWLEDGMENTS

When the invitation came from the Library of American Landscape History to prepare a revised and expanded edition of Shipman's biography (first published in 1996), I welcomed the opportunity to revisit the work of this distinguished designer and update the preservation status of her gardens. This book owes its inception to pioneering research by Daniel W. Krall, Professor Emeritus, Department of Landscape Architecture, Cornell University, who dedicated many years to unraveling the career of Ellen Shipman. Krall's knowledge of her projects, working methods, and design intent is unsurpassed, and his generosity in sharing both his files and the frustration of the pursuit of Shipman is deeply appreciated. Other experts who provided essential information include Deborah Kay Meador, whose thesis work documents Shipman's Cornish years and whose bibliography and client listing served as models for this book. Deborah Van Buren's dissertation and published writings on the Cornish Colony and her interview with Shipman's longtime associate Frances McCormic were invaluable. Noel Dorsey Vernon's interview with Eleanor Christie was useful in understanding Shipman's office procedures.

The book could not have been written without the encouragement of Shipman's grandchildren, the late Nancy Angell Streeter and Nicholas B. Angell, who patiently answered my relentless queries about their grandmother's personal life and generously shared family mementos. I would also like to thank Nancy Streeter's daughters, Meg Streeter Lauck, Ellen Shipman Rhodes, and Ruth C. Streeter, who were encouraging in the preparation of this new edition.

Many people and institutions were helpful in my search for documents and resources or provided illustrations, including Suzy Berschbach, Grosse Pointe War Memorial; Leslie Bottaro, head gardener, Greenville Country Club; Virginia Colby, Cornish Historical Society; Lorna Condon, Historic New England; Joyce Connolly, Archives of American Gardens, Smithsonian Institution; Lenora Costa, curator of collections, Longue Vue House & Gardens; William Louis Culberson, Sarah P. Duke Gardens; Jean Dodenhoff, Grosse Point Historical Society; John Dryfhout, former superintendent, Saint-Gaudens National Historic Site; Elaine Engst, former curator of manuscripts, Rare and Manuscripts Collections, Cornell University Library; Janet Evans, Pennsylvania Horticultural Society Library; Amy Graham, horticultural director, Longue Vue House & Gardens; Reine Hauser, former executive director, Graycliff Conservancy; Michael A. Jehle, Nantucket Historical Association; Vicky Jones, Special Collections, University of Oregon; Holly Keris, acting director, Cummer Museum of Art & Gardens; Jane Knowles, Schlesinger Library, Radcliffe College; Paul C. Lasewicz, archivist, Aetna Life; Lucy Lawliss, former superintendent, Fredericksburg and Spotsylvania National Military Park; Bonnie Lepard, former executive director, Tregaron Conservancy; Karen Marzonie, director of landscapes, Henry Ford Estate; Amy McDonald, Duke University Archives; Mona McKindley, gardener, Longfellow House–Washington's Headquarters National Historic Site; John Franklin Miller, former director, Stan Hywet Hall; Liz Muller, curator of collections, Rare and Manuscripts Collections, Cornell University Library; Brent Newman, Edison & Ford Winter Estates; Nancy Norwalk, former curator, Philip Read Memorial Library; Lynn Parseghian, executive director, Tregaron Conservancy; Chris Pendleton, president, Edison & Ford Winter Estates; Walter Punch, former librarian, Massachusetts Horticultural Society Library; Catha Grace Rambusch, Catalog of Landscape Records, Wave Hill; Lydia H. Schmalz, former curator of collections, Longue Vue House & Gardens; James M. Shea, former site manager, Longfellow House–Washington's Headquarters National Historic Site; Glenn Stach, Tregaron Conservancy; Orla Swift, Sarah P. Duke Gardens; Carol Traynor, Society for the Preservation of Long Island Antiquities; Lt. Col. Rudy T. Veit, U.S. Military Academy, West Point; Donna Werling and Helen Hopkins, Fair Lane, Dearborn, Michigan; Hugh Wilburn, former librarian, Frances Loeb Library, Harvard University; Robert Wooler, excecutive director, Graycliff Conservancy; Kristen Zimmerman, registrar, Cummer Museum of Art & Gardens; and Catherine Zusy, New Hampshire Historical Society.

Others who shared information or documents pertaining to Shipman include Jeff Allen, Kelly Allegrezza, Noni Ames, Philip Archer, Chris Beagan, Virginia Lopez Begg, Craig Bergmann, Paul Bergmann, Charles Birnbaum, the late Ann Bloom, the late Sarah Boasberg, Lucinda Brockway, Dona Caldwell, William Cary, Margaret Carpenter, Staci Catron, Richard Channick, Leslie Rose Close, Christopher Combs, Peggy Cornett, Hope Cushing, Bobbie Dolp, Lake Douglas, Reed Engle, Catherine Evans, Betsy Fitzsimmons, the late Christopher Gray, Robert Grese, Mac Griswold, Gerald Halligan, Susan Haltom, Ce Ce Haydock, Robin Heller, Mark Alan Hewitt, the late Martha Hill, Elizabeth Igleheart, Beate Jensen, Barbara Johnstone, Richard Karberg, Robin Karson, Richard Kenworthy, Joanne Lawson, Maggie Lidz, Carolyn Marsh Lindsay, Tom Matthews, Diane K. McGuire, Lauren G. Meier, Arthur Miller, Keith N. Morgan, Bill Noble, Jill Nooney, James O'Day, Patricia O'Donnell, Sean O'Rourke, Janice Parker, Marion Pressley, James Prise, Robin Reed, Helen Rollins, the late Janet Seagle, James Speck, McDonald Sprague, Elizabeth Stone, David Streatfield, W. Barry Thomsen, Patricia Thorpe, Maria Tousimis, Gay Tucker, Spenser Tunnell, Joseph Tyree, George Waters, Christopher Vernon, David Warren, Sam Watters, Thomas Wedell, Eleanor Weller, Katherine Grayson Wilkins, Carleton B. Wood, and Cynthia Zaitzevsky.

Thanks are due to the many people who welcomed me into their Shipman gardens or provided access to them. These include Michael Bloomberg and Ellen Shapiro, Max Blumberg and Eduardo Araujo, John and Neville Bryan, Annick Cooper, Jerome Gratry, Douglas and Karen Heaton, Lars Leicht, Jim and Lucy Owen, John and Kelly Palasics, Melinda Penn, Jean and Scott Peterson, Clara M. Rankin, John Shannon, Mary Ann Streeter, and Lucy Ireland Weller.

Deep thanks are due to Robin Karson, executive director of the Library of American Landscape History, for developing and guiding this project, both its original incarnation and this new edition. Carol Betsch, LALH managing editor, improved the text with her copyediting. Sarah Allaback, LALH senior manuscript editor, aided enormously in assembling the illustrations. Jonathan Lippincott is responsible for the beautiful new design.

INDEX